EGYPT
and the
NILE

EGYPT
and the
NILE
through writers' eyes

EDITED BY
DEBORAH MANLEY
SAHAR ABDEL-HAKIM

The American University in Cairo Press

First published in Egypt in 2008 by
The American University in Cairo Press
113 Sharia Kasr el Aini, Cairo, Egypt
www.aucpress.com

This edition published by arrangement with Eland Publishing Ltd

Dar el Kutub No. 27018/07
ISBN 978 977 416 174 2

Dar el Kutub Cataloging-in-Publication Data

Manley, Deborah
Egypt and the Nile: Through Writers' Eyes / edited by Deborah Manley and Sahar Abdel-Hakim.—Cairo: The American University in Cairo Press, 2008
p. cm.
ISBN 977 416 174 2
1. Egypt—description and travel I. Manley, Deborah (ed.) II. Abdel-Hakim, Sahar (jt. ed.)
916.2

Printed in Egypt

Contents

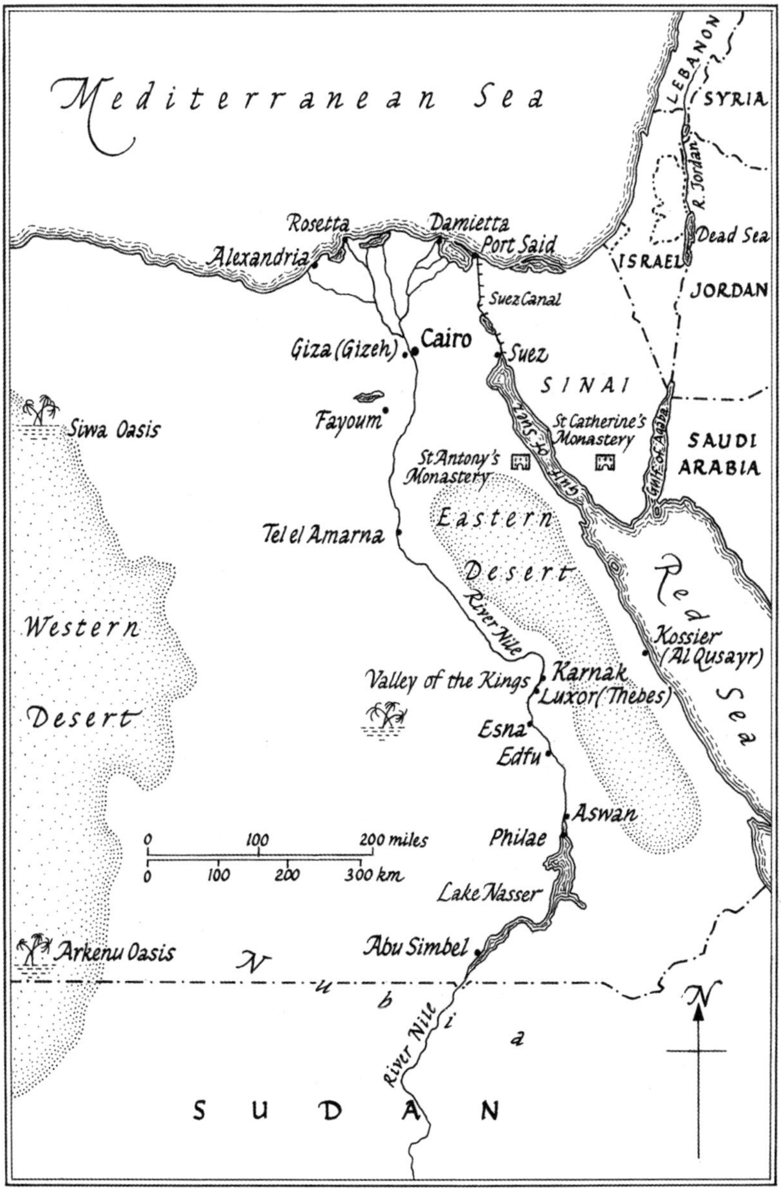

Mediterranean Sea
LEBANON
SYRIA
R. Jordan
Dead Sea
ISRAEL
JORDAN
Rosetta
Damietta
Port Said
Alexandria
Suez Canal
Cairo
Giza (Gizeh)
Suez
SINAI
Fayoum
Siwa Oasis
St Catherine's Monastery
Gulf of Suez
Gulf of Aqaba
SAUDI ARABIA
St Antony's Monastery
Eastern Desert
Tel el Amarna
Red Sea
River Nile
Western Desert
Kossier (Al Qusayr)
Karnak
Valley of the Kings
Luxor (Thebes)
Esna
Edfu
Aswan
Philae
0 100 200 miles
0 100 200 300 km
Lake Nasser
Abu Simbel
Arkenu Oasis
Nubia
N
River Nile
SUDAN

Introduction

Egypt has a history and a culture that is more strongly alive into the distant past than that of almost any other country. We are all made aware of Egypt's ancient past as children. We learn about the inundation and the pyramids and mummies and the great empty temples. Our imaginations are caught by the extraordinary story of this country along the banks of the Nile. In this collection we – one a citizen of Egypt, the other a frequent traveller to it – have brought together writers' voices to give a comprehensive view of this enduring civilisation.

You might say that if you have not been to Egypt at least once, you have hardly travelled. There is so much there to see and reflect upon, from the ancient past to the very present. We have brought together the experiences of early travellers, from both Arabic-speaking and other countries, the voices of those who came during the flowering of tourism in the Victorian era, and the interpretations and understanding of the Egyptians themselves of their own culture. For it is the experience of the people whose daily life both mirrors that distant past, and who are creating the present and the future, that gives a deeper sense of the country. Some accounts are mythical or fictional; some are tales told by village story-tellers, some the experience of our contemporaries and some records of life experiences accumulated over centuries.

As well as the ancient Egypt familiar from childhood, we examine the country's more recent history. In the Mediterranean and the wider world, Egypt has always been pivotal as trade and traders moved between East and West. Pilgrims too travelled through Egypt on their way to Mecca or to St Catherine's

Monastery in Sinai and the other monasteries in the Egyptian deserts. For some writers like Ibn Jubayr in the twelfth century and Ibn Battuta a century later, their travels started with pilgrimage but continued as wider journeys. In 1798 Napoleon's army and their accompanying scholars pushed their way through the country – and then left. But in their discovery of the Rosetta Stone and their publication of the vast *Description of Egypt,* illustrating in text and pictures the flora and fauna, the people and their achievements, they awakened even greater interest in Egypt in other parts of the world. For another few decades the hieroglyphics which paper the walls of every temple and tomb were still just that – 'hidden writing' – but scholars were beginning to decipher the names and cartouches of the pharaohs. Then, after thousands of years, the book of Egypt was opened again with the key of the Rosetta Stone.

Right through the nineteenth century and onwards, a growing number of travellers came to wander and wonder at, and often to write about, Egypt. And Egypt always outstrips their expectations. The pyramids rise higher above us than we imagined; the great temple at Karnak near Luxor absorbs and ignores cruise-shipfuls of tourists, the vast figures of Ramses guarding the temple at Abu Simbel are mightier and more enigmatic than any statues we know, and the tombs on the west bank at Luxor still make us catch our breath at their very freshness. And increasingly writers have travelled further from the Nile across Egypt to the places described by Ahdaf Soueif in fiction and others in travel accounts.

The great discoveries from the past continuously brought, and bring, Egypt into the world's news. Little knowing what to expect as he struggled up the soft drift of sand on the shoulder of the mountain at Abu Simbel and turned and saw the great figures of Pharaoh Ramses II, the words of the Swiss explorer, Jean Louis Burckhardt, in 1813, are spine-tingling:

> I fell in with what is yet visible of four immense colossal statues cut out of the rock… they stand in a deep recess excavated in the mountain; but it is greatly to be regretted that they are almost entirely buried beneath the sands, which are blown down here in torrents.

A few years later, on 1 August 1817, a young Italian Muslim (Giovanni Finati) became the first recorded person to enter the great temple of Abu Simbel for centuries. And the discoveries kept coming – and tourists came to share them and returned home to tell the tale of what they had seen.

We have chosen for this collection the experience of Florence Nightingale's days at Abu Simbel from all the many accounts. But the Abu Simbel early travellers knew is not the one you see today. In the 1960s the High Dam was built across the Nile and the river and the country changed forever. The peoples of the world came together through the United Nations to lift the great temple of Abu Simbel above the flood. Less well known is that many smaller temples along the river were also moved back from the rising waters. The temples on the island at Philae were moved from one island to another. And the annual inundation of the Nile was replaced by a human-controlled flow.

The Nile is still the pathway through Egypt, linking the shores of the Mediterranean to the heart of Africa, and even today if we move by road or rail from one city to another, we see rural life along the Nile continuing in its ageless manner. Yes, some farmers may have a tractor, indeed many have a pickup truck, but for many others the ass and the camel still serve their needs as the most sensible engines and means of transport. There are two great changes since the long-ago past: in every village the mosque's minaret points heavenwards and at night, the hydroelectric power that flows from the High Dam lights up each village so that the Nile's route through the desert lands of Egypt can be seen clearly from space. Another deep-seated change has been brought by travel itself: the continuing movement from the countryside to the cities – and from the cities to the oil-countries. It is recognised that travel and cultural mixing have brought – and are bringing – more changes than all the political movements put together.

Always in Egypt there was – and is – so much to see. There is the meeting of the peoples of the world in the great cities as Robert Curzon described on his first evening in Alexandria in 1833, and as the Nobel Prize-winning novelist Naguib Mahfouz expressed in his novel, *Miramar*, and there is the community experience of

Ramadan witnessed by Amitav Ghosh. Max Rodenbeck was drawn back to Cairo and Egypt to drink – at least in theory – the waters of the Nile. Ahmed Hassanein went out into the deserts of his ancestors to rediscover his own past there; William Dalrymple, too, explored another past in the Eastern Desert; Jean Said Makdisi explored the strains placed on her adopted country by the modern world. It is not only in the cities that one sees the results of the population explosion of Egypt which has multiplied the flow of people from the country to the town. Along the Nile there is always a human presence: a man fishing, women coming down to catch a ferry (no longer carrying water jars to fill but gas cylinders instead), children swimming or driving the beasts to water or, like a bright frieze on their way to school, waving at the Nile steamers as they pass. But this presence never seems oppressive or unmanageable.

From around the world travellers – and tourists – come to look, admire, eat the local food, comment, learn, sunbathe, visit the sites, photograph, buy and send postcards home, and rejoin their cruise ship or fly home again, having hardly touched or been touched by the life of their destination. Most do not speak the language. Nor are they aware of any part of Egypt's modern history, except those parts that are famed. This division of tourists and people can be especially marked where the tourist goes – or is taken – to tourist centres where many citizens have hardly been since their school days. The tourist centres have become inevitable honey-pots for those who live off the tourism and serve the transient population with undiscriminating charm. Were tourists to travel like the Indian student Amitav Ghosh travelled, they might understand rather more about both ancient and modern Egypt.

What we have set out to do in this book is to provide a new and more comprehensive view of Egypt through the many voices past and present and to bring the diversity and the continuity of Egypt together to give a picture of this country, its many places, its long history and its people.

Editorial Note

To put each writer in chronological context, we have given the approximate year in which each extract was written or published. We have also written brief biographies to provide some background for each. These are to be found, listed alphabetically, at the end of the book, as is a chronology of the journeys made by the writers. We have not tried to regularise the spelling of names and places, but have retained those of the originally published texts.

1

Egypt and the Nile

Ra and his Children

Roger Lancelyn Green

From the plethora of confused and confusing ancient legends discovered on papyri, stone and paper, the children's writer Roger Lancelyn Green re-narrates the story of creation as the ancient Egyptians told it.

BEFORE THE LAND of Egypt rose out of the waters at the beginning of the world, Ra the Shining One came into being. He was all-powerful, and the secret of his power lay in his Name which was hidden from all the world. Having this power, he had only to name a thing, and that thing too came into being.

'I am Khepera at the dawn, and Ra at noon, and Tum in the evening,' he said – and as he said it, behold, he was the sun rising in the east, passing across the sky and setting in the west. And this was the first day of the world.

When he named Shu, the wind blew. The rain fell when he named Tefnut the spitter. After this he spoke the name of Geb, and the earth rose above the waters of the sea. He cried, 'Nut!' – and that goddess was the arch of the sky stretching over the earth with her feet on one horizon and her hands on the other. Then he named Hapi, and the sacred River Nile flowed through Egypt to make it fruitful.

Then Ra went on to name all the things on earth, which grew into being at his words. Last of all he spoke the words for 'Man' and 'Woman', and soon there were people dwelling throughout the land of Egypt.

After this Ra himself took on the shape of a man and became the first Pharaoh of Egypt. For thousands of years he reigned over the land, and there was peace and plenty. The Nile rose each year and flooded the fields; then it sank back into its channel, leaving the rich coating of mud which made sure of fine crops as the cool spring turned into the baking summer. There were no lean years when the Nile did not rise high enough; nor were there any years when the floods rose too high or lasted too long. It was the golden age of the world, and ever afterwards the Egyptians spoke of the good things 'which happened in the time of Ra'.

At last, however, even Ra grew old: for it was decreed that no man should live for ever, and he had made himself a man to rule over Egypt. And when he was old and his bones were like silver, his flesh like gold and his hair like lapis lazuli, he could no longer rule well over the people of Egypt, nor fight against Apophis, the Dragon of Evil who had grown out of the evil vapours in the darkness of the night and sought ever to devour all that was good and bright and kissed by the sun.

Presently the evil of Apophis entered into the souls of the people of Egypt and many of them rebelled against Ra and did evil in his sight, worshipping the Dragon of Darkness instead of the Eye of Day.

Ra perceived these things and the plots which the evil among men were preparing against his divine majesty. Then he spoke to his attendants, saying, 'Gather together the high gods who are my court. Summon Shu and Tefnut, bid Geb and Nut hasten to the council hall – send even for Nun, the spirit of the waters out of which I arose at the beginning of the world. Gather them secretly: let not the evil among men know that I am aware of their doings.'

Then the gods came into the presence of Ra, bowing in turn before him and kissing the ground at his feet in token of loyalty.

When all were gathered Nun spoke for them, saying, 'Life, health, strength be to you, Ra, Pharaoh of Egypt, maker of all things! Speak to us so that we may hear your divine will.'

Then Ra answered, 'Nun, eldest of all things, and all ye gods whom I have called into being – look upon mankind, whom also I made at a glance of my all-seeing Eye, naming them in the beginning that they might appear upon the earth and multiply to be my servants in life and in death. See, they have plotted against me, they have done evil things – the wicked among them gather even now in Upper Egypt to work further ill in my sight. Tell me, shall I slay them all with a burning glance from my Eye?'

Nun answered, speaking for all the gods: 'Ra, greater than I out of whom you came in the beginning; you who are mightier than all the gods you have created – if you send forth the burning glance of your Eye to slay mankind, it will turn all the land of Egypt into a desert. Therefore make a power that will smite men and women only; send out that which will burn the evil but not harm the good.'

Then answered Ra, 'I will not send forth the burning glance of my Eye. Instead I will send Sekhmet against mankind!'

As he spoke the name, Sekhmet leapt into being, in form as a mighty lioness of gigantic size. Away she sped into Upper Egypt, and slaughtered and devoured mankind until the Nile ran red with blood and the earth beside it became a great red marsh.

Before long the most wicked among men had been slain by Sekhmet, and the rest prayed to Ra for mercy. And Ra wished to spare them, for he had no desire to slay all of mankind and leave himself the ruler of a desolate earth with no human beings to serve him.

But, having tasted blood, Sekhmet would not cease from her hunting. Day by day she stalked through the land of Egypt slaying all whom she met; and night by night she hid herself among the rocks on the edge of the desert, waiting for the sun to rise so that she might hunt once more.

Then said Ra, 'Sekhmet cannot be stayed except by a trick. If I can deceive her and save mankind from her sharp teeth and from her claws, I will give her greater power yet over them so that her heart shall rejoice and she shall not feel that honour has been taken from her.'

So Ra summoned before him swift and speedy messengers and commanded them, saying, 'Run like the shadow of a body – swifter and more silently than the body itself – to the island of Elephantine that lies in the Nile below the First Cataract. Bring me the red ochre that is found there alone – bring it with speed.'

Away sped the messengers through the darkness and returned to Heliopolis, the city of Ra, bearing loads of the red ochre of Elephantine. There, by Ra's command, all the priestesses of the Temple of the Sun, and all the maidservants of the royal court were set to crushing barley and making beer. Seven thousand jars did they make and, by the command of Ra, they mingled the red ochre of Elephantine with it so that it gleamed in the moonlight red as blood.

'Now,' said Ra, 'carry this upstream to protect mankind. Carry it to where Sekhmet means to slaughter men when day returns, and pour it out upon the earth as a trap for her.'

Day dawned and Sekhmet came out into the sunlight from her lair among the rocks and looked about her, seeking whom she might devour. She saw no living thing. But, in the place where yesterday she had slain many men, she saw that the fields were covered to the depth of three hands' breadths with what seemed to be blood.

Sekhmet saw and laughed with a laugh like the roar of a hungry lioness. Thinking that it was the blood she had shed upon the previous day, she stooped and drank greedily. Again and again she drank, until the strength of the beer mounted to her brain and she could neither hunt nor kill.

As the day drew to its close she came reeling down to Heliopolis where Ra awaited her – and when the sun touched the horizon she had not slain a single man or woman since the evening before.

'You come in peace, sweet one,' said Ra, 'peace be with you and a new name. No longer are you Sekhmet the Slayer: you are Hathor the Lady of Love. Yet your power over mankind shall be greater even than it was – for the passion of love shall be stronger than the passion of hate, and all shall know love, and all shall be your victims. Moreover, in memory of this day, the priestesses of love shall drink the beer of Heliopolis made red with the ochre of

Elephantine on the first day of each year at a great festival in honour of Hathor.'

So mankind was saved by Ra, and given both a new delight and a new pain.

From *Tales of Ancient Egypt,* 1967

The Story of the Nile

Ahmad bin Tuwayr al-Janna

NOW I WILL mention something of the story of the Nile, recorded in the 'Unbored pearl of marvels' (Kharidat al-'Aja'ib). I have only done so because in it is explained the tradition of the four rivers in the world which come from Paradise. Two rivers are manifest, and two are concealed. As for the first they are the Nile and the Euphrates, and as for the latter, they are the Jaxartes and Oxus (Sayhun and Jayhun). The Prophet, the blessing and peace of God be upon him, said it.

Let me quote the Kharidat al-'Aja'ib: It is said that there was a man of the offspring of Esau, son of Jacob son of Abraham 'the friend of God', upon them be blessing and peace, named Ha'id. When he entered Egypt and saw its marvels, the idea came to him that he would not leave the river Nile until he reached its source, or die. He marched for thirty years in inhabited tracks and thirty in deserted wastes until he reached a green sea. He saw that the Nile divided that sea. He mounted a pack animal there, a beast which God Almighty had made subservient to him, and for a long while it took him over a far distance.

He found himself in a land of iron. Its mountains and its trees were of iron. Then he came upon a land of copper. Its mountains and its trees were of copper. Then he entered a land of silver. Its mountains and trees were of silver. Then he came upon a land of gold. Its mountains and trees were of gold. At length he came to a wide wall of gold. In it was a high domed structure of gold. It had four doors. Water came down from that wall and stayed in that domed structure, and then came out of the four doors. Three of the waters watered the earth with abundance, but one of them – the fourth – flowed on the surface of the ground. It was the Nile. The other three were the Jaxartes, the Oxus and the Euphrates.

Then an angel of beautiful countenance came to him and said, 'Peace be upon you, oh, Ha'id, this is Paradise.' Then he said to him, 'The sustenance of Paradise will come to you, and you will prefer it to any worldly thing.' While he was there a bunch of grapes was brought to him. It was of three colours – pearl, green amethyst and ruby. The angel said, 'Oh, Ha'id, this is the green fruit of Paradise.' Ha'id took it and retired and saw a person under an apple tree. He spoke to him and made his acquaintance. He said to him, 'Oh, Ha'id, will you not eat of these apples?' He replied, 'I have of the food of Paradise, I do not need your apples.' The other said, 'Truly, you have spoken, oh, Ha'id; I know it is from Paradise and know of the one who brought it to you. He is my brother, and these apples are also from Paradise.'

That old man continued thus with him until he ate of the apples. No sooner had he bitten upon the apples than he saw that angel who was biting his finger and saying to him, 'Do you know who the old man is?' He said, 'No.' He said, 'By God, he it is who sent out your father Adam from Paradise. If you had been content with the bunch of grapes, then the people of the world would have eaten of them as long as the world lasts, and they would not be exhausted. This is your own doing. Return to your abode.' Thus he spoke. Ha'id wept and repented. He travelled until he entered Egypt, and he began to tell the people about what marvels he saw in his journey. So ends my quotation from the Kharidat al-'Aja'ib. I have introduced it to explain and confirm the authentic tradition of the issuing of the Nile from Paradise.

From *The Pilgrimage of Ahmas, c.*1835

The Family Life of the Dead

Lady Evelyn Cobbold

Peasant life changes little over many centuries. Familiar seasonal tasks are performed by farmers each year: grain needs to be planted and nourished and harvested; beasts must be fed and tended; fish are still caught in rivers much as they have ever been; rulers still rule people. Thus, in the tombs of ancient Egypt, we recognise the tasks being performed by the ancient peasants and the formalities performed by their masters. Lady Evelyn Cobbold, en route for the Fayoum in 1911, records the familiarity with which she recognised the activities of five thousand and more years ago.

WE BREAK UP camp early to visit this great Necropolis of the dead. We go first to the tomb of Ti, companion and counsellor of the king, 'pleasing to the heart of his Lord'.

As we descend into the mysterious silence of the tomb, an Arab guardian lights candles, whose feeble rays enable us to see dimly the marvellous drawings on the walls, in those rooms unlighted from above.

As was the custom in those days, men of importance had many honorary titles, and Ti's exact station and calling are uncertain. It is evident that he possessed great power. His statue in the Cairo Museum shows him as a man of unusual intelligence and energy. With head upheld he seems to be striding through the world, knowing how to take and use the best things in life.

It is well named 'the happy tomb of Ti'. In the exquisite bas-reliefs which cover the seven rooms of his *mastaba* there is such restraint, proportion, above all such delicate modelling, such perfect rendering of every animal, bird and reptile, that each one is at once an individual portrait and a type. And the genius which grasped the individual in the race achieved, perhaps, the most notable work of art before the days of Greece, with a note of vivacious energy and pagan gaiety which men may well have had when the world was young.

The busy toilers of old Egypt are hard at work digging and tilling the Nile soil, gathering in the corn, slaving to satisfy the demands of their exacting masters.

Here we see the making of beer and bread, working in metal, building of boats, the catching and salting of fish; flax being cut, tied in sheaves on the backs of donkeys, unloaded, trodden by oxen, and counted by scribes, with their papyrus, ink palettes, and cases of reed pens; Courts of Justice being held, with the *fellaheen* brought for judgement. An orderly procession of cattle, birds, antelopes, game, marches onward to be changed by the magical formulæ into food for the Ka of Ti.

We see Ti seated with his wife, Nefer-Hoteps, beside him, watching the slow dancing of the East; Ti at his table eating, with a menu above his head of the food, drink, clothes, and perfumes which are at his disposition. There are sacrificial bulls for Ti, incense for Ti, statues of Ti in their shrines; a whole world filled with a serene ardour and activity. Through all these centuries, with what buoyancy of life has each followed his appointed task in the 'happy tomb of Ti'.

From *Wayfarers in the Libyan Desert,* 1912

The Downfall of the Nile

Pierre Loti

The Nile and Egypt are both part of one story. Here the French naval officer, novelist, travel writer – and often scornful eccentric – wonders at the past and pours his rage on the present. Although the Egypt of his idyll can never be recovered, much has been done to stop the worst excesses of Egypt's industrial revolution. But the 'enslaving of the old Nile' by dams and steam pumps, and later by bigger dams and electric pumps, cannot be reversed. Thus, the annual inundation of the Nile is now not even a memory. Nor is the man-driven equipment that raised the water to the thirsty land for millenia. Yet the river bank is still enchanting.

SOME THOUSANDS of years ago, at the beginning of our geological period, when the continents had taken, in the last great upheaval, almost the forms by which we now know them, and when the rivers began to trace their hesitating courses, it happened that the rains of a whole watershed of Africa were precipitated in one formidable torrent across the uninhabitable region which stretches from the Atlantic to the Indian Ocean, and is called the region of the deserts. And this enormous waterway, lost as it was in the sands, by and by regulated its course: it became the Nile, and with untiring patience set itself to its proper task of river, which in this accursed zone might well have seemed an impossible one. First it had to round all the blocks of granite scattered in its way in the high plains of Nubia; and then, and more especially, to deposit, little by little, successive layers of mud, to form a living artery, to create, as it were, a long, green ribbon in the midst of this infinite domain of death.

How long ago is it since the work of the great river began? There is something fearful in the thought. During the five thousand years of which we have any knowledge the incessant deposit of mud has scarcely widened this strip of inhabited Egypt, which at the most ancient period of history was almost as it is today. And as for the granite blocks on the plains of Nubia, how many thousands of years did it need to roll them and to polish them thus? In the times of the Pharaohs they already had their present rounded forms, worn smooth by the friction of the water, and the hieroglyphic inscriptions on their surfaces are not perceptibly effaced, though they have suffered the periodical inundation of the summer for some forty or fifty centuries!

It was an exceptional country, this valley of the Nile; marvellous and unique; fertile without rain, watered according to its need by the great river, without the help of any cloud. It knew not the dull days and the humidity under which we suffer, but kept always the changeless sky of the immense surrounding deserts, which exhaled no vapour that might dim the horizon. It was this eternal splendour of its light, no doubt, and this easiness of life, which brought forth here the first fruits of human thought. This same Nile, after having so patiently created the soil of Egypt, became also the father of that people, which led the way for all the others – like those early branches that one sees in spring, which shoot first from the stem, and sometimes die before the summer. It nursed that people, whose least vestiges we discover today with surprise and wonder; a people who, in the very dawn, in the midst of the original barbarity, conceived magnificently the infinite and the divine; who placed with such certainty and grandeur the first architectural lines, from which afterwards our architecture was to be derived; who laid the bases of art, of science, and of all knowledge.

Later on, when this beautiful flower of humanity was faded, the Nile, flowing always in the midst of its deserts, seems to have had for mission, during nearly two thousand years, the maintenance on its banks of a kind of immobility and desuetude, which was in a way a homage of respect for these stupendous relics. While the sand was burying the ruins of the temples and the battered faces of the colossi, nothing changed under this sky of changeless blue. The same cultivation proceeded on the banks as in the oldest ages; the same boats, with the same sails, went up and down the thread of water; the same songs kept time to the eternal human toil. The race of *fellahs*, the unconscious guardian of a prodigious past, slept on without desire of change, and almost without suffering. And time passed for Egypt in a great peace of sunlight and of death.

But today the foreigners are masters here, and have wakened the old Nile – wakened to enslave it. In less than twenty years they have disfigured its valley, which until then had preserved itself like a sanctuary. They have silenced its cataracts, captured its precious water by dams, to pour it afar off on plains that are become like marshes and already sully with their mists the crystal clearness of the sky. The ancient rigging no longer suffices to water the land under cultivation. Machines worked by steam, which draw the water more quickly, commence to rise along the banks, side by side with new factories. Soon there will scarcely be a river more dishonoured than this, by iron chimneys and thick, black smoke. And it is happening apace, this exploitation of the Nile – hastily, greedily, as in a hunt for spoils. And thus all its beauty disappears, for its monotonous course, through regions endlessly alike, won us only by its calm and its old-world mystery.

Poor Nile of the prodigies! One feels sometimes still its departing charm, stray corners of it remain intact. There are days of transcendent clearness, incomparable evenings, when one may still forget the ugliness and the smoke. But the classic expedition by *dahabiya*, the ascent of the river from Cairo to Nubia, will soon have ceased to be worth making.

Ordinarily this voyage is made in the winter, so that the traveller may follow the course of the sun as it makes its escape towards the southern hemisphere. The water then is low and the valley parched. Leaving the cosmopolitan town of modern Cairo, the iron bridges, and the pretentious hotels, with their flaunting inscriptions, it imparts a sense of sudden peacefulness to pass along the large and rapid waters of this river, between the curtains of palm trees on the banks, borne by a *dahabiya* where one is master and, if one likes, may be alone.

At first, for a day or two, the great haunting triangles of the pyramids seem to follow you, those of Dashur and that of Sakkarah succeeding to those of Gizeh. For a long time the horizon is disturbed by their gigantic silhouettes. As we recede from them, and they disengage themselves better from neighbouring things, they seem, as happens in the case of mountains, to grow higher. And when they have finally disappeared, we have still to ascend slowly and by stages some six hundred miles of river before we reach the first cataract. Our way lies through monotonous desert regions where the hours and days are marked chiefly by the variations of the wonderful light. Except for the phantasmagoria of the mornings and evenings, there is no outstanding feature on these dull-coloured banks, where may be seen, with never a change at all, the humble pastoral life of the *fellahs*. The sun is burning, the starlit nights clear and cold. A withering wind, which blows almost without ceasing from the north, makes you shiver as soon as the twilight falls.

One may travel for league after league along this slimy water and make head for days and weeks against its current – which glides everlastingly past the *dahabiya*, in little hurrying waves – without seeing this warm, fecundating river, compared with which our rivers of France are mere negligible streams, either diminish or increase or hasten. And on the right and left of us as we pass are unfolded indefinitely the two parallel chains of barren limestone, which imprison so narrowly the Egypt of the harvests: on the west that of the Libyan desert, which every morning the first rays of the sun tint with a rosy coral that nothing seems to dull; and in the east that of the desert of Arabia, which never fails in the evening to retain the light of the setting sun, and looks then like a mournful girdle of glowing embers. Sometimes the two parallel walls sheer off and give more room to the green fields, to the woods of palm-trees, and the little oases, separated by streaks of golden sand. Sometimes they approach so closely to the Nile that habitable Egypt is no wider than some two or three poor fields of corn, lying right on the water's edge, behind which the dead stones and the dead sands commence at once. And sometimes, even, the desert chain closes in so as to overhang the river with its reddish-white cliffs, which no rain ever comes to freshen, and in which, at different heights, gape the square holes leading to the habitations of the mummies. These mountains, which in the distance look so beautiful in their rose-colour, and make, as it were, interminable backcloths to all that happens on the river banks, were perforated, during some five thousand years, for the introduction of sarcophagi and now they swarm with old dead bodies.

And all that passes on the banks, indeed, changes as little as the background.

First there is that gesture, supple and superb, but always the same, of the women in their long black robes who come without ceasing to fill their long-necked jars and carry them away balanced on their veiled heads. Then the flocks which shepherds, draped in mourning, bring to the river to drink, goats and sheep and asses all mixed up together. And then the buffaloes, massive and mud-coloured, who descend calmly to bathe. And, finally, the great labour of the watering of the traditional *noria*, turned by a little bull with bandaged eyes and, above all, the *shadûf*, worked by men whose naked bodies stream with the cold water.

The *shadûfs* follow one another sometimes as far as the eye can see. It is strange to watch the movement – confused in the distance – of all these long rods which pump the water without ceasing, and look like the swaying of living antennæ. The same sight was to be seen along this river in the times of the Ramses. But suddenly, at some bend of the river, the old Pharaonic rigging disappears, to give place to a succession of steam machines, which, more even than the muscles of the *fellahs*, are busy at the water-drawing. Before long their blackish chimneys will make a continuous border to the tamed Nile.

Did one not know their bearings, the great ruins of this Egypt would pass unnoticed. With a few rare exceptions they lie beyond the green plains on the threshold of the solitudes. And against the changeless, rose-coloured background of these cliffs of the desert, which follow you during the whole of this tranquil navigation of some six hundred miles, are to be seen only the humble towns and villages of today, which have the neutral colour of the ground. Some openwork minarets dominate them – white spots above the prevailing dullness. Clouds of pigeons whirl round in the neighbourhood. And amongst the little houses, which are only cubes of mud, baked in the sun, the palm trees of Africa, either singly or in mighty clusters, rise superbly and cast on these little habitations the shade of their palms which sway in the wind. Not long ago, although indeed everything in these little towns was mournful and stagnant, one would have been tempted to stop in passing, drawn by that nameless peace that belonged to the Old East and to Islam. But, now, before the smallest hamlet – amongst the beautiful primitive boats, that still remain in great numbers, pointing their yards, like very long reeds, into the sky – there is always, for the meeting of the tourist boats, an enormous black pontoon, which spoils the whole scene by its presence and its great advertising inscription: 'Thomas Cook & Son (Egypt Ltd.)'. And, what is more, one hears the whistling of the railway, which runs mercilessly along the river, bringing from the Delta to the Soudan the hordes of European invaders. And to crown all, adjoining the station is inevitably some modern factory, throned there in a sort of irony, and dominating the poor crumbling things that still presume to tell of Egypt and of mystery.

And so now, except at the towns or villages which lead to celebrated ruins, we stop no longer. It is necessary to proceed farther and for the halt of the night to seek an obscure hamlet, a silent recess, where we may moor our *dahabiya* against the venerable earth of the bank.

And so one goes on, for days and weeks, between these two interminable cliffs of reddish chalk, filled with their hypogea and mummies, which are the walls of the valley of the Nile, and will follow us up to the first cataract, until our entrance into Nubia. There only will the appearance and nature of the rocks of the desert change, to become the more sombre granite out of which the Pharaohs carved their obelisks and the great figures of their gods.

We go on and on, ascending the thread of this eternal current, and the regularity of the wind, the persistent clearness of the sky, the monotony of the great river, which winds but never ends, all conspire to make us forget the hours and days that pass. However deceived and disappointed we may be at seeing the profanation of the river banks, here, nevertheless, isolated on the water, we do not lose the peace of being a wanderer, a stranger amongst an equipage of silent Arabs, who every evening prostrate themselves in confiding prayer.

And, moreover, we are moving towards the south, towards the sun, and every day has a more entrancing clearness, a more caressing warmth, and the bronze of the faces that we see on our way takes on a deeper tint.

And then too one mixes intimately with the life of the river bank, which is still so absorbing and, at certain hours, when the horizon is unsullied by the smoke of pit-coal, recalls you to the days of artless toil and healthy beauty. In the boats that meet us, half-naked men, revelling in their movement, in the sun and air, sing, as they ply their oars, those songs of the Nile that are as old as Thebes or Memphis. When the wind rises there is a riotous unfurling of sails, which, stretched on their long yards, give to the *dahabiyas* the air of birds in full flight. Bending right over in the wind, they skim along with a lively motion, carrying their cargoes of men and beasts and primitive things. Women are there draped still in the ancient fashion, and sheep and goats, and sometimes piles of fruit and gourds, and sacks of grain. Many are laden to the water's edge with those earthenware jars, unchanged for three thousand years, which the *fellaheens* know how to place on their heads with so much grace – and one sees these heaps of fragile pottery gliding along the water as if carried by the gigantic wings of a gull. And in the far-off, almost fabulous, days the life of the mariners of the Nile had the same aspect, as is shown by the bas-reliefs on the oldest tombs; it required the same play of muscles and of sails; was accompanied no doubt by the same songs, and was subject to the withering caress of this same desert wind. And then, as now, the same unchanging rose coloured the continuous curtain of the mountains.

But all at once there is a noise of machinery, and whistlings, and in the air, which was just now so pure, rise noxious columns of black smoke. The modern steamers are coming, and throw into disorder the flotillas of the past: colliers that leave great eddies in their wake, or perhaps a wearisome lot of those three-decked tourist boats, which make a great noise as they plough the water, and are laden for the most part with ugly women, snobs and imbeciles.

Poor, poor Nile! which reflected formerly on its warm mirror the utmost of earthly splendour, which bore in its time so many barques of gods and goddesses in procession behind the golden barge of Amen, and knew in the dawn of the ages only an impeccable purity, alike of the human form and of architectural design! What a downfall is here! To be awakened from that disdainful sleep of twenty centuries and made to carry the floating barracks of Thomas Cook & Son, to feed sugar factories and to exhaust itself in nourishing with its mud the raw material for English cotton-stuffs.

From *The Downfall of the Nile,* 1909

Give me Arabic!

Dr Robert Richardson

O! FOR THE GIFT of tongues is most fervently prayed by the traveller, who feels himself transported into the midst of grand Cairo, with an anxiety to know this boast of the Saracenic conquest, and to converse with the inhabitants of this wonderful city, celebrated as the largest, richest, and most populous in the universe. Greek and Latin to the dogs! Give me Arabic and Turkish; but above all, give me Arabic that I may speak, and hear, and know if the people among whom I have come, think and feel, love and hate, like those whom I have left. It is an easy matter to call on spirits from the vasty deep; but no easy matter to make them come at the call. The days of inspiration are gone, and the object for which it was imparted accomplished; and hard labour is now the lot of man before he can speak in a language different from his own. With the prospect of residing here for but a few days, or at the very utmost of hibernating during the months of winter, it would have been an unprofitable waste of time to set about learning the language, previously to holding any intercourse with the people; for before we could have acquired it, the opportunity of using it would have been superseded by our departure, and we should have known a little of Arabic, but nothing of the Arabians, or inhabitants of Cairo. It was requisite, however, to know something of the language, seeing it was impossible, without both a great deal of expense and formality, to have an interpreter always at hand. And, therefore, I set myself, as soon as possible, to acquire a store of vocables, which might enable me to name the object which I wished to obtain, or about which I wished to be informed; in order to accomplish this, I wrote down the Arabic word for every object as it came in my way, or occurred to my recollection, and committed them to memory, as a task which I often repeated in the course of the day, and always at night when I laid my head upon my pillow, and in the morning before I arose.

It is inconceivable how words accumulated, and how much in a very little time I could understand of their conversation. Seeing my anxiety to learn, the Arabs, from the highest to the lowest, were equally willing to teach, and having once acquired as much Arabic as enabled me to ask the name of this, that, or the other object, I in a little time became pretty independent, and could go on with a native, and add to my store of words, though no interpreter was present. Besides the advantage of being able to hold an intercourse with the natives, this was a source of never-failing amusement, the mind was constantly on the whet, and I never felt languid in the presence of an Arab. Without being able to utter a few words in the vernacular tongue, a man may adopt their dress, shoulder his pipe, cultivate his beard with all the paraphernalia of the eastern costume; yet still he smells as an exotic, and is but an unwelcome guest in their most ordinary coteries; being viewed not only as a stranger, but as a man that wishes to continue so.

From *Travels along the Mediterranean,* 1822

2
Alexandria and the Delta

An Alexandrian Street
Robert Curzon

Alexandria was for centuries a world-class port, drawing in trade from all around the Mediterranean and beyond, and linking trade across the desert to the East from deep Egypt and the rest of Africa. With trade came people. On his first night in Egypt in 1833, Robert Curzon sat at a window of his room and contemplated humanity and the street below.

IT WAS TOWARDS the end of July 1833 that I took a passage from Malta to Alexandria in a merchant vessel called the *Fortuna*; for in those days there were no steam-packets traversing every sea, with almost the same rapidity and accuracy as railway carriages on shore. We touched on our way at Navarino to sell some potatoes to the splendidly dressed and half-starved population of the Morea, numbers of whom we found lounging about in a temporary wooden bazaar, where there was nothing to sell. In various parts of the harbour the wrecks of the Turkish and Egyptian ships of war, stripped of their outer coverings, and looking like the gigantic skeletons of antediluvian animals, gave awful evidence of the destruction which had taken place not very long before in the battle between the Christian and Mohammedan fleets in this calm, land-locked harbour.

On the 31st we found ourselves approaching the castle of Alexandria, and were soon hailed by some people in a curious-looking pilot-boat with a lateen sail. The pilot was an old man with a turban and a long grey beard, and sat cross-legged in the stern of his boat. We looked at him with vast interest, as the first live specimen we had seen of an Arab sailor. He was just the sort of man that I imagine Sinbad the Sailor must have been.

Having by his directions been steered safely into the harbour, we cast anchor not far from the shore, a naked dusty plain, which the blazing sun seemed to dare anyone to cross, on pain of being shrivelled up immediately. The intensity of the heat was tremendous; the pitch melted in the seams of the deck; we could scarcely bear it even when we were under the awning. Malta was hot enough, but the temperature there was cool in comparison to the fiery furnace in which we were at present grilling. However, there was no help for it; so, having got our luggage on shore, we sweltered through the streets to an inn called the Tre Anchore – the only hotel in Africa, I believe, in those days. It was a dismal little place, frequented by the captains of merchant vessels, who, not being hot enough already, raised the temperature of their blood by drinking brandy and water, arrack, and other combustibles, in a dark oven-like room below stairs.

We took possession of all the rooms upstairs, of which the principal one was long and narrow, with two windows at the end, opening on to a covered balcony or verandah: this overlooked the principal street and the bazaar. Here my companion and I soon stationed ourselves, and watched the novel and curious scene below; and strange indeed to the eye of an European, when for the first time he enters an Oriental city, is all he sees around him. The picturesque dresses, the buildings, the palm trees, the camels, the people of various nations, with their long beards, their arms, and turbans, all unite to form a picture which is indelibly fixed in the memory. Things which have since become perfectly familiar to us were then utterly incomprehensible, and we had no one to explain them to us, for the one waiter of the poor inn, who was darting about in his shirt-sleeves after the manner of all waiters, never extended his answers to our questions beyond 'Si, Signore', so we got but little information from him; however, we did not make use of our eyes the less for that.

Among the first things we noticed was the number of half-naked men who went running about, each with something like a dead pig under his arm, shouting out 'Mother! mother!' with a doleful voice. These were the *sakis,* or water-carriers, with their goatskins of the precious element, a bright brass cupful of which they sell for a small coin to the thirsty passengers. An old man with a fan in his hand made of a palm branch, who was crumpled up in the corner of a sort of booth among a heap of dried figs, raisins, and dates, just opposite our window, was an object of much speculation to us how he got in, and how he would ever manage to get out of the niche into which he was so closely wedged. He was the merchant, as the *Arabian Nights* would call him, or the shopkeeper as we should say, who sat there cross-legged among his wares waiting patiently for a customer, and keeping off the flies in the meanwhile, as in due time we discovered that all merchants did in all countries of the East. Soon there came slowly by a long procession of men on horseback with golden bridles and velvet trappings, and women muffled up in black silk wrappers: how they could bear them, hot as it was, astonished us. These ladies sat upon a pile of cushions placed so high above the backs of the donkeys on which they rode that their feet rested on the animals' shoulders. Each donkey was led by one man, while another walked by its side with his hand upon the crupper. With the ladies were two little boys covered with diamonds, mounted on huge fat horses, and ensconced in high-backed Mameluke saddles made of silver gilt. These boys we afterwards found out were being conducted in state to a house of their relations, where the rite of circumcision was to be performed. Our attention was next called to something like a four-poster bed, with pink gauze curtains, which advanced with dignified slowness preceded by a band of musicians, who raised a dire and fearful discord by the aid of various windy engines. This was a canopy, the four poles of which were supported by men, who held it over the heads of a bride and her two bridesmaids or friends, who walked on each side of her. The bride was not veiled in the usual way, as her friends were, but was muffled up in Cashmere shawls from head to foot. Something there was on the top of her head which gleamed like gold or jewels, but the rest of her person was so effectually wrapped up and concealed that no one could tell whether she was pretty or ugly, fat or thin, old or young; and although we gave her credit for all the charms which should adorn a bride, we rejoiced when the villainous band of music which accompanied her turned round a corner and went out of hearing.

Some miserable-looking black slaves caught our attention, clothed each in a piece of Isabel-coloured canvas and led by a well-dressed man, who had probably just bought them. Then a great personage came by on horseback, with a number of mounted attendants and some men on foot, who cleared the way before him, and struck everybody on the head with their sticks who did not get out of the way fast enough. These blows were dealt all round in the most unceremonious manner; but what appeared to us extraordinary was, that all these beaten people did not seem to care for being beat. They looked neither angry nor affronted, but only grinned and rubbed their shoulders, and moved on one side to let the train of the great man pass by. Now, if this were done in London, what a ferment would it create! What speeches would be made about tyranny and oppression! What a capital thing some high-minded and independent patriot would make of it! How he would call a meeting to defend the rights of the subject! And how he would get his admirers to vote him a piece of plate for his noble and glorious exertions! Here nobody minded the thing; they took no heed of the indignity; and I verily believe my friend and I, who were safe up at the window, were the only persons in the place who felt any annoyance.

The prodigious multitude of donkeys formed another strange feature in the scene. There were hundreds of them, carrying all sorts of things in panniers; and some of the smallest were ridden by men so tall that they were obliged to hold up their legs that their feet might not touch the ground. Donkeys, in short, are the carts of Egypt and the hackney-coaches of Alexandria.

In addition to the donkeys, long strings of ungainly-looking camels were continually passing, generally preceded by a donkey, and accompanied by swarthy men clad in a short shirt, with a red and yellow handkerchief tied in a peculiar way over their heads, and wearing sandals; these savage-looking people were Bedouins, or Arabs of the desert. A very truculent set they seemed to be, and all of them were armed with a long crooked knife and a pistol or two, stuck in a red leathern girdle. They were thin, gaunt and dirty, and strode along looking fierce and independent. There was something very striking in the appearance of these untamed Arabs: I had never pictured to myself that anything so like a wild beast could exist in human form. The motions of their half-naked bodies were singularly free and light, and they looked as if they could climb, and run, and leap over anything. The appearance of many of the older Arabs, with their long white beard and their ample cloak of camel's hair, called an *abba*, is majestic and venerable. It was the first time that I had seen these 'Children of the Desert', and the quickness of their eyes, their apparent freedom from all restraint, and their disregard of any conventional manners, struck me forcibly. An English gentleman in a round hat, and a tight neck-handkerchief and boots, with white gloves and a little cane in his hand, was a style of man so utterly and entirely unlike a Bedouin Arab, that I could hardly conceive the possibility of their being only different species of the same animal.

After we had dined, being tired with the heat and the trouble we had in getting our luggage out of the ship, I resolved to retire to bed at an early hour, and on going to the window to have another look at the crowd, I was surprised to find that there was scarcely anybody left in the streets, for these primitive people all go to bed when it gets dark, as the birds do; and except a few persons walking home with paper lanterns in their hands, the place seemed almost entirely deserted.

From *Visits to Monasteries of the Levant,* 1849

Alexandria: the City of Words

Michael Haag

To his guidebooks on Egypt, Michael Haag brings deep knowledge and love, both of ancient and modern history and of people and place. With him as your guide, you may be able to get a real understanding of Egypt.

I FIRST WENT TO Alexandria in 1973, shortly before the October war, when visitors and guidebooks were scarce. Instead, in a Cairo bookshop I bought a neglected copy of Lawrence Durrell's *Justine* and began rereading it as the train drove through the widening Delta.

It is strange to explore a city through the pages of a novel. I was not led to Pompey's pillar or round the Greco-Roman Museum, but to the mirrors and splintered palms of the Cecil Hotel, the café tables at Pastroudis, and along Tatwig Street towards its vanished child bordellos. I was sad to have missed Justine at the Cecil, but then I had not expected to meet Cleopatra either. I knew that Alexandria had changed.

The city was much as Durrell describes her in his Introduction to this edition. The Suez fiasco of 1956 had unhappily though not surprisingly led to a convulsive rejection of the western presence in Egypt. And even earlier the Second World War must have tolled the death of an era when 'Alexandria was the foremost port of Egypt, and a hive of activity for the country's cotton brokers ... with wide streets flanked by palms and flame trees, large gardens, stylish villas, neat new buildings, and above all, room to breathe. Life was easy. Labour was cheap. Nothing was impossible, especially when it involved one's comfort' (as Jacqueline Carol remembers in her appropriately titled *Cocktails and Camels*). We do not get away with it so easily now.

Of course for that sort of world you could have gone to Los Angeles. What made Alexandria special was its cosmopolitan population: Greeks, Italians, British, French, Armenians, White

Russians mixing with one another, though rarely mixing with Egyptians. Cavafy, for example, never visited an Egyptian house and knew hardly any Arabic, and this in a city where fifty thousand Greeks (and eighty thousand foreigners in all) lived among nearly half a million Egyptians. Still, the families of many of these foreigners had lived in Alexandria for generations, and the Greeks particularly had rooted their culture, as they had long ago, on this distant littoral.

Forster wrote to a friend in 1917: 'The Greeks are the only community here that attempt to understand what they are talking about, and to be with them is to re-enter, however imperfectly, the Academic world. They are the only important people east of Ventimiglia – dirty, dishonest, unaristocratic, roving, and warped by Hellenic and Byzantine dreams – but they do effervesce intellectually, they do have creative desires, and one comes round to them in the end.'

Forster's great discovery was the poet Constantine Cavafy. Before they met, Forster wrote: 'One can't dislike Alex … because it is impossible to dislike either the sea or stones. But it consists of nothing else as far as I can gather: just a clean cosmopolitan town by some blue water.' But later, in his Preface to this book, he writes of another dimension: 'The "sights" of Alexandria are in themselves not interesting, but they fascinate when we approach them through the past.' It was Cavafy who supplied the imaginative link between past and present, as Forster acknowledges by placing *The God Abandons Antony* between his History and his Guide.

But Cavafy did more than resurrect an historical city. As he himself wrote in 1907: 'By now I've got used to Alexandria,' – he was born and had lived there almost all his life – 'and it's very likely that even if I were rich I'd stay here. But in spite of this, how the place disturbs me. What trouble, what a burden small cities are – what a lack of freedom.' Yet in 1910 he published *The City*; these are its last few lines:

> You'll always end up in this city. Don't hope for things elsewhere:
> There's no ship for you, there's no road.
> Now that you've wasted your life here, in this small corner,
> you've destroyed it everywhere in the world.

Alexandria has not wasted your life, that you have done yourself. The city is what you make her, as you would make any city, and so there is no escape in blaming Alexandria for your misfortunes. The poet made Alexandria a metaphor on which later he, Forster and Durrell would build many possible Alexandrias.

Forster says Alexandria was suspiciously like a funk-hole, but this was a funk-hole in which he found love, and much else. He notes the peculiarity of the site's geography, to which the city owed its founding and the direction of its development, physically, culturally and historically. On the verge of sea and land, Greece and Egypt, neither simply one nor the other, the city mediated between opposites. Reconciling the irreconcilable became the essence of her existence, as when early Christian Alexandria disputed man's relationship with and exact distance from God. She has always been an explosive city, known for her riots and passions, struggling to contain great tensions.

In a 1923 review in the *Times Literary Supplement* of Forster's *Pharos and Pharillon* (*Alexandria* has never been published until now in Britain, but the review can serve to comment on it) Middleton Murry says: 'To this dubious race' of people with a strange angle of vision 'Mr Forster indisputably belongs. Being a dubious character, he goes off to a dubious city, to that portion of the inhabited world where there is most obviously a bend in the spiritual dimension … where the atmosphere is preternaturally keen and there is a lucid confusion of the categories. At this point a spinning eddy marks the convergence of two worlds, and in the vortex contradictions are reconciled. It is nothing less than a crack in the human universe. Mr Forster wanders off to put his ear to it. He finds Mr Cavafy already engaged in the enterprise. So they listen together.'

Following a novel through the streets of Alexandria may lead you to strange places but, like following Bloom through Dublin, you get glimpses of the city that really matter. *Alexandria* still works well as a guide, not least because it works like a novel, or like Cavafy's poetry, commanding time and space and intimacies. On another visit I had it with me. Near the Ramleh tram terminus I came to what in Forster's day was a 'featureless spot' (now, as it happens, the square which lies before the Cecil Hotel) and discovered that here Cleopatra began the Caesarium in honour of Antony. And then, told to look at p.28 of the History, I read: 'Voluptuous but watchful, she treated her new lover as she had treated her old. She never bored him, and since grossness means monotony she sharpened his mind to those more delicate delights, where sense verges into spirit. Her infinite variety lay in that. She was the last of a secluded and subtle race, she was a flower that Alexandria had taken three hundred years to produce and that eternity cannot wither, and she unfolded herself to a simple but intelligent Roman soldier.'

Yes, I had arrived far, far too late at the Cecil Hotel 'stripped of all its finery and echoing like a barn with the seawind sweeping under the doors and through the windows', and like Durrell and like Antony before him I reflected on that exile to which we are abandoned by the passage of time.

This is what haunts you in Alexandria. If more of the ancient city survived it would haunt you less. Unlike Rome or Athens with their monuments extant, Alexandria is all intimation: here (some spot) is where Alexander lay entombed; here Cleopatra committed suicide; here the Library, the Serapeum, etc... and there is nothing physically there. 'I stepped laughing out into the street once more to make a circuit of the quarter which still hummed with the derisive, concrete life of men and women... I began to walk slowly, deeply bemused, and to describe to myself in words this whole quarter of Alexandria for I knew that soon it would be forgotten and revisited only by those whose memories had been appropriated by the fevered city, clinging to the minds of old men like traces of perfume upon a sleeve: Alexandria, the capital of Memory.' (*Justine*, p.152)

Forster's *Alexandria*, with time in one section, place in the other, and its many invitations to flip between the two, is a Guide to Memory, as the *Alexandria Quartet* is in a sense the novel of the guide – *Justine*, *Balthazar* and *Mountolive* the spatial dimensions, while *Clea* unleashes time. Not since the foreign community has been expelled from the city has Alexandria ceased being the capital of memory. Naguib Mahfouz, the outstanding Arab novelist who has made Cairo his literary universe, chose Alexandria as the setting for his criticism of the Nasser regime's excesses and failures.

'Alexandria. At last, Alexandria, Lady of the Dew. Bloom of white nimbus. Bosom of radiance, wet with sky-water. Core of nostalgia steeped in honey and tears' (*Miramar*, p.1).

The pride and confidence Egypt won in the 1973 war led to the inauguration that year of the Open Door (*Infitah*) policy inviting foreign investment, and to the 1979 peace treaty with Israel. As Alexandria suffered after the Suez invasion, so rapprochement with the West and liberalisation at home have slowly revived something of the city's former sparkle. Lawrence Durrell's description of Alexandria in 1977 is now, I think, overly severe, and in any case can only apply to that formerly European part of the city, to those eighty thousand memories. The old Arab quarter along the silted-up Heptastadion remains colourful and warm as it has always been, even when it only lived on the edge of foreign consciousness.

On one side of Midan Ramleh is a Greek taverna, on the other, beneath what were once the offices of the Third Circle of Irrigation where Cavafy worked, is a nightclub, Athinaios, where some of the city's remaining Greeks still gather, listening to rough, wailing, amplified *rembetika* music and smashing plates with abandon. All round lies Iskanderia. For someone who knew it as a cosmopolitan city and remembers old haunts and old friends now vanished, the uncomprehended Arabic of its people today may only translate into emptiness.

But there would be nothing new in this alienation: 'No, I don't think you would like it,' Durrell wrote to Miller in spring 1944, '… this smashed-up broken-down shabby Neapolitan town, with its Levantine mounds of houses peeling in the sun. A sea flat, dirty brown and waveless rubbing the port. Arabic, Coptic, Greek, Levant French; no music, no art, no real gaiety. A saturated middle European boredom laced with drink and Packards and beach-cabins. NO SUBJECT OF CONVERSATION EXCEPT MONEY. Even love is thought of in money terms… No, if one could write a single line of anything that had a human smell to it here, one would be a genius.'

From the introduction to E. M. Forster's
Alexandria: a History and a Guide, 1982 edition

Alexandria, I am here

Naguib Mahfouz

Pension Miramar, in the minds of many, now stands for Alexandria. Although the hotel only existed in fiction, it has become more real than many of the real places in Alexandria. It is Alexandria. Like the city, it houses visitors from different national and cultural backgrounds and is run by an old Greek-Alexandrian woman, who is the 'Madonna'. Nostalgic hotel residents rally around her periodically to revive their memories, relive the past in the present and carry on with their lives in mixed Alexandrian fashion.

ALEXANDRIA. AT LAST. Alexandria, Lady of the Dew. Bloom of white nimbus. Bosom of radiance, wet with sky water. Core of nostalgia steeped in honey and tears.

The massive old building confronts me once again. How could I fail to recognize it? I have always known it. And yet it regards me as if we had shared no past. Walls paintless from the damp, it commands and dominates the tongue of land, planted with palms and leafy acacias, that protrudes out into the Mediterranean to a point where in season you can hear shotguns cracking incessantly.

My poor stooped body cannot stand up to the potent young breeze out here. Not anymore.

Mariana, my dear Mariana, let us hope you're still where we could always find you. You must be. There's not much time left; the world is changing fast and my weak eyes under their thinning white brows can no longer comprehend what they see.

Alexandria, I am here.

On the fourth floor I ring the bell of the flat. The little judas opens, showing Mariana's face. Much changed, my dear! It's dark on the landing; she does not recognize me. Her white face and golden hair gleam in the light from a window open somewhere behind her.

'Pension Miramar?'

'Yes, monsieur?'

'Do you have any vacant rooms?'

The door opens. The bronze statue of the Madonna receives me. In the air of the place is a kind of fragrance that has haunted me.

We stand looking at each other. She is tall and slim, with her golden hair, and seems to be in good health, though her shoulders are a little bowed and the hair is obviously dyed. Veins show through the skin of her hands and forearms; there are telltale wrinkles at the corners of her mouth. You must be sixty-five at least, my dear. But there is still something of the old glamour left. I wonder if you'll remember me.

She looks me over. At first she examines me; then the blue eyes blink. Ah, you remember! And my self comes back to me.

'Oh! It's you.'

'Madame.'

We shake hands warmly – 'Goodness me! Amer Bey! Monsieur Amer!' – and she laughs out loud with emotion *(the long feminine laugh of the fishwives of Anfushi!)*, throwing all formality to the winds. Together we sit down on the ebony settee beneath the Madonna, our reflections gleaming on the front of a glassed bookcase that has always stood in this hall, if only as an ornament. I look around.

'The place hasn't changed a bit.'

'Oh, but it has,' she protests. 'It's been redecorated a number of times. And there are many new things. The chandelier. The screen. And the radio.'

'I'm so glad to have found you here, Mariana. Thank heaven you're in good health.'

'And so are you, Monsieur Amer – touch wood.'

'I'm not at all well. I'm suffering from colitis and prostate trouble. But God be thanked all the same!'

'Why have you come here now? The season's over.'

'I've come to stay. How long is it since I saw you last?'

'Since … since … did you say "to stay"?'

'Yes, my dear. I can't have seen you for some twenty years.'

'It's true. You never turned up once during all that time.'

'I was busy.'

'I bet you came to Alexandria often enough.'

'Sometimes. But I was too busy. You know what a journalist's life is like.'

'I also know what men are like.'

'My dear Mariana, you are Alexandria to me.'

'You're married, of course.'

'No. Not yet.'

'And when will you marry, monsieur?' she asks teasingly.

'No wife, no family. And I've retired.' I reply somewhat irritably. 'I'm finished.' She encourages me to go on with a wave of her hand. 'I felt the call of my birthplace. Alexandria. And since I've no relations I've turned to the only friend the world has left me.'

'It's nice to find a friend in such loneliness.'

'Do you remember the good old days?'

'It's all gone,' she says wistfully.

'But we have to go on living,' I murmur.

When we start discussing the rent, however, she can still drive as hard a bargain as ever. The pension is all she has; she has had to take in winter guests, even if they are those awful students; and to get them she is forced to depend on middlemen and waiters in the hotels. She says it all with the sadness of humbled pride; and she puts me in number six, away from the seafront on the far side, at a reasonable rent, though I can retain my room in the summer only if I pay at the special summer rate for vacationers.

We settle everything in a few minutes, including the obligatory breakfast. She proves as good a businesswoman as ever, notwithstanding sweet memories and all that. When I tell her I've left my luggage at the station, she laughs.

'You were not so sure you'd find Mariana. Now you'll stay here with me forever.'

I look at my hand and think of the mummies in the Egyptian Museum.

My room is pleasant enough, quite as good as any of the seaward rooms I used to occupy in the past. I have all the furniture I need. Comfortable, old-fashioned chairs. But there is no place for the books; I'd better leave them in the box and take out only a few at a time. The light here is not very good, a sort of constant twilight. My window opens onto a big air shaft, and the service stairs are so close that I can hear alley cats chasing up and down and cooks and chambermaids carrying on their affairs.

I made the round of all the rooms where I used to stay in summer; the pink, the violet, and the blue, all vacant now. There was a time when I stayed in each a summer or more, and though the old mirrors, the rich carpets, the silver lamps, and the cut-glass chandeliers are gone, a certain faded elegance lingers still on the papered walls and in the high ceilings, which are adorned with cherubs.

Mariana sighs and I see her false teeth.

'Mine was a very select pension.'

'Glory be to Him who remaineth.'

'These days, my guests in winter are mostly students. And in summer I take just anybody.'

'Amer Bey, will you please put in a good word for me?'

'Your Excellency,' I said to the Pasha, 'the man is not very efficient, but he lost his son in the Cause and should be nominated for the seat.'

He backed my proposal. God rest his soul. My great master. He loved me and read everything I wrote with the keenest interest.

'You', he said to me once, 'are the nation's throbbing cur.'

He said cur for core, God rest his soul, and it became a standing joke. A few old colleagues from the National Party heard the story and they'd always greet me with 'Hello, you cur!' Those were the days – the glory of working for the Cause, independence, the nation! Amer Wagdi was someone indeed – full of favours for friends, but a man to be feared and avoided by enemies.

In my room I reminisce, read, or sleep. In the hall I can talk to Mariana or listen to the radio. If I need further entertainment there is the Miramar Café downstairs. It is not likely that I should see anyone I know, even in the Trianon. All my friends are gone. The good old days are over.

Alexandria, I know you in winter: you empty your streets and your squares at sunset, leaving them to solitude, wind, and rain, while your inner rooms are filled with chatter and warmth.

'"... that old man shrouding his mummified form in a black suit that dates from the Flood." None of your long-winded rhetoric, please!' said that nonentity of an editor, so typical of these days. 'Give us something a jet-age traveller can read.'

A jet-age traveller. What would you know, you fat moronic puppet? Writing is for men who can think and feel, not mindless sensation seekers out of nightclubs and bars. But these are bad times. We are condemned to work with upstarts, clowns who no doubt got their training in a circus and then turned to journalism as the appropriate place to display their tricks.

I sit in an armchair wearing my dressing gown. Mariana reclines on the ebony settee beneath the statue of the Madonna. Dance music is being played on the European programme. I would rather listen to something different, but I hate to disturb her. She is completely absorbed in the music, just as she always used to be, nodding her head to its beat.

'We've always been friends, Mariana.'

'Yes, always.'

'But we never made love, not once.'

'You went in for your plump countrywomen. Don't deny it.'

'Except for that one incident. Do you remember?'

'Yes, you brought home a Frenchwoman and I insisted that you sign the register as Monsieur and Madame Amer.'

'I was discouraged by the multitude of your aristocratic admirers.'

She beams with pleasure. Mariana, let's hope I may be the first of us two to go; no more shifting quarters. There you are, a living proof that the past was no illusion, even from the days of my great master down to the present moment.

'My dear sir, I'd like to say goodbye.' He looked at me, as usual not bothering to disguise his impatience. 'At my age, I think I should retire.'

'We shall certainly miss you,' he answered with ill-concealed relief, 'but I hope you'll have a good time.'

That was all. A page of the newspaper's history turned without a word of goodbye, a farewell party, or even a jet-age snippet at the bottom of a page. Nothing. The buggers! A man has no value to them at all unless he plays football or something.

As she sits there under the statue of the Madonna, I look at her and say, 'Helen in her prime would not have looked as marvellous!'

She laughs. 'Before you arrived, I used to sit here all alone waiting for someone, anyone I knew, to come through the door. I was always in dread of…of getting one of my kidney attacks.'

'I'm sorry. But where are your people?'

'They've gone, every one of them.' She purses her lips, showing her wrinkles. 'I couldn't leave – where should I go? I was born here. I've never even seen Athens. And after all, who'd want to nationalize a little pension like this?'

'Let us be true to our word and devoted to our work and may love, not law, control man's dealings with man.' Look at us now. It was a kindness of God to give you death when he did – with a couple of statues as your memorial.

'Egypt's your home. And there's no place like Alexandria.'

The wind plays outside. The darkness steals up quietly. She rises, switches on two bulbs of the chandelier, and returns to her seat.

'I was a lady,' she says. 'A lady in the full sense of the word.'

'You're still a lady, Mariana.'

'Do you still drink the way you used to?'

'Just one drink at dinner. I eat very little. That's why I can still move around.'

'Monsieur Amer, I don't know how you can say there's no place like Alexandria. It's all changed. The streets nowadays are infested with *canaille.*'

'My dear, it had to be claimed by its people.' I try to comfort her and she retorts sharply.

'But *we* created it.'

'And you, do you still drink the way you did in the old days?'

'No! Not a drop. I've got kidney trouble.'

'We should make two fine museum pieces. But promise me you won't go before I do.'

'Monsieur Amer, the first revolution killed my first husband. The second took my money and drove out my people. Why?'

'You've got enough, thank God. *We* are your people now. This sort of thing is happening everywhere.'

'What a strange world.'

'Can't you tune the radio to the Arabic station?'

'No. Only for Umm Kulthum.'

'As you wish, my dear.'

'Tell me, why do people hurt one another? And why do we grow old?'

I smile, not saying a word. I look around at the walls, which are inscribed with Mariana's history. There is the Captain's portrait, in full dress, heavy-whiskered – her first husband, probably her first and only love, killed in the Revolution of 1919. On the other wall, above the bookcases, is the portrait of her old mother, a teacher. At the opposite end of the hall, beyond the screen, is her second husband, a rich grocer, 'the Caviar King', owner of the Ibrahimiya Palace. One day he went bankrupt and killed himself.

'When did you start this business of the pension?'

'You mean, when I was forced to open a boarding-house? In 1925. A black year.'

'Here I am, almost a prisoner in my house, and the hypocrites queue up to flatter the King.'

'All lies, Your Excellency.'

'I thought the Revolution had cured them of their weaknesses.'

'The true heart of the nation is on your side. Shall I read you tomorrow's editorial?'

She sits there massaging her face with a piece of lemon.

'I was a lady, Monsieur Amer. Living the easy life and loving it. Lights, luxury, fine clothes, and big parties. I would grace a salon with my presence. Like the sun.'

'I saw you then.'

'You saw me only as a landlady.'

'But you were still like the sun.'

'My guests did belong to the elite. But that has never consoled me for such a comedown.'

'You're still a lady. In every sense.'

She shakes her head. 'What happened to all your old friends in the Wafd?'

'What was fated to happen.'

'Why did you never marry, Monsieur Amer?'

'Sheer bad luck. I wish I had a family. And you as well!'

'Neither of my husbands could give me children.'

More than likely it was you who couldn't conceive. A pity, my dear. Isn't the whole purpose of our existence to bring children into the world?

That big house in Khan Gaafer, which slowly turned into a hotel: it looked like a little castle, its old courtyard standing where a path now runs to Khan al-Khalili. The image of the place is engraved in my memory – the ancient houses around it, the old Club – and in my heart. *A memorial to the ecstasy of first love. Burning love. Broken. Frustrated.* The turban and the white beard and the cruel lips saying 'No.' Blindly, fanatically dealing the blow, killing love, whose power has been with us for a million years, since even before the birth of faith.

'Sir, may I ask for your daughter's hand?' Silence. Between us stood a cup of coffee, untouched. 'I am a journalist. I have a good income. My father was the keeper of the mosque of Sidi Abu al-Abbas al-Morsy.'

'He was a pious man, God rest his soul,' he said, taking up his prayer beads. 'My son, you were one of us. You studied in al-Azhar once. But don't let us forget that you were expelled.'

That old story, when would they forget it?

'Sir, that was a long time ago. They'd expel you for the least thing – for being young and full of spirit, for playing in an orchestra, or just for asking innocent questions.'

'Wise men accused you of a terrible crime.'

'Who can judge a man's faith, when only God sees through our souls?'

'Those who take God's words for a guide.'

Goddamnit! Who can be sure of his faith? To His prophets God revealed Himself once, but we need to see Him even more: when we consider our place in this enormous house we call the world, our heads begin to reel.

From *Miramar*, 1978

The Evenings of Ramadan

Amitav Ghosh

As a student of anthropology researching the history of an Indian trader and his slave who had travelled in the Middle East hundreds of years earlier, the Indian Amitav Ghosh landed in a small village in Lower Egypt. At Lataifa he encountered the medieval customs his predecessors had come across, living alongside modern aspirations and discontents. His account focuses on how the traditional and the modern blend, coexist and interact in the lives of the twentieth-century fellahin.

SOON THE MONTH of Ramadan arrived and I began to think of taking a holiday. First I would go to Alexandria, I decided, to talk to Doctor Issa, and to see whether I could make arrangements for moving out of Abu-'Ali's house. After that I would go to Cairo: I had spent one night there when I first arrived, but I had seen nothing other than the airport, and the station. Now at last, the time had come to pay the city a proper visit.

As the days passed the thought of my trip became ever more exciting. We were then well into Ramadan, and I was one of the handful of people in the hamlet who were not fasting. I had wanted to join in the fast, but everyone insisted, 'No, you can't fast, you're not Muslim – only Muslims fast at Ramadan.' And so, being reminded of my exclusion every day by the drawn, thirsty faces around me, the thought of Cairo and Alexandria, and the proximity of others among the excluded, grew ever more attractive.

From the very first day of the lunar month the normal routines of the village had undergone a complete change: it was as though a segment of time had been picked from the calendar and turned inside out. Early in the morning, a good while before sunrise, a few young men would go from house to house waking everyone for the *suhûr*, the early morning meal. After that, as the day progressed, a charged lassitude would descend upon Lataifa. To ease the rigours of the fast people would try to finish all their most pressing bits of work early in the morning, while the sun was still low in the sky; it was impossible to do anything strenuous on an empty stomach and parched throat once the full heat of the day had set in. By noon the lanes of the hamlet would be still, deserted. The women would be in their kitchens and oven-rooms, getting their meals ready for the breaking of the fast at sunset. The men would sit in the shade of trees, or in their doorways, fanning themselves. Their mouths and lips would sometimes acquire thin white crusts, and often, as the hours wore on, their tempers would grow brittle.

I often wondered whether there were any people in the village who were occasionally delinquent in their observance of the fast. It was true that the most vulnerable people – pregnant women, young children, the sick, the elderly, and so on – were exempted by religious law, but even for those of sound body the fast must have been very hard: those were long, fiercely hot summer days, and it must have been difficult indeed to last through them without food, water or tobacco. Yet I never once saw a single person in Lataifa breaking the fast, in any way: there were occasional rumours that certain people in such and such village had been seen eating or drinking, but even those were very rare.

In every house as the sun sank slowly towards the horizon, the women would lay out their trays and serve the food they had cooked during the day. Their families would gather around, ravenous now, with cool, tall glasses of water resting in front of them. They would sit watching the lengthening shadows, tense and still, listening to their radios, waiting for the sheikhs of the mosque of al-Azhar in Cairo to announce the legal moment of sunset. It was not enough to see the sun going down with one's eyes; the breaking of the fast was the beginning of a meal of communion that embraced millions of people and the moment had to be celebrated publicly and in unison.

When the meal was finished and the trays had been cleared away, the men would wash and change and make their way to the mosque, talking, laughing, replete with a sense of well-being which the day's denials had made multiply sweet. I would go up to my room alone and listen to the call of the muezzin and try to think of how it must feel to know that on that very day, as the sun travelled around the earth, millions and millions of people in every corner of the globe had turned to face the same point, and said exactly the same words of prayer, with exactly the same prostrations as oneself. A phenomenon on that scale was beyond my imagining, but the exercise helped me understand why so many people in the hamlet had told me not to fast: to belong to that immense community was a privilege which they had to re-earn every year, and the effort made them doubly conscious of the value of its boundaries.

In the evenings, after the prayers, the hamlet would be full of life and laughter. Where at other times of the year the lanes and paths were generally empty by eight o'clock, they were now full of bustle and activity: children going from house to house, chanting and demanding gifts, and people visiting their families and staying up late, gossiping and joking with their friends.

From *In an Antique Land,* 1993

Rosetta: The Home of the Stone

E. M. Forster

The name Rosetta is forever linked with the trilingual stone which holds a proud place in the British Museum and made it possible for the hieroglyphs – or secret language – of ancient Egypt to be read in the modern world.

ROSETTA ITSELF was founded in AD 870 by El Motaouakel, one of the Abbaside Caliphs of Egypt. The date is most significant. By 870 the Canopic mouth of the Nile had dried up, and isolated Alexandria from the Egyptian water system. Shipping passed back to the Bolbitiné mouth, and frequented it again for nearly a thousand years. 'El Raschid', as the Arabs named the new settlement, became the western port of Egypt, Damietta being the eastern. It was important in the Crusades; St Louis of France (1049) knew it as 'Rexi'. In the seventeenth and eighteenth centuries it was practically rebuilt in its present form; the mosques, dwelling houses, cisterns, the great warehouses for grain that line the river bank, all date from this period. It evolved an architectural style, suitable to the locality. The chief material is brick, made from the Nile mud, and coloured red or black, there was no limestone to hand, such as supplied Alexandria: with the bricks are introduced courses of palm wood, antique columns &c., and a certain amount of *mashrabiyeh* work and faience. The style is picturesque rather than noble and may be compared with the brick style of the North German Hansa towns. Examples of it are to be found throughout the Delta and even in Alexandria herself, but Rosetta is its headquarters. In architecture, as in other matters, the town kept in touch with Cairo; an Oriental town, scarcely westernised even today. So long as Alexandria lay dormant, it flourished; at the beginning of the nineteenth century its population was thirty-five thousand, that of Alexandria five thousand.

In 1798 Napoleon's troops took Rosetta, in 1801 the British and Turks retook it, in 1807 the reconnoitring expedition of General Frazer was here repulsed. These events, unimportant in themselves, were the prelude to an irreparable disaster: the revival of Alexandria, on scientific lines, by Mohammed Ali. As soon as he developed the harbours there and restored the connection with the Nile water systems by cutting the Mahmoudieh Canal, Rosetta began to decay exactly as Bolbitiné had decayed two thousand years before. The population now is fourteen thousand as against Alexandria's four hundred thousand, and it has become wizen and puny through inbreeding. The warehouses and mosques are falling down, the costly private dwellings of the merchants have been gutted, and the sand, advancing from the south and from the west, invades a little farther every year through the palm groves and into the streets. One can wander aimlessly for hours (it is best thus to wander) and can see nothing that is modern, nor anything more exciting than the arrival of the fishing fleet with sardines. It is the East at last, but the East outwitted by science, and in the last stages of exhaustion.

The main street of Rosetta starts from the railway station and runs due south, parallel to the river, so it is easy to find one's way. In it is the only hotel, kept by a Greek; those who are not fastidious can sleep here: the rest must manage to see the sights between trains. The hotel has a pleasant garden, overlooked by the minaret of a mosque.

In the main street, to the right: Mosque of Ali-el-Mehalli, built 1721, but containing the tomb of the Saint, who died in the sixteenth century. A large but uninteresting building, with an entrance porch in the 'Delta' style – bricks arranged in patterns, pendentives, &c.

Further down, to the left, by the covered bazaars: Entrance with old doors to a large ruined building, probably once an '*okel*', or courtyard, for travellers and their animals; one can walk through it and come out the other side through a fine portal, in the direction of the river. All this part of the town is most picturesque. The houses are four or five storeys high, and have antique columns fantastically disposed among their brickwork. The best and oldest example of this domestic architecture is the House of Ali-el-Fatairi, in the Haret-el-Ghazl, with inscriptions above its lintels that date it 1620; its external staircase leads to two doors, those of the men's and women's apartments respectively. Other fine houses are those of Cheikh Hassan el Khabbaz in Rue Dahliz el Molk; Osman Agha, at some crossroads, carved wood inside, date 1808; Ahmed Agha in the Chareh el Ghabachi to the west of the town, invaded by sand.

From *Alexandria: a History and a Guide,* 1922

3
Cairo and the Pyramids

Mother of Cities
Ibn Battuta

I ARRIVED AT length at Cairo, mother of cities and seat of Pharaoh the tyrant, mistress of broad regions and fruitful lands, boundless in multitude of buildings, peerless in beauty and splendour, the meeting-place of comer and goer, the halting-place of feeble and mighty, whose throngs surge as the waves of the sea, and can scarce be contained in her for all her size and capacity. It is said that in Cairo there are twelve thousand water-carriers who transport water on camels, and thirty thousand hirers of mules and donkeys, and that on the Nile there are thirty-six thousand boats belonging to the Sultan and his subjects, which sail upstream to Upper Egypt and downstream to Alexandria and Damietta, laden with goods and profitable merchandise of all kinds. On the bank of the Nile opposite Old Cairo is the place known as The Garden, which is a pleasure park and promenade, containing many beautiful gardens, for the people of Cairo are given to pleasure and amusements. I witnessed a fête once in Cairo for the sultan's recovery from a fractured hand; all the merchants decorated their bazaars and had rich stuffs, ornaments and silken fabrics hanging in their shops for several days. The mosque of 'Amr is highly venerated and widely celebrated. The Friday service is held in it, and the road runs through it from east to west. The *madrasas* [college mosques] of Cairo cannot be counted for multitude.

From *Travels in Asia and Africa,* 1325-54

A Note on Misr and Cairo and some of their wonderful monuments

Ibn Jubayr

On his journey from Valencia to Mecca, Ibn Jubayr passed through Egypt in 1183 and recorded his impressions of the country which, to him, was both soaked in history but still very much alive.

WE SHALL BEGIN by mentioning the monuments and blessed shrines, which for their beneficence are preserved by Great and Glorious God. Of such is the great tomb in Cairo in which is kept the head of Husayn, the son of 'Ali ibn Abi Talib, may God hold them in favour. It is in a silver casket and over it has been built a mausoleum so superb as to be beyond description and beyond the powers of the mind to comprehend. It is covered with various kinds of brocades, and surrounded by white candles that are like large columns; smaller ones are placed, for the most part, in candlesticks of pure silver and of gilt. Silver lamps are hung from it and its whole upper part is encircled with golden spheres like apples, skilfully executed to resemble a garden and holding our eyes in spell by its beauty. There too are various kinds of marble tessellated with coloured mosaics of rare and exquisite workmanship such as one cannot imagine nor come near to describing. The entrance to this garden [mausoleum] is by a mosque like to it in grace and elegance, with walls that are all marble in the style we have just described. To the right and left of the mausoleum are two chambers of exactly the same style and both leading into it. A brocade covering of exquisite workmanship is hung over all.

A strange thing we noticed as we entered this blessed mosque was a stone set in the wall which faces him who enters. It is very black and shining, reflecting the image of a man like a new-polished Indian mirror.

We observed men kissing the blessed tomb, surrounding it, throwing themselves upon it, smoothing with their hands the *Kiswah* [covering] that was over it, moving round it in a surging throng, calling out invocations, weeping and entreating Glorious God to bless the hallowed dust, and offering up humble supplications such as would melt the heart and split the hardest flint. A solemn thing it was, and an awe-inspiring sight; God granted that we should share in the blessings of that venerable shrine. This is but a flash, a fragment of its description, only indicating what lies beyond; for it does not behove the wise man to apply himself to its description, since he must find himself incapable and incompetent. To be short, I do not believe that in all existence there is a more superb work or more exquisite and wonderful building. May God in His grace and favour sanctify the noble bones that are within it.

The night of that day we passed in the cemetery known as al-Qarafah. This also is one of the wonders of the world for the tombs it contains of prophets – God's benedictions upon them – of the kindred of Muhammad – May God hold them in His favour – of his Companions, of the followers of the Companions, of learned men and ascetics, and of saintly men renowned for their miracles and of wonderful report. We shall describe only those we saw ourselves…

Al-Qarafah is remarkable for being all built with mosques and inhabited shrines in which lodge strangers, learned men, the good and the poor. The subsidy for each place comes monthly from the Sultan; and likewise is it for the theological colleges [*mudaris*] in Misr and Cairo. We were assured that the cost of all this exceeds two thousand Egyptian dinars, or four thousand mu'mini, a month. It was told us that the mosque of 'Amr ibn al-'As has a daily income of about thirty Egyptian dinars, which is spent on benefits connected with it and the stipends of its officials, custodians, imams, and readers.

Amongst the things we saw in Cairo were four congregational mosques superbly built and of beautiful design, as well as many other mosques. In one of these congregational mosques one day the preacher delivered the *khutbah* according to the (orthodox) Sunni practice and included in it invocations for the Companions of the Prophet – may God hold them in His favour – for the followers of the Companions and others, for the 'Mothers of the Faithful' wives of the Prophet – may God bless and preserve them – and for his two noble uncles Hamzah and al-'Abbas – may God hold them in His favour. He discoursed so sweetly and gave so moving a sermon as to humble the hardest heart and cause the tearless eye to flow. He came to the *khutbah* dressed in black according to the 'Abbaside usage. His costume was a black *burdah* topped by a *taylasan* of fine black cloth which in the Maghreb we call *ihram*, and a black turban, and he was girded with a sword. When he had ascended the pulpit, at the first step, he struck it with the end of his scabbard a blow which those present heard as it were a call to silence. He did it again when halfway up, and a third time at the end of his climb. He then saluted the congregation right and left, standing between two black banners, white-checkered, that were planted at the top of the pulpit. His invocations on that day were to the 'Abbaside Imam, Abu al-'Abbas Ahmad al-Nasir li din Ilah ibn al-imam Abu Muhammad al-Hasan al-Mustadi' billah ibn al-Imam Abu 'l-Muzaffar Yusuf al-Mustanjid billah, and then to the reviver of his dynasty, Abu 'l-Muzaffar Yusuf ibn Ayyub Salah al-Din [Saladin], and then to the Sultan's brother and heir to the throne, Abu Bakr Sayf al-Din [Safadin].

We also looked upon the building of the citadel, an impregnable fortress adjoining Cairo which the Sultan thinks to take as his residence, extending its walls until it enfolds the two cities of Misr and Cairo. The forced labourers on this construction, and those executing all the skilled services and vast preparations, such as sawing the marble, cutting the huge stones, and digging the fosse that girdles the walls noted above – a fosse hollowed out with pick-axes from the rock to be a wonder amongst wonders of which trace may remain – were the foreign Rumi prisoners whose numbers were beyond computation. There was no cause for any but them to labour on this construction. The Sultan has constructions in progress in other places and on these too the foreigners are engaged so that those of the Muslims who might have been used in this public work are relieved of it all, no work of that nature falling on any of them.

Another of the things we saw, doing honour to the Sultan, was the *maristan* [hospital] in the city of Cairo. It is a palace, goodly for its beauty and spaciousness. This benefaction he made so that he might deserve a heavenly reward, and to acquire merit. He appointed as intendant a man of science with whom he placed a store of drugs and whom he empowered to use the potions and apply them in their various forms. In the rooms of this palace were placed beds, fully appointed, for lying patients. At the disposal of the intendant are servants whose duty it is, morning and evening, to examine the condition of the sick, and to bring them the food and potions that befit them.

Facing this establishment is another specially for women, and they also have persons to attend them. A third which adjoins them, a large place, has rooms with iron windows, and it has been taken as a place of confinement for the insane. They also have persons who daily examine their condition and give them what is fitting for them. All these matters the Sultan oversees, examining and questioning, and demanding the greatest care and attention to them. In Misr there is another hospital of precisely the same model.

Between Misr and Cairo is the great mosque which takes its name from Abu 'l-'Abbas Ahmad ibn Tulun. It is one of the old congregational mosques, of elegant architecture, and of large proportions. The Sultan made it a retreat for the strangers from the Maghreb [the western part of North Africa and Spain], where they might live and receive lectures; and for their support he granted a monthly allowance. A curious thing, told us by one of their prominent men, was that the Sultan had entrusted to them their own management, and allows no other hand over them. They themselves produce their own leader, whose orders they obey and to whom they appeal in sudden contingency. They live in peace and satisfaction, devoted exclusively to the worship of their Lord, and finding, in the favour of the Sultan, the greatest help to the good on whose path they are set.

There is no congregational or ordinary mosque, no mausoleum built over a grave, nor hospital, nor theological college, where the bounty of the Sultan does not extend to all who seek shelter or live in them. He is helped in this by grants from the public treasury.

Amongst the beneficent acts that proclaim his care for all the affairs of the Muslims was his ordering the building of a school which he assigned to those preachers of the Book of Great and Glorious God who teach exclusively the children of the poor and orphans. For their needs he grants an adequate allowance.

Another of the Sultan's benefactions, and a monument of enduring usefulness to Muslims, are the bridges he has begun to construct seven miles west of Misr at the end of a causeway that begins at high-Nile beside Misr. This causeway is like a mountain stretched along the ground, over which it runs for a distance of six miles until it reaches the aforesaid bridges. These have about forty arches of the biggest type used in bridges, and reach the desert which extends from them to Alexandria. It is one of the most excellent measures taken by a prudent king in readiness against any sudden onslaught by an enemy coming through the breach of Alexandria at the time of the Nile's overflow, when the countryside is in flood and the passage of soldiers thereby prevented. He prepared this as a passageway for any time it may be needed. May God by His favour avert from the lands of the Muslims all apprehension and danger. To the Egyptians, the construction of these bridges is a warning of a coming event, for they see in it an augury that the Almohades [a fundamentalist dynasty from Morocco] will conquer it and the eastern regions. But God is the Knower of His hidden affairs. There is no God but He.

Near to these new bridges are the ancient pyramids, of miraculous construction and wonderful to look upon, four-sided, like huge pavilions rearing into the skies; two in particular choke the firmament. The length of one of them from one angle to another is three hundred and sixty-six paces. They have been built with immense hewn rocks, arranged above each other in an awesome fashion and wonderfully joined having nothing between them that (like cement) would serve to bind them. Their tips seem to the eye to be pointed, but it may be that the ascent to them is possible with danger and difficulty, and that their pointed tops may be found to be broad and level. If men sought to tear them down they must fail. There is dispute concerning them, some saying that they are the tombs of 'Ad and his sons [a pre-Islamic tribe associated with tyranny and corruption]; others have different views. To be short, none but Great and Glorious God can know their story.

One of the two large pyramids has a door, up to which one climbs a *qamah* or more from the ground, and through which entry is made to a large chamber about fifty spans wide and about the same in length. Inside that chamber is a long hollow block of marble resembling what is commonly called *al bilah* [the pillar], and which is said to be a tomb. God best knows the truth of this. Below the large pyramid is another which from one angle to another measures one hundred and forty paces. Below this smaller pyramid are five smaller ones, three contiguous and two nearby and connected.

Near to these pyramids at about a bow-shot's distance, is a strange figure of stone [the Sphinx] rising up like a minaret in the form of a man of fearsome aspect. Its face is to the pyramids and it has its back to the *qiblah* where the Nile falls and (is called) Abu 'l-Ahwal [the Father of Dread]...[1]

Another of the generous deeds of this Sultan close to God Most High, and of the memorials he has left in happy remembrance of him both in religion and in the world, was his annulling of the customs duty imposed as a tax on pilgrims during the 'Ubaydin [Fatimid] dynasty. The pilgrims had suffered distress from its harsh exactment and were much wasted by it, and felt wronged by this humbling and crushing device. At times there came some who had with them no more than the bare cost of the journey, or had not even this provision, but they were

[1] Ibn Jubayr is uncharacterisitcally careless in his description of the pyramids. For example ther are six not five smaller pyramids, and the Sphinx faces the Nile not the Pyramids.

compelled to pay the fixed tax, which was seven and a half Egyptian dinars, or fifteen mu'mini dinars, a head. Those who could not suffered the most painful punishment at 'Aydhab, which city is like its name without the 'y'. [Dropping the 'y' in 'Aydhab gives 'adhab, meaning 'punishment'.] Among the various inflictions devised was hanging by the testicles, or such foul acts. May God protect us from the abuse of His decrees…

Thus did he make a most happy reform, lightening the way of the pilgrim, who had been abandoned, with no one to whom he could turn. God, at the hands of this just Sultan, was sufficient to deliver the Muslims from grievous case and a most painful state. Thanks should follow to him from all who believe that the pilgrimage to the sacred mosque (in Mecca) is one of the five fundamental pillars of Islam; until (his name) shall be spread throughout all lands; and in all countries and all regions prayers should be offered up for him. God who rewards all who do good, and whose power is great, will not fail to reward one who wrought so worthily.

From *The Travels of Ibn Jubayr, c.*1190

The Gossip of Cairo
Amin Maalouf

In 1986 the Arab-French writer, Amin Maalouf, published his novel Leo the African, *a fictional account based on the travel narrative of the sixteenth-century traveller Leo Africanus (also known as Hassan Ibn al-Wazzan). In it he reconstructs the figure of the adventurous traveller, builds a dazzling picture of Mediterranean society at the time and reimagines the fluidity and intimacy of travel in those days.*

CAIRO AT LAST! In no other city does one forget so quickly that one is a foreigner. The traveller has scarcely arrived before he is caught up in a whirlwind of rumours, trivialities, gossips. A hundred strangers accost him, whisper in his ear, call him to witness, jostle his shoulder the better to provoke him to the curses or the laughter which they await. From then on he is let into the secret. He has got hold of one end of a fantastic story, he has to know the sequel even if it means staying until the next caravan, until the next feast day, until the next flood. But, already, another story has begun.

That year, when I disembarked, worn out and haggard a mile from my new home, the whole town, although scarred by the plague, was poking fun without restraint at the 'noble eye', meaning that of the monarch. The first syrup seller, guessing my ignorance and delighting in it, took it upon himself to tell me about it forthwith, pushing away his thirsty clients with a disdainful air. The account which merchants and notables gave me later on was no different from that of this man.

'It all began,' he told me, 'with a stormy interview between Sultan Qansuh and the caliph.'

The caliph was a blameless old man who lived peacefully in his harem. The sultan had treated him harshly and insisted that he should abdicate, on the pretext that his sight was failing, that he was already almost blind in his left eye and that his signature on the decrees was just a scrawl. Apparently Qansuh wanted to frighten the Commander of the Faithful in order to extort a few tens of thousands of dinars from him in exchange for keeping him in office. But the old man did not go along with this game. He took a piece of glazed paper and without trembling wrote out a deed of abdication in favour of his son.

The whole matter would have gone no further, merely another act of injustice that would have been soon forgotten, had the sultan himself one morning not felt pain in his left eye. This had happened two months before my arrival, when the plague was at its most deadly. But the sovereign was losing interest in the plague. His eyelid kept closing. Soon it would close so firmly that he had to hold it open with his finger to be able to see at all. His doctor diagnosed ptosis and recommended an incision.

My informant offered me a goblet of rose syrup and suggested that I should sit down on a wooden box, which I did. There was no longer a crowd around us.

'When the monarch refused categorically, his doctor brought before him a senior officer, the commander of a thousand, who had the same disease, and operated on him forthwith. The man returned a week later with his eye completely restored.'

It was useless. The sultan, said my narrator, preferred to have recourse to a female Turkish healer, who promised to cure him without surgery, only applying an ointment based on powdered steel. After three days of treatment the disease spread to the right eye. The old sultan no longer went out, no longer dealt with any business, did not even manage to carry his *noria* on his head, the heavy long-horned headdress which had been adopted by the last Mameluke rulers of Egypt. To such an extent that his own officers, convinced that he was going to lose his sight, began to look around for a successor.

The very evening before my arrival in Cairo, rumours of a plot were spreading through the city. They had naturally reached the ears of the sultan, who decreed a curfew from dusk to dawn.

'Which is why,' finished the syrup vendor, pointing out the position of the sun on the horizon, 'if your house is far off, you really ought to run, because in seven degrees anyone caught in the streets will be flogged in public until the blood runs.'

Seven degrees was less than half an hour. I looked around me; there was no one there except soldiers, on every street corner, peering nervously at the setting sun. Not daring either to run or to ask the way for fear of being suspected, I merely walked along the river bank, quickening my pace and hoping that the house would be easily recognizable.

Two soldiers were coming towards me, with enquiring steps and looks, when I saw a path on my right. I turned into it without hesitation, with the strange impression of having done so every day of my life.

I was at home. The gardener was sitting on the ground in front of the door, his face immobile. I greeted him with a wave and made a great show of taking out my keys. Without a word, he drew aside to let me in, not appearing at all surprised to see a stranger going into his master's house. My self-assurance reassured him. However, feeling obliged to explain the reason for my presence, I took out of my pocket the deed signed by the Copt. The man did not look at it. He could not read, but trusted me, resumed his place and did not move.

The next day, when I went out, he was still there, so that I did not know whether he had spent the night there or whether he had resumed his post at dawn. I walked about in my street, which seemed extremely busy. But all the passers-by looked at me. Although I was used to this annoyance which afflicts all travellers, I felt the sensation particularly strongly, and put it down to my Maghribi clothing. But it was not that. A greengrocer stepped out of his shop to come over and give me advice:

'People are astonished to see a man of your rank walking about humbly on foot in the dust.'

Without waiting for my reply, he hailed a donkey-driver, who offered me a sumptuous beast, equipped with a fine blanket, and left me a young boy as an orderly.

So mounted, I made a tour of the old city, stopping especially at the famous mosque of Amr and at the textile market, before pushing on towards New Cairo, from which I returned with my head full of murmurings. Henceforth this excursion would take place every day, taking a longer or shorter time according to my mood and what there was for me to do, but always fruitful. I used to meet various notables, officers, palace officials and do business. Already in the first month I arranged to have a load of Indian crepe and spices for the benefit of a Jewish merchant in Tlemcen conveyed in a camel caravan chartered by some Maghribi traders. At my request, he sent back a casket of amber from Massa.

Between two deals, people confided in me. In this way I learned a week after my arrival that the sultan was now in a better mood. Persuaded that his illness was a chastisement from the Most High, he had summoned the four Grand Qadis of Egypt, representing the four rites of the Faith, to reproach them for having let him commit so many crimes without reprimanding him. He had, it was said, burst into tears before the judges, who were dumbfounded by the sight; the sultan was indeed a stately man, very tall and very stout, with an imposing rounded beard. Swearing that he bitterly regretted his treatment of the old caliph, he had promised that he would immediately make amends for the wrong he had done. And he had dictated forthwith a message for the deposed pontiff which he had had conveyed at once by the commander of the citadel. The note was worded thus: 'I bring you the greetings of the sultan, who commends himself to your prayers. He acknowledges his responsibility for his behaviour towards you and his wish not to incur your reproach. He was unable to resist an evil impulse.'

That very day the provost of the merchants came down from the citadel, preceded by torch-bearers who went around the city announcing: 'According to a decree of His Royal Majesty the Sultan, all monthly and weekly taxes and all indirect taxes without exception are abolished, including the rights upon the flour mills of Cairo.'

The sultan had decided, whatever the cost, to attract the Compassion of the Most High towards his eye. He ordered that all the unemployed of the capital, both men and women, should be assembled in the hippodrome, and gave each of them two half-fadda pieces as alms, which cost four hundred dinars altogether. He also distributed three thousand dinars to the poor, particularly those who lived in the mosque of al-Azhar and in the funerary monuments of Karafa.

After having done all this Qansuh summoned the Qadis once more and asked them to have fervent prayers for the healing of his noble eye said in all the mosques. Only three of the judges could answer his call; the fourth, the Maliki Qadi, had to bury that day two of his young children who had fallen victim to the plague.

The reason why the sultan set such store by these prayers was that he had eventually accepted that he should be operated on, and this took place, at his request, on a Friday just after the midday prayer. He kept to his room until the following Friday. Then he went to the stands of Ashrafiyya, had the prisoners kept in the four remand prisons, in the keep of the citadel and in the Arkana, the prison of the royal palace, brought forth, and signed a large number of releases, particularly of favourites who had fallen in disgrace. The most famous beneficiary of the noble clemency was Kamal al-Din, the master barber, whose name quickly went the rounds of Cairo, provoking several ironical comments.

A handsome youth, Kamal al-Din had long been the sultan's favourite. In the afternoons, he used to massage the soles of his feet to make him sleep. Until the day when the sultan had been afflicted by an inflammation of the scrotum which had necessitated bleeding, and this barber had spread the news across the city with graphic details, incurring the ire of his master.

Now, he was pardoned, and not only pardoned but the sultan even excused himself for having ill-treated him, and asked him, since this was his particular vice, that he should go about and tell the whole city that the august eye had been cured. In fact the eyelids were still covered with a bandage, but the sovereign felt sufficiently strong to have his audience once more. The more so since a series of events of exceptional gravity had come to pass. He had just received, one after the other, an envoy from the Sharif of Mecca and a Hindu ambassador who had arrived in the capital a few days earlier to discuss the same problem: the Portuguese had just occupied the island of Kamaran, they were in control of the entrance to the Red Sea and had landed troops on the coast of Yemen. The sharif was afraid that they would attack the convoys of Egyptian pilgrims who usually passed through the ports of Yanbu' and Jidda, which were now directly threatened. As for the Hindu emissary, he had come in great pomp, accompanied by two huge elephants caparisoned in red velvet; he was particularly concerned about the sudden interruption of trade between the Indies and the Mameluke Empire brought about by the Portuguese invasion.

The sultan pronounced himself most concerned, observing that the stars must have been particularly unfavourable for the Muslims that year, since the plague, the threat to the Holy Places and his own illness had all occurred at the same time. He ordered the inspector of granaries, the Amir Kuchkhadam, to accompany the Hindu ambassador in procession back as far as Jidda, and then to stay there in order to organize an intelligence service to report on the intentions of the Portuguese. He also promised to arm a fleet and command it himself if God granted him health.

It was not before the month of Sha'ban that Qansuh was seen wearing his heavy *noria* again. It was then understood that he was definitively cured, and the city received the order to rejoice. A procession was organized, at the head of which walked the four royal doctors, dressed in red velvet pelisses trimmed with sable, the gift of a grateful sovereign. The great officers of state all had yellow silk scarves, and cloths of the same colour were hanging from the windows of the streets where the procession passed as a sign of rejoicing. The Grand Qadis had decorated their doors with brocaded muslin dotted with specks of amber, and the kettledrums resounded in the citadel. As the curfew had been lifted, music and singing could be heard at sunset in every corner of the city. Then, when the night became really dark, fireworks sprang forth on the water's edge, accompanied by frenzied cheering.

On that occasion, in the general rejoicing, I suddenly had an overwhelming urge to dress in the Egyptian fashion. So I left my Fassi clothes, which I put away carefully against the day when I would leave, and then put on a narrow gown with green stripes, stitched at the chest and then flared to the ground. On my feet I wore old-fashioned sandals. On my head I wrapped a broad turban in Indian crepe. And it was thus accoutred that I called for a donkey, on which I enthroned myself in the middle of my street, surrounded by a thousand neighbours, to follow the celebrations.

I felt that this city was mine and it gave me a great sense of well-being. Within a few months I had become a real Cairene notable. I had my donkey-man, my greengrocer, my perfumer, my goldsmith, my paper-maker, prosperous business dealings, relations with the palace and a house on the Nile.

I believed that I had reached the oasis of the clear springs.

From *Leo the African,* 1986

Going Home

Taha Hussein

Most journeys are reported by things seen. Taha Hussein was blind. His daily journey home from the Al-Azhar University to the room where he lived was illustrated only by sounds and odours and touch. Yet we can 'see' his route through Cairo's back streets as clearly as if we were with him, although he writes as if of a person observed.

FOR THE FIRST TWO or three weeks of his stay in Cairo he was lost in bewilderment. All he knew was that he had left the country behind him and settled in the capital as a student attending lectures at the Azhar. It was more by imagination than by sense that he distinguished the three phases of his day.

Both the house he lived in and the path that led to it were strange and unfamiliar. When he came back from the Azhar he turned to the right through a gateway which was open during the daytime and shut at night; after evening prayer there was only a narrow opening left in the middle of the door. Once through it, he became aware of a gentle heat playing on his right cheek, and a fine smoke teasing his nostrils; while on the left he heard an odd gurgling sound which at once puzzled and delighted him.

For several days, morning and evening, he listened curiously to this sound, but lacked the courage to inquire what it might be. Then one day he gathered from a chance remark that it came from the bubbling of a *narghile* smoked by tradesmen of the district. It was provided for them by the proprietor of the café from which the gentle heat and the fine smoke-cloud issued.

He walked straight on for a few steps before crossing a damp, roofed-in space in which it was impossible to stand firmly because of the slops thrown there by the café proprietor. Then he came out into an open passageway; but this was narrow and filthy and full of strange, elusive smells, which were only moderately unpleasant early in the day and at nightfall, but as the day advanced and the heat of the sun grew stronger, became utterly intolerable.

He walked straight on through this narrow passage; but rarely did he find it smooth or easy. More often than not his friend would have to push him either this way or that so as to avoid some obstacle or other. Then he would continue in the new direction, feeling his way towards a house either to left or right, until he had passed the obstacle and taken the old direction again. He hurried along nervously at his companion's side, breathing the nauseous smells, and half-deafened by the medley of sounds that came from all sides at once, left and right, above and below, to meet in mid-air, where they seemed to unite above the boy's head, layer upon layer, into a single fine mist.

There was in fact a remarkable variety of sounds. Voices of women raised in dispute, of men shouting in anger or peaceably talking together; the noise of loads being set down or picked up; the song of the water-carrier crying his wares; the curse of a carter to his horse or mule or donkey; the grating sound of cart-wheels; and from time to time this confused whirl of sounds was torn by the braying of a donkey or the whinnying of a horse.

As he passed through this babel, his thoughts were far away, and he was scarcely conscious of himself or of what he was doing; but at a certain point on the road he caught the confused sound of conversation through a half-open door on the left; then he knew that a pace or two further on he must turn to the left up a staircase which would bring him to his lodging.

It was an ordinary sort of staircase, neither wide nor narrow, and its steps were of stone; but since it was used very frequently in both directions, and no one troubled to wash or sweep it, the dirt piled up thickly and stuck together in a compact mass on the steps, so that the stone was completely covered up, and whether you were going up or coming down the staircase appeared to be made of mud.

Now whenever the boy went up or down a staircase he was obliged to count the steps. But long as were the years he stayed in this place, and countless the times he negotiated this staircase, it never occurred to him to count the number of its steps. He learnt at the second or third time of climbing it that after going up a few steps he had to turn a little to the left before continuing his ascent, leaving on his right an opening through which he never penetrated, though he knew that it led to the first floor of the building in which he lived for so many years.

This floor was not inhabited by students, but by workers and tradesmen. He left the entrance to it on his right, and went on up to the second floor. There his harassed spirit found rest and relief; lungfuls of fresh air drove away the sense of suffocation with which he had been oppressed on that filthy staircase; and then too there was the parrot, whistling on without a break, as if to testify before all the world to the tyranny of her Persian master, who had imprisoned her in an abominable cage, and would sell her tomorrow or the day after to another man who would treat her in exactly the same way. And when he was rid of her and had laid hands on the cash, he would buy a successor for her who would be cooped up in the same prison pouring forth the same curses on her master, and waiting as her sister had waited to be passed on from hand to hand, and from cage to cage, while everywhere she went that plaintive cry of hers would delight the hearts of men and women.

When our friend reached the top of the staircase he breathed in the fresh air that blew on his face, and listened to the voice of the parrot calling him towards the right. He obeyed, turning through a narrow corridor, past two rooms in which two Persians lived. One of these was still a young man, while the other was already past middle age. The one was as morose and misanthropic as the other was genial and good-natured.

At last the boy was home. He entered a room like a hall, which provided for most of the practical needs of the house. This led on to another room, large but irregular in shape, which served for social and intellectual needs. It was bedroom and dining-room, reading-room and study, and a room for conversation by day or by night. Here were books and crockery and food; and here the boy had his own particular corner, as in every room he occupied or visited at all frequently.

This place of his was on the left inside the door. After advancing a pace or two he found a mat spread on the ground, and above that an old but quite serviceable carpet. Here he sat in the daytime, and here he slept at night, with a pillow for his head and a rug to cover him. On the opposite side of the room was his elder brother's pitch, a good deal higher than his own. He had a mat spread on the ground, and a decent carpet on top of that, then a felt mattress, and above that a long, wide piece of bedding stuffed with cotton, and finally, crowning all, a coverlet. Here the young sheikh[2] would sit with his close friends. They were not obliged to prop up their backs against the bare wall, as the boy did, having cushions to pile up on the rugs. At night this couch was transformed into a bed on which the young sheikh slept.

This was all the boy ever learnt about his immediate surroundings. The second phase of his life consisted in the tumultuous journey between his home and the Azhar. He went out through the covered passage till he felt the heat of the café on his left cheek, and heard the bubbling of the *narghile* on his right. In front of him was a shop which played an important part in his life; it belonged to El-Hagg Firûz, who supplied the neighborhood with most of the necessities of life. In the morning he sold boiled beans, prepared in the usual variety of ways. But El-Hagg Firûz used to boast the special virtues of his beans – and raise their prices accordingly. He had plain beans, beans in fat, beans in butter, beans in every kind of oil; he added, if required, all sorts of spices. As for the students, they adored these beans, and often made far too large a meal of them. So by mid-morning they were already dull in the head, and at the noon lecture they slept.

When evening came El-Hagg Firûz sold his customers their supper: cheese, olives, milled sesame, or honey. To the more luxurious he supplied boxes of tunny or sardines. And to a few of them perhaps, as night approached, he sold things which have no name, and nothing to do with food, things spoken of in a whisper, yet passionately vied for.

The boy used to overhear these whisperings; sometimes he half understood, but as a rule the whole transaction was a mystery to him. As the days passed by and he grew older, he came to see through these subtle hints and ambiguities. What he learnt then

[2] Sheikh, unusually meaning 'elder', here means 'scholar.'

obliged him to overhaul his standards of judgement, and to revise his valuation both of people and of things...

On leaving the covered passage, then, the boy found himself in front of El-Hagg Firûz's shop; his friend would take him a few paces in that direction to greet El-Hagg Firûz and to inquire if there was a letter for him or not; the reply would bring either smiles or frowns to his face. Then he turned away to the left, and walked straight forwards down the long narrow street crowded with passers-by. It was full of students, merchants, tradesmen, labourers; carts drawn by donkeys, horses or mules; carters shouting out warnings or curses at the men, women or children blocking their path. Then on each side of the street were different kinds of shops, in many of which was prepared the meagre diet of the poor. The smells that issued from them were abominable, but that did not prevent them from delighting most of the passers-by, whether they were students, labourers or porters. Some of them turned aside to these shops and bought a scrap of food to gulp down on the spot, or take home and eat, either alone or with others. And some of them, assailed by this battery of smells, remained unmoved. They were tempted but did not yield. Their eyes saw, their nostrils smelt, their appetite was stirred; but, alas, their pockets were empty. They passed on with yearning in their souls and with bitterness and resentment in their hearts; yet at the same time they were content with their lot and accepted it with resignation.

In some other shops a quiet, unhurried trade was transacted, almost without any words passing at all. If anything was said, it was under the breath, so as scarcely to be heard. In spite of this – or perhaps for this very reason – the trade in question brought great wealth and prosperity to those who practised it. To all appearances the majority of these shops dealt only in coffee and soap, though some of them also sold sugar and rice.

As he passed through all this a warm interest stirred in the boy. But he would have understood practically nothing had not his friend from time to time volunteered an explanation. He continued on his way, sometimes walking firmly forwards, sometimes swerving aside. When the road was clear he marched with a sure step, but stumbled and faltered on its edges when it was crowded or twisty. At last he came to a spot where he had to turn a little to the left and then plunge into a lane as narrow and crooked and filthy as could be. Its atmosphere was foul with an abominable medley of smells, and from time to time weak, hollow voices which reflected its misery and wrong echoed back cries for charity to the footfalls of passers-by, begging at the sound of steps, as if life had only been perceptible through the ears. They were answered by other voices: the thin, harsh, strangled cries of those winged creatures which love darkness and desolation and ruins. Often enough these noises were accompanied by the flutter of wings, which sometimes, to his horror, shaved past his ear or his face. Instinctively his hand would fly up for protection, and for sometime afterwards his heart would be throbbing with apprehension.

On he walked with his friend along this narrow, dark, twisting alley, now rising, now descending, now going straight on, now turning to left or right. And all the time these loathsome sounds assailed him, sometimes from in front, and sometimes from behind, but never without dismaying him. After a time he felt his heart lighten and his lungs expand, and knew that the moment of release had come. He heaved one sigh of relief, loaded with all the weight of his anxiety and distress.

Now he breathed freely and easily, as if he were taking in great draughts of life from the fresh air which flowed over him as he left the bat-ridden alley. On he went along the road, which twisted treacherously under his feet for a few moments, then became firm again so that he could step forward easily and with confidence. His heart thrilled with joy at the strange harmony of sounds which came to his ears as he walked along the pleasant, peaceful street. On one side of him was the Mosque of Sayyidna-l-Hussein and on the other a series of small shops. How often he would stop at one of these during the days that followed, and what good things he tasted there! Soaked figs and their juice in summertime, and in winter *bassbûssa*,[3] which diffused a warm glow of well-being through the body. Sometimes he would stop at a Syrian retailer's to choose from a variety of foods, hot or cold, salt or sweet. Their taste gave him inexpressible pleasure, yet if they were offered him now he would be afraid they might make him ill, or even poison him.

[3] A nut cake.

He continued along this street until he came to a place where the voices grew louder and more numerous. He realised that the roads divided here and that he could branch right or left, go straight on, or turn about. 'Here are the crossroads,' said his companion. 'If you go right you reach the Sikka El-Gadida, then the Musky, then 'Ataba El-Khadra. To the left you have Sharia El-Darrâssa. But we must go straight on into Sharia El-Halwagi, the street of learning and hard work. It is so narrow that if you stretched out your arms left and right you could almost touch both walls. Now you are walking between a number of small bookshops. There are books of every kind in them, new and old, good and bad, in print or manuscript.'

How many a pleasant and rewarding halt did our friend make in that narrow street, which remained fixed in his memory later on, after his life had changed its course.

But this time he must hurry past. His guide had to be at the Azhar before the lecture began. Here they were, arrived at the Barbers' Gate. He took off his sandals, laid them one on top of the other, then picked them up in his hand as he followed his companion. A little further on he stepped over a shallow threshold into the quiet courtyard of the Azhar, and felt a cool morning breeze blow refreshingly upon his face. And so he entered the third phase of this new life of his.

This third phase of his existence was the one he loved best of all. In his own room he endured all the pains of exile. It was like a foreign country to him, and he never became familiar with its contents, except perhaps those nearest to him. He did not live in it in the same sense that he had lived in his country home or in other familiar rooms where nothing was unknown to him. He passed his days there in exile from people and things alike, and in such anguish of heart that the oppressive air he breathed there brought him no rest or refreshment, but only heaviness and pain.

Nor was there any doubt of his preferring these hours in the Azhar to the agitated journey back and forth, whose hazards drove him almost to despair. It was not only his steps that were confused and unsteady; his very heart was overwhelmed by that unnerving perplexity which perverts a man's purposes and drives him blindly onwards, not only along the material road which he needs must follow, but also along the free paths of the mind, feckless and without a plan. Not only was he distracted by the hubbub and tumult that eddied around him. He was distressed at the unsteadiness of his walk and the impossibility of harmonising his own quiet, faltering steps with the firm and even brutal pace of his companion.

It was only in the third phase of his day that he found rest and security. The fresh breeze that blew across the court of the Azhar at the hour of morning prayer met him with a welcome and inspired him with a sense of security and hope. The touch of this breeze on his forehead, damp with sweat from that feverish journey, resembled nothing so much as the kisses his mother used to give him during his early years, when he chanted verses from the Koran to her, or entertained her with a story he had heard at the village school; or when, as a pale, delicate infant, he abandoned the corner in which he had been reciting the litany from the *sura* Ya-Sin to go and carry out some household task or other.

Those kisses revived his heart and filled him not only with tenderness but with hope and confidence. The breeze which welcomed him in the court of the Azhar, no less, brought rest after weariness, calm after tumult, a smile after gloomy looks. However, he as yet knew nothing of the Azhar, and had not the least idea what he would find there. But it was enough for him to brush with his bare feet the ground of that court, to feel on his face the caress of its morning breeze, and to realise that around him the Azhar was preparing to awake from its drowsiness, that its inertia would soon give place to activity. He began to recover consciousness of himself, as life returned to him. He felt the conviction of being in his own country, amongst his own people, and lost all sense of isolation, all sadness. His soul blossomed forth, and with every fibre of his being he yearned to discover … well, what? Something he was a stranger to, though he loved it and felt irresistibly drawn towards it – knowledge. How many times had he heard this word, and longed to find out its hidden meaning! His impression of it was vague enough, to be sure; but of this he was convinced, that knowledge had no limits and that people might spend their whole lives in acquiring a few drops of it. He too wished to devote his whole life to it and to win as much of it as he could, however little that might be. His father and the learned friends who came to visit him had spoken of knowledge as a boundless ocean, and the child had never taken this expression for a figure of speech or a metaphor, but as the simple truth. He had come to Cairo and to the Azhar with the intention of throwing himself into this ocean and drinking what he could of it, until the day he drowned. What finer end could there be for a man of spirit than to drown himself in knowledge? What a splendid plunge into the beyond!

All these thoughts suddenly thronged into his young spirit, filling it and taking possession of it, blotting out the memory of that desolate room, of the turbulent, twisty road, and even of the country and its delights. They convinced him that it was no mistake or exaggeration to be consumed with love for the Azhar as well as with regret for the country.

The boy paced on with his companion until he had crossed the court and mounted the shallow step which is the threshold of the Azhar itself. His heart was all modesty and humility, but his soul was filled with glory and pride. His feet stepped lightly over the worn-out mats that were laid out across the floor, leaving a bare patch here and there, as if on purpose to touch the feet which passed over them with something of the benediction attached to that holy ground. The boy used to love the Azhar at this moment, when worshippers were finishing their early-morning prayer and going away, with the marks of drowsiness still in their eyes, to make a circle round some column or other and wait for the teacher who was to give a lecture on tradition or exegesis, first principles or theology.

At this moment the Azhar was quiet, and free from the strange intermingled murmurs that filled it from sunrise until evening prayer. You could only hear the whispered conversations of its inmates or the hushed but steady voice of some young man reciting the Koran. Or you might come upon a worshipper who had arrived too late for the common service, or had gone on to perform extra prayers after completing the statutory number. Or maybe you would hear a teacher beginning his lecture in the languid tone of a man who has awakened from sleep and said his prayers but has not yet eaten anything to give him strength and energy. He starts in a quiet, husky voice: 'In the name of God, the merciful, the compassionate: Praise be to God, father of the worlds. May His peace and blessing be upon our lord Muhammad, the most noble of the prophets, upon his family and his companions. These are the words of the author of the Book, may God rest his soul and grant us the fruits of his learning. Amen!'

From *The Stream of Days: A Student at the Azhar,* 1948

An Orientation

Max Rodenbeck

> Every year a little deposit of mud is left by the Nile on its banks, and every year sees deposited upon the counters of the London booksellers the turbid overflow of journalizing travel. Alas! It has not the usefulness of the leavings of this sacred river.

From *A Nile Journal,* Thomas Gold Appleton, 1876

MR APPLETON IS RIGHT, which is why when a friend urged me to write a book about Cairo, I said tsk and went back to my waterpipe. Yes, I agreed, this was a magnificent city, and one whose story has rarely been told with sympathy or truth. But books about cities, I argued, were of two kinds. They were either travelogues or histories, and I knew that, while a travel story could barely skim the surface of Cairo's depth, a straight history was sure to founder in the immensity of the city's past.

Besides, there was the question of where to begin in a tale so vast in scope as Cairo's. Fourteen centuries ago, when the Muslim conquerors of Egypt made this their capital? Or several millennia earlier, when great cities had already bloomed and faded here at the apex of the Nile Delta? And where to end? This place I had known since childhood was changing elusively fast. Between my starting and finishing its portrait Cairo was certain to slip out of the frame.

Then, perhaps I had come to know the city all too well. If Cairo was, in the words of its great novelist the Nobel laureate Naguib Mahfouz, like meeting your beloved in old age, then was I to tell about her wrinkles, her bad breath and worse taste, and her unfortunate habit of shouting at the servants? Because just as one could expand on the city's wonders – its pyramids and minarets and showbiz glitter – one could also mutter over its noise and pollution and sheer, bewildering, annoying clutter.

The fact was that after a twelve-year stretch of living in Cairo, most of which was spent in enchantment, I was falling out of love. The city was changing, and what it was changing into disturbed me, as it disturbed most Cairenes that I knew. I felt increasingly estranged from what was becoming a harder, more impatient, less tolerant city of ugly new buildings – a place far removed from other Cairos I had known.

I first arrived here at the age of two. What I remember is heady colour bursts of bougainvillea crimson, jacaranda violet and flame-tree red, and the glistening blackness of olives at the Greek grocer. I remember the crackling urgency of backgammon dice in cafés and the tooting insistence of human, animal and motorized traffic. I recall the glamour of seeing *Lawrence of Arabia* open at that art deco jewel of a cinema, the Metro on Sulayman Pasha Street, and the sheer fun of hurling potatoes into the gap-toothed maw of a hippo at the zoo (still elegant then, with its pathways in Portuguese mosaic and lemonade served beside the still-lush lotus ponds). I remember the peculiarity of that cartoon mountainscape of pyramids on the western horizon, and the taxis – those high-sprung jalopies in harlequin black and white whose radios moaned a single song by the city's great diva Umm Kulsoum, then at the climax of her fortunes. 'You are my life,' she crooned over and over, as the Nile's sunset sheen flickered through the treacly jungle of banyan trees lining the Corniche. 'You are my life that dawned with your light.'

I didn't understand the words then. That particular light dawned much later, when I returned to study Arabic here, worked as a reporter, and discovered the Mother of the World – as Egyptians fondly call their capital – in all her shambolic grandeur and operatic despair. The city seduced me. Her depth seemed limitless, whether by the measure of time or the fortunes of her people or the mystery of their ways. Layers overlapped effortlessly, the ancient and the new, the foreign and the native, the rich and the poor. Worlds mingled in the bookstalls along the edge of the Azbakiyya Gardens: the works of Enver Hoxha next to a score by Puccini beside an Armenian body-building manual on top of *The Thousand and One Nights*. They mingled in the streets, where a barefoot incense man swirled his censer from shop to shop collecting a *shillin* or *bariza* from their keepers in exchange for a blessing. Brandy-swilling leftists at the Café Riche spun tall plots to tease eavesdropping, hookah-puffing secret police. Refugees out of Africa rented their bodies at the Borsalino discotheque to key-jangling spivs and Israeli agents and German engineers and backpackers straying from the road to Kathmandu. On the weathered marble floor of a fourteenth-century mosque, under the coffered and gilded ceiling, a turbanned sheikh dozed over his holy book. Young couples cooed at the chipped tables of the venerable Groppi Tea Rooms. They ignored their neighbours, the painted old birds in laddered stockings who had lost the will to migrate back to Salonica or Trieste or wherever it was they had come from, and so reminisced in ragged Levantine French about Cairo's Roaring Forties – and when the waiter turned his back slipped scarce sugar cubes into their tattered Hermès handbags.

In time the old birds at Groppi went extinct, along with most of the variegated cosmopolitans whose world had closed in after the 1952 revolution. The Nileside banyans fell to road-widening schemes. Secret police began to do their mufti in beards and robes. They now hunted not harmless leftist barflies, but the new breed of violent zealots who buzzed with pious anger and chiselled busily at Cairo's old civility. A chorus of full-volume Koranic cassette sellers invaded the Azbakiyya bookstalls. Instead of weeding out these noisy intruders, the dullard city government abolished the market altogether.

I grew wary of exploring the city. Each successive visit to its old core – the zone of grand medieval mosques and palaces and bazaars –

brought fresh evidence of further decay: marble buckled off walls, ancient minarets toppled into neighbouring houses; and in the markets plastic shoes and pharaonic T-shirts replaced camel-hide slippers and satin kaftans. Strolling one day downtown – in what used to be the 'European' Quarter – I discovered one favourite café transformed into a tawdry jeans outlet and another replaced by a burger bar called Madonna's. The National Hotel, whose crusty, broken-keyed piano bar once boasted a preposterous coterie of Second World War vintage prostitutes, was bought and torn down by an 'Islamic' investment company. When its pyramid scheme went bust the site remained a gaping parking lot.

It was not just my own proprietorial sensibilities that made this breakneck defoliation sad. Everyone from Shukri the ironing man to Ahmad the tailor to Dr Sabri the dentist felt it, and moaned about it. The weather had never been humid like this, they agreed. The streets had never looked so scruffy. The Cairene character itself, they chimed, had altered. People were now sanctimonious, rude and grasping where once they lived only for laughs. Those who could were simply leaving. Embarrassed clusters of would-be émigrés huddled outside foreign consulates. Even Usta Mahmud the mechanic, a gruff fellow more interested in feeding stray cats than in servicing cars, took off to live with his son in Jersey City, New Jersey.

After a particularly scorching, frustrating summer I joined the exodus.

'He who drinks the water of the Nile is destined to taste its sweetness again.' The proverb is something of a cliché to Egyptians, but I couldn't help recalling it as my plane touched down at Cairo three years later. The idea of the place had made me uneasy, but all hesitation evaporated with the first sniff of the city's hot night air, with the welcoming image of a soldier sleeping in an airport corridor and the familiar feel of playful bustle as taxi hustlers swooped like seagulls on to the crowd of dazed travellers at the airport's exits. As the impressions flooded in, I knew without a doubt I was home. The place was tatty, yes. It was grubby and noisy too. But Cairo fitted snug as an old shoe.

Right away I knew, too, that I must write this book. There lurked a faint recollection of how the ancient gods had kept Menelaus dawdling by the Nile on his way home from the Trojan War. 'And so he tarried, for he had not paid their due of sacrifice', is how Homer explained the strange reluctance of Odysseus's friend to return to Sparta. I felt that in some similar sense I owed an offering, however flawed, to this city which had given me many stories and whose people had been so unfailingly kind.

Besides, my brief *hejira* had renewed my appreciation of Cairo. Other places may have been neater, quieter and less prone to wrenching change, but they all lacked something. The easy warmness of Cairenes, perhaps, and their indomitable insouciance; the complexities and complicities of their relations; their casual mixing of sensuality with moral rigour, of razor wit with credulity. or perhaps it was the possibility this city offered of escape into other worlds: into the splendours of its pharaonic and medieval past say, or out of its bruising crowds on to the soft, gentle currents of the Nile – even if the tapering lateen sails of the river feluccas did now advertise Coca-Cola.

And then, reading into Cairo's past, I saw how foolish it was to fret about its future. How silly to imagine that this great town – this *Ur-Stadt* if there ever was one – could ever decay beyond repair. The fact was that not one generation in Cairo's five millennia of incarnations had failed to whine about decline, and still the city endured.

Cairo's ancient stone guardian, the Sphinx himself, had been known to complain of neglect. According to the 3,000-year-old stone inscription between his paws, the Sphinx appeared in a dream to a young prince who, exhausted by a desert gazelle hunt, had fallen asleep in his shadow. 'My manner is as if I were ailing in all my limbs,' moaned the idol. 'The sand of the desert upon which I stand has reached me.' The Sphinx vowed that if the prince dusted him off he could have the god's kingdom on earth, 'at the head of the living'. The Sphinx kept his promise. The prince was to rule Egypt as the pharaoh Tutmosis IV.

The plaintive tone echoed in medieval times, when Cairo was reborn as the greatest of Muslim cities. Here is a certain Sheikh Badr al-Din al-Zaytuni, complaining in verse about the sultan's closure of the Birkat al-Ratl, a seasonal lake outside the great city walls where fifteenth-century Cairenes had whiled away autumn evenings on torchlit pleasure boats:

> The eater of opium found constant delight…
> While the mirth of the drunkard was at its height.
> Goblets brimmed beneath the full moon…
> While poets sang to the gentlest of tunes.
>
> Now time has erased these haunts…
> O eyes, shed tears of grief, O heart endure
> And God's favour bless those days of joy when Cairo was secure.

And here was the French novelist Pierre Loti, who reckoned at the turn of the last century that the city had grown too modern. It had lost its *Thousand and One Nights* allure: 'What is this? Where are we fallen? Save that it is more vulgar than Nice, or the Riviera … [the] great town – which sweats gold now that men have started to buy from it its dignity and its soul – is become a place of rendezvous and holiday for all the idlers and upstarts of the whole world …'

Loti was wrong. Cairo may have lived through periods of bad as well as good taste. (Actually, much of what Loti saw as vulgarity is now considered fine stuff and worthy of preservation – like the *beaux arts* and neo-Islamic architecture of the European Quarter.) The city may have plundered many of its own riches or wantonly scarred them or let them tumble into ruin. But it has never sold its dignity or its soul. This is, after all, the place that endowed the world with the myth of the phoenix.

From *Cairo: The City Victorious,* 1998

The World around Me

Jean Said Makdisi

Domestic life in Cairo in the 1950s had its own special flavour. The Palestinian Jean Said Makdisi moved to Cairo with her family in the aftermath of the 1948 war, and spent her childhood there. She invites her reader to visit her flat in Zamalek (now a mostly modern, upper-class cosmopolitan residential area) where three generations of Arab women lived: her grandmother, mother, and herself as a child. There you smell Egyptian mouloukhia *and taste Syrian* kibbeh, *are served* foul m'dammas *for breakfast and* moujaddara *for lunch. There too one learns about women's diplomatic power in the family: they are the neck that turns the heads of the family round.*

I WAS IN MY mid-teens when the world in which I was brought up came to an abrupt end. The nationalization of the Suez Canal in 1956 was one of the great moments in modern Arab history, and I am proud to say that I was part of that moment. I have always felt myself to be, in many ways, a daughter of Suez. The Suez crisis awakened me to history and politics, and marked the end of my childhood. At first I was exhilarated by the experience, and reacted to events with a joy and immediacy that, today, looking back at it, I find astounding. Later, I would gradually be recalled, restrained, reminded of my domestic duties; eventually I would re-learn the lesson that I was not meant to be part of the world which defied power greater than itself, which vigorously and courageously searched for and pursued justice. The older I grew, the less directly involved I became in the political events surrounding me, and the less vocal I became in expressing my reactions. That remained true until very recently, when, propelled by the direct and shattering experiences of the Lebanese war, I learned to speak up on politics.

During the Suez crisis, school was closed and there was nothing to do all day long but follow the news. Because my parents were absorbed in their adult concerns, I was left to my own devices, freed from the exigencies of polite manners and the usual security and affection. In this state of unaccustomed, and totally exhilarating, freedom, I received the world of Suez unedited: no neat explanations intervened between it and me, smoothing out the questions. I was now the oldest child left at home, as Edward and Rosemarie were away at university; I was too patronizing then of my younger sisters to engage with them in any sort of meaningful talk.

I was only a fifteen-year-old schoolgirl, but I shared from my own room the excitement when the Canal was nationalized. Gamal Abdel Nasser was a great orator. He could keep huge crowds spellbound for hours on end, castigating them, telling them stories, making them laugh – he had an extraordinary sense of humour – moving them to a new awareness, not so much of patriotic chauvinism, but of their rightful place in history. His particular oratorical style provided a democratic sense of participation in the events of the day. Later I would become aware of his responsibility in founding a state security system that was typical of the post-independence third world, oppressive, tyrannical and unjust. But at the time, he was just a liberator.

Though we never joined the crowds on the streets – our parents would never have allowed us to, and we never dreamed of asking – my friends and I, especially my neighbours Nadia and Huda Gindy, listened to his speeches on the radio at home. We discussed the issue, especially as our English school remained closed well after the summer had ended. As threats and ultimatums flew between Cairo and London, and the clouds of the tripartite invasion gathered, the mood of excitement and finality grew.

One day in the autumn I was sitting at the piano with Cherry at my side munching away and yelling, '*Répetez, répetez*', when the doorbell rang. My parents were out, and my younger sisters were in their room, playing. I opened the door to find a man from the US embassy who told me to tell my father that he should prepare his family for the immediate evacuation of US citizens from Egypt. When my parents came home an hour or two later and I delivered the message, they went into their bedroom to hold a conference. I stood at the door and listened to them as they debated the matter in low voices.

Clearly, war was imminent. Danger was around the corner. Their primary concern was the safety of the family. But then they started to have doubts. What about their friends? What about the neighbours? What about the employees of the Standard Stationery Company? What about Egypt itself? Were they to abandon their friends, turn their backs on their employees? Were they to leave Egypt in its moment of danger? They had enjoyed life there while all was well: were they to leave now, when it was threatened? And Palestine – Palestine was turning into a lesson for everyone. Palestine weighed heavily on them. If you leave, you do not go back – all you have left are the photograph albums, if you're lucky.

The matter was soon settled: we were staying, not running away. Standing there listening, I was vastly relieved. I was not as aware of the dangers, but I was aware of the excitement, and I did not want to go. Most of all, I was deeply impressed by my parents' feeling of solidarity with Egypt and their friends – I never forgot it. It was one of the things about them that I always admired.

In the meantime, as we waited for the invasion, I was still allowed to go to the cinema with my friends. In the past, the programme had always been preceded by the royal anthem; now it was preceded by stirring nationalist songs and martial music as well. The deep voice of Um Kulthoum was raised as a banner, as was that of Abdel Halim Hafeth, and both came to symbolize the fervently nationalistic mood of the time. As the Suez war began, and the Israelis, British and French invaded Egypt, fever pitch was reached. The marching song '*Allahu akbar*', with its deeply rousing words sung by a vigorous male chorus, still rings in my ears. I was to hear it again during the 1982 Israeli invasion of Lebanon, when once more it became a battle hymn.

The invasion came, and the excitement reached a paroxysm. Though the attacks were mostly on the Canal area, air-raid sirens wailed even in Cairo. At night, we had blackouts. As in those earlier times in my childhood – the Second World War and the Palestine war – we sat in the corridors during air raids, and Joyce, who specialized in this reaction, vomited regularly. This time, however, I was old enough to follow events and understand them.

There is no question in my mind that part of the influence of this event lay precisely in the fact that I was a child of British imperial schooling. The war touched my life and my sensibilities, directly and tangibly. For me the word 'imperialism' was never abstract or polemical: it was as real as real life, and real experience. It appeared to me in the guise of the people I knew, the history lessons I had taken, the language I spoke and all the songs and dances I had been taught.

As a result of the war, the English School, along with all British and French interests in Egypt, was nationalized. Our old teachers were ordered out of the country: my friends and I went on a round of farewell visits. We looked at our teachers with new and amazed eyes. Those we visited did not express the slightest regret that Britain, among others, had invaded Egypt, the country in which they had lived and worked all those many years.

What, then, was the meaning of all those hymns, prayers, sermons and rules of behaviour they had taught us with such zeal? What about loyalty, team spirit and all the other rules that comprised the elaborate code of honour we had been taught? Probably only a naive teenager with no knowledge of the world could raise such questions. Perhaps, in spite of my many experiences since then, I have remained a sixteen-year-old girl at heart. Perhaps I have chosen to be this because I preferred my reaction then to the compromises and accommodations that have since overtaken our world. Better, I think, the honour, belief and trust of a sixteen-year-old schoolgirl than the worn-out rationalizations, the passivity and the forgotten pride of the present.

My reaction was not, of course, an individual matter. For once, I was exactly in tune with the world around me. And if the whole Arab world reacted then with the exuberance of unity, the excitement of shared loyalty and pride, the self-assurance of supporting correct actions, those heady days of Suez stand in my personal memory, as well as in the collective memory, as a permanent reprimand to today's general indifference and corruption.

My total freedom was short-lived, however, though my mental freedom continued to the end of the crisis. As the long weeks without school continued, with no end in sight, my mother enrolled me in two sets of activities that were meant, I suppose, to fill my time usefully. She certainly considered them to be part of my education. First I was sent on two or three mornings a week, together with Claude Dirlik and Linda Fahoum, as apprentices to the *atelier* of one of the great dressmakers of Cairo, Madame Sophie. She was a large pleasant woman, who governed her employees with a rod of iron, while indulging us, the dilettantes, speaking to us sweetly, laughing and spoiling us. We learned how to take measurements correctly, to make patterns, to cut the material – so this was the 'Cutting Out' of Teta's time! – laying it down flat on the table; we learned how to pin it together, sew it and finish it.

On the alternate free mornings, I was sent to study another useful skill: shorthand and typing. 'Let her do something useful,' I overheard my parents say. 'Who knows? Perhaps some day she will have to go out to work.' Here again the Palestine experience, which had forced many exiled families in vastly reduced circumstances to send their daughters out to work, informed their judgement. Among the secretaries my father employed in his business, some at least were from Palestinian families in straitened circumstances.

The war ended, the British, French and Israelis withdrew, the excitement abated and at last school reopened. Like all the other English and French schools in Egypt, it had been nationalized and was now called Madrassat al-Nasr (Victory School). Instead of English teachers, we now had Egyptians, some of them trained at British universities.

The first lesson after Suez was conducted in Arabic. It was short, but utterly spellbinding. The new teacher spread a map of the area, including Palestine, on the board. Though it was probably the first time I had ever seen one, I still looked around at my classmates with a triumphant air of proprietorship and exceptional knowledge. Very simply and briefly, he recounted the story of the British occupation of Egypt, the history of the Suez Canal, the Egyptian labour that went into building it, the benefits denied to Egypt and appropriated by Europe, and the reasons for the nationalization of the Canal. As part of this outline he talked a little about Palestine, tracing some of the events leading to its fall. He told us of the connection with Egypt: that Abdel Nasser had been an officer in the Egyptian army during the Palestine war; how King Farouq had betrayed his own soldiers by sending them faulty weapons; and how Abdel Nasser had come to recognize that both the king and the British had to go for Egypt to become strong and healthy, and to save the Arab world.

I was fascinated. For the first time in my life, I had been made to understand, in however sketchy a manner, the world around me. The experience I had lived through had now acquired a comprehensible framework. Thus, for a brief moment, I felt myself tied directly and consciously into history.

From *Teta, Mother and Me,* 2004

Through Cairo and to the Pyramids

H. J. Ross

Travellers who go to Egypt expect to see the Pyramids which rise like hills to the west of the Nile. Over the centuries the route out to them has changed and has become built over, but the Pyramids still have the power to astonish. Only when you have been there can you truly understand their magnificence. Here Ross describes that journey in 1852.

THE 'BARRAGE' OF THE NILE is a superb work, a worthy monument of engineering skill, spanning that wild race of mighty waters. Far in the distance rose the twin summits of the Pyramids of Ghizeh, no novel object, as my mind was familiar with their appearance. Then came the garden of Shoubrah, the Pasha's river steam fleet, *dahabiehs,* or Nile boats, their white expanse of graceful sail swelling in the breeze like the wings of a seagull; then the quaint, tumble-down edifices of Boulak, their latticed balconies of many patterns tottering over the brown waters of father Nile; then the transit quay, up the high flight of steps to gain the bank, into an omnibus! And with four greys at full gallop, along high embanked roads shaded by avenues of fine 'Lebbek' acacias, past rich gardens and verdant fields on either side, through the tall portals of European fortifications, past Saracenic mosques and Arab minarets of beautiful design into the Ezbekiyeh, an immense square laid out in fine gardens cut by carriage drives and walks, and fenced with hedges of pomegranate and myrtle, to the British hotel.

The next morning he went with a party to the Pyramids. The ladies started at five and drove as far as Old Cairo, and the two young men and I made outriders on donkeys. We crossed to Ghizeh, where all mounted donkeys, and away we trotted and cantered with janissaries and Indian servants as escort, the ragged donkey boys screeching behind us, through groves of date-palms, and broad fields of grain and lupins till we reached the sand, across which at a little distance we came to the sandy hills upon which are the mighty masses of the Pyramids. I will tell the truth, however; I did not think them so immense when I stood at their base. The great Pyramid especially covers so much ground and slopes upwards in such beautiful proportion that the mind does not grasp its magnitude. But the stones of which it is built and which seem so commonplace, on inspection are found to be enormous, and one then begins to discover what is the size of the mass which has been reared. I walked round its base and learned its dimensions, then got up to the portal, and from that walked along the edge with two Arabs, to the angle up which I was to ascend. I scarcely liked the footing along the ledge of the course of masonry which made my path, hanging over a height much too great to be agreeable. Then began the ascent: each Arab grasped one of my hands and dragged me up the steep incline and over the tall grades of stone, until my knees lost their strength and my chest its breath. I halted in a kind of grotto a long way up, perspiration streaming from every pore, my lungs labouring, and I turned dizzy when I looked down at where I had come from, and gazed upwards at what yet was to be surmounted. Again went the scramble up and up, until I sat on the great stones at the top, placing myself in the centre, where I could not see the sides of the steep I had just climbed. I preferred looking at the stretch of the desert, the further Pyramids of Abou Seer and Sakhara, the Nile with its verdant belt, the groves of Cairo, and the blue dome and tall minarets of Mohammed Ali Pasha's new mosque, standing on the citadel hill, a prominent object seen far away. I felt dead beat. At last came the descent, and as I stood on the extreme pinnacle and prepared to descend the first huge step of the gigantic staircase and saw the little pigmies below, I clutched my two Arabs with most earnest grasp, for one descends with one's back to the Pyramid, and the idea of being precipitated headlong down its side was by no means pleasant. All I know is that when I did get down my knees were powerless, and I had great difficulty in walking. I was never so tired in my life. We then rambled about among the tombs which were nothing particular, and then went to the Sphynx. It is a magnificent thing. A hasty glance at its mutilated features conveys nothing, but when one gazes long and earnestly upon it, its beauty dawns upon the senses with a feeling of sadness and surprised admiration of the extraordinary race which created these unparalleled monuments.

We then had breakfast on a ledge over the portal which leads to the entrails of the artificial mountain, and each recounted his or her impressions and experiences. I went in, and it was as much as I could do to stoop sufficiently, and yet get through its steep descents and ascents along difficult ways into the chamber where is the sarcophagus of that ancient monarch Suphis, or Cheops. I did not enter, much less ascend the second Pyramid, which is at a sharper angle and at the top has still the smooth casing left. We then went to Colonel Vyse's tomb, another nervous undertaking. Through the sand of the desert sinks into the rock a fosse, in a quadrangle of seventy-five feet deep and several feet wide; across this, and uniting the two walls of rock, is a wall a few feet wide but some seven feet below the level of the desert, and to get down upon this bridge and to walk across it, and clamber up on the other side is disagreeable, for on either side yawns a horrid grave for him whose foot should slip. When you reach you find yourself upon another broader wall girting a square, cut down fifty feet deep, and in the bottom of this great tomb lies an enormous square sarcophagus of black basalt, its lid sculptured as usual into a gigantic mummy. It is so large, and the depth is so great, that it is impossible to raise it, and so it remains in peace, an unattainable treasure to the many museums desirous of possessing it.

I was very glad to have seen this extraordinary sepulchre, hewn as usual on a scale which no other nation has attempted to imitate, but was also glad to find myself safe across its perilous bridge, which reminded me of the one suspended over hell and leading to paradise, across which the children of Islam have to pass, and from which the wicked tumble into the bottomless pit.

From *Letters to the East,* 1902

Tombs and Paradise

Constance Sitwell

Now hardly known, Constance Sitwell was an impressionable young woman with a gift for creating an atmosphere of time and place frozen forever in her words.

I AM SITTING ON the windowsill in my room eating sugar-cane. It is so juicy and fresh one could go on nibbling at it all day. The Soudanese servant, in a green cap and full green trousers, just now brought in a basket-full cut up into pieces, and set it down on the floor with a wide smile. My window is high above the ground; beneath, the whitewashed walls of the hotel ache in the midday glare; across the sand I can see the two great Pyramids, all their colour bleached out by the fierce light. But early this morning they looked very different. Just as the sun rose I came to this window and saw them standing there drowsily splendid, a tigerish gold set on the tigerish sand.

When first I drew near the Great Pyramid it was with a feeling of real shrinking. My mind was bludgeoned and I lifted bewildered eyes; it was almost painful to realize that this was the work of men's slight hands. One wanders along the base, wondering inanely at the vast blocks so perfectly placed along the bottom courses, one stops at the corners to gaze inanely at the fabulous line that goes slanting up and up into the sapphire blue.

The sun beat down on that stupendous slope of stone, and up on it a scattering of tiny men were crawling like sluggish flies; and presently I too started to climb up; we were making for the small opening that leads downwards to the King's Chamber. We reached it at last and the Bedouin in fluttering garments who was our guide slid down the polished shaft, at the bottom of which he lit some magnesium wire which showed a narrow gleaming passage going steeply down into the core. The unnatural light played pallidly upon the smooth dark stone as we followed after him. How hot it was in the thick darkness! As we plunged deeper into that stifling fastness of stone an awful oppression seized me, and at last when we came to the solemn bat-infested chamber which contains the royal sarcophagus the sense of the weight pressing downwards became almost more than I could bear. There was something terrible in the thought of the monstrous walls that surround the little empty tomb of sombre reddish granite.

That was my first impression, but later the pyramids grew very familiar. In the evening of the day before we started up the Nile I found my way to a little pyramid, half-ruined, nearby, and I climbed on to a rock at its base to sit and draw there. A tiny Arab boy came along behind. He was dressed in black with an old black cloak and had a round dirty-white cap on his head. His face was round too, and his broad smile always ready. When I sat on the sand he jerked off his ragged cloak in an instant and spread it on the ground, and while I sketched he sat holding my paint-box in one hand and a paint-brush in the other.

He had some friends who joined us; a boy from Tunis with pale golden-brown skin, and a diminutive donkey-boy dressed in a stained garment of yellow who dragged the dusty donkey behind him without even one necklet of beads to adorn it. He was seven years old, he said; his donkey looked a hundred. His small wrinkled face was as yellow as his dress, and his name, he told me with some importance as he lit a cigarette, was Abbas. I thought I should never forget that preternaturally old little creature who never smiled but puffed brazenly at his cigarette.

The boy from Tunis said that he could divine the future. He stared at me and then drew the sun's disc with rays spreading all round it in the powdery sand. Stooping lower and lower over the circle of his sun with an absorbed face he kept counting these rays, and muttering words that the others tried to translate. Having reached his conclusion he straightened himself and pronounced, 'Not happy, if too much thinking.' I thanked him but replied that I did not agree. For a moment, after taking my coin, he looked at me in silence, then kicking away the traces of his sun with his hard feet, he walked off apparently heading for the empty desert.

The plain stretching away below us had a veil, a bloom, on it now. The stripes of shrill green and yellow mustard, so garish in the full daylight, were a little dimmed. Far away, with a low line of pale blue hills running behind them, lay the four pyramids of Sakhara. Far away and faint they looked, wedge-shaped, rosy on the sunlit side and lilac in the shadow; the desert below shimmered in violet and gold and a group of lebbek trees with three palms amongst them stood up against it purple-black. A sound of monotonous singing drifted up through the dreamy evening air. It came from the valley below, and a few moments later a straggling procession appeared. I asked my little Arab what it was. He spread out his hands helplessly.

'Man getting married?' I suggested.

'No,' said the boy gravely, trying to explain. 'No; man finished.'

We watched the little file draw nearer; the funeral was evidently that of a poor man. It was led by a group of mourners in scanty, filthy garments who looked like beggars; two or three of them held one another's hands, for they were blind; and as they hobbled along they chanted in cracked voices the familiar chant to Allah. Next came another throng who were rather better clothed. 'Friends,' said the boy. There followed a company wearing turbans of dull indigo and carrying rather forlorn black flags. These, my companion told me, were 'Darwish'; and he pointed out the Koran which, under a piece of silk, was being borne along immediately in front of a sort of stretcher-bier. This was carried by four unconcerned-looking men, and upon it one could see the stiff dead form beneath a faded

Persian shawl which was its only covering. After it came women with dishevelled hair and idly wandering looks, who in forced voices kept up a ceaseless wail, and this ended the procession.

A Mohammedan donkey-boy who could talk English had joined us and he too watched, leaning against his donkey with one arm round its neck. I pointed at the procession that was passing out of sight and said, 'Man finished.'

He looked at me surprised.

'Not finished,' was his reply, spoken with unexpected vigour. 'He good man – he Mohammedan; he will be white bird in heaven; he will drink sweet waters, he will find the Tuba tree of gold, he will have a horse. There will be honey and milk and fountains of wine, and to him will be given a woman of Paradise who lives in a big pearl. He will never get old, and afterwards when Israfel shall sound his trumpet he will have again his camels.'

His camels! Well, paradise would not be paradise to him without them, I suppose. And my eyes fell upon a row of turbanned men who had come up silently and were sitting on a ridge of sand a little way off. They had their camels still! The strange contemptuous animals were couched on the ground near them and, with their heads held high, dark against the burning horizon, they looked as if they would be disdainful even of Paradise. Pieces of cloth, patched and striped, orange, maroon, and plum colour, were thrown about the men and their beasts. The light touched them and the pointed saddles with a fierce glow.

'So he will have his camels again,' I said, turning once more to the boy. 'And what about his wife?'

At this question he smiled rather scornfully and shook his head; then jumping on his donkey he thumped it with his fist and off they went down the incline.

My little Arab glanced at me with rather an apologetic air as he gathered together the sketching things. Standing up, he drew his thin cape round him and led the way down the crumbling stones, for it was time to go home.

From *Lotus and Pyramid*, 1928

4
Up the Nile

Up the Nile, 1943 and 1993
Dame Penelope Lively

Penelope Lively lived in Egypt as a child and returned half a century later with memories she compared with the world she came into.

TO ME, KHARTOUM had plenty of superficial resemblances to Cairo, in the cultural sense, but was stiflingly hot, and unquestionably distant.

It was a distance that was again defiantly physical. The journey was a re-creation in tangible and vivid form of that dominant and significant winding black line on the map. We moved slowly down the Nile, from Cairo to Aswan and there we got on to a train which crawled on and down to Wadi Halfa and then across the neck of the Nile's great bulge to the left and then moved parallel with it again until at last we arrived at Khartoum. It took a long time. Ten days? About that, I should think but, like those Mediterranean journeys, it became a separate unit of time, distinct from ordinary life, a capsule in which one was suspended in slow motion trundling for ever down and down, into another place. It was travel, as travel should be, and since I have never been back to

Khartoum, I am left with one surviving correct impression of the relation between time and space.

It would have been possible to fly. There was a flying-boat service which plied between Cairo and Khartoum, and indeed further still down into the continent, but it was expensive and was used mainly by those on official business or in a hurry. We had time enough to spare. We negotiated the Nile as people had always done, and probably not a great deal faster. We boarded a Nile steamer and chugged slowly down through Upper Egypt, until we got to Aswan and the limits of the Nile's navigability in this type of craft. Ahead lay the cataracts, and the narrowing of the river.

I have done that journey since, in a tourist cruise-boat. The steamer we took in 1943 was a passenger craft with three or four decks, as firmly hierarchical as the trains to Alexandria. There was the upper deck, which was first class and on which we rode. Individual cabins, dining and sitting saloons, a deck with awnings. Below was the second class, with sparser versions of these amenities, and below that yet was a pullulating free-for-all where people swarmed unconfined over open decks, cooking, sleeping, arguing. The boat hugged one bank, so that the other seemed so far away that you could barely see it. This was a wider, untamed Nile, not like the constrained and confined river which flowed through Cairo. And it went on, and on, and on. The steamer stopped frequently, for long periods. It would tie up for half a day at some riverside halt where people would pour on and off the lower deck and others proffered goods from the quayside: baskets of eggs, live chickens, oranges. Up in the higher regions, there was a certain amount of fretfulness. My mother muttered about the flying-boat. Lucy remarked that we might as well have walked, the time it was taking. And then at last we would be on the move again, after a great production over hoisting of gangways and casting off. I would settle down with my eyes glued to the muddy bank and the slopping shallows, waiting for crocodiles. So far as I was concerned, we were leaving the civilised world and heading into jungle country.

What I saw then – or did not see – is overlaid now by that subsequent visit, when I sat on the deck of a cruise-boat and saw that incomparable Nile landscape with all the intrusions of adult understanding and experience. I saw how beautiful it is. Brilliantly coloured – emerald-green, ochre, feathered all over with the silver-blue of palms, splashed with the jewelled dots of figures in *galabiyas* of vermilion, salmon-pink, midnight-blue, *eau-de-Nil* (actually the *eau* of the Nile is a sort of greyish-buff). The soft light of the afternoon, with the desert hills beyond the cultivation pale buff and lilac, the palms throwing long quivering reflections on the water. Evening, the hills now pink and shedding a glow on to the river. The violent descent of night, when the sky turns a heavy peach colour and the river is suddenly blue, and within ten minutes it is quite dark. The birds: flocks of egrets like shredded white paper flying low over the water as the sun goes down, flights of brightly coloured ducks exactly like those in tomb wall-paintings. A black ibis in silhouette on a spit of sand; a pelican patrolling the shore; a fish-eagle with golden head and shoulders perched on an overhanging branch. And the abiding interest of the river bank – clusters of mud huts like models of a prehistoric village, a man working a *shaduf*, women carrying water jars, children swinging from the huge leaves of a palm, and waving to the boat.

Back then, I must have seen all this, but differently. In the first place, I did not know that it was beautiful. It was profoundly familiar, and beauty to me would have implied something special and exotic. More significantly, I could not see it in terms of anything else. A perception of landscape is something learned – it depends upon individual knowledge and experience. At the age of ten, a mud hut to me was a mud hut, and could not be seen in the light of prehistory. A *shadûf* was a *shadûf*, and not a remarkable and ancient piece of engineering whereby water is raised from one level to another. Women carrying water jars were just that, without implications about health or economic circumstance. I probably noted the birds, but was far more interested in those potential crocodiles.

From *Going Back*, 1994

In the Fayoum: The Beauty Around

Lady Evelyn Cobbold

In 1911 the young Lady Evelyn Cobbold set off with a friend from Cairo on an expedition to the Fayoum – an area within a much larger depression surrounded by low mountains. Here it is cooler and lush, fertile crops can flourish, watered by ancient canals from the Nile.

SUNDAY, MARCH 5TH – This morning reveals to us that we are camped in a 'Garden of Allah', an opening in a forest of palm trees.

In the soft sand beneath grow all manner of lovely flowers: saxifrages with yellow-green, grey-green and blue-green foliage; mesambrianthemums with starry orange or purple-red blossom; pomegranates with shiny leaf and pink flower; while more marvellous than all else are the scarlet hibiscus that riot and spread in reckless fashion dazzling to the eyes.

Beautiful birds perch in the trees; hoopoes, golden orioles, and other brilliantly plumaged denizens of this country flutter about, seeming to know no fear. A stream gives a delicate sound of running water; a road, leading we know not where, surges with a continual flow of animated life. Horsemen in gracefully draped burnouses, with guns slung across their shoulders, mounted on their little Arab steeds, with high-peaked saddles and gay trappings, dash by. Ladies of the harem, veiled and muffled in voluminous black silk, amble along on donkeys. Long strings of camels more or less heavily burdened file past. The women of the people wrapped in their dark *hulalieyehs* swell the population of the road, while the small *gamin*, clad in orange or blue, flits about, adding colour to the scene.

Directly opposite our tents is a large sycamore tree, giving shade to a well and a marabout's tomb. Bamboos, prickly pears and mish-mish grow rampant beside it, and here are always to be found a few grave, bearded Arabs, smoking their *narghilehs*. Through long vistas in the far distance we can see the gold of the desert crossed with long stripes of blue shadow, caused by the white clouds floating above in the azure sky. This is indeed a day of content, and we lie absorbed in the beauty around. The magic of the sun gives of its warm, rich life; the magic of the flowers allures with sweet, seductive scent; the magic of the East holds us in its mysterious thrall.

From *Wayfarers in the Libyan Desert,* 1911

Digging with Nefertiti

Mary Chubb

Working at Tel el Amarna in 1930, Mary Chubb came new to Egypt and to archaeology. To her there was no necessity to focus only on research. She was fascinated, too, by the people with whom she worked; the work they were doing and the wonders of their finds, and the long-ago people who had once owned these trinkets and treasures, and walked in these places.

SOON WE APPROACHED THE DIG. But we heard it before we rounded a spur of protruding trees and saw it, looking like a newly disturbed anthill. There were occasional shouts, and bursts of strange singing. The work seemed to be in two places. The North Suburb was divided by a dry wadi at one point, which ran at right angles to the river; John had said it might even have been a canal in ancient times so that supplies could come by boat into the heart of the suburb. Most of the workmen, judging by the noise and the dust, were digging beyond this wadi; but a small group of them with about twenty children, and one *Gufti* in charge, had begun to tackle the south-west corner of the suburb to the north of the wadi. John was there talking to the *Gufti*, and we joined him.

He told us that the house he had begun lay in square T.34. We stood watching the digging. The sand still filled the rooms to a height of about three feet, so that the work went quickly; for as yet it was a simple matter of clearing down until floor level was nearly reached, where naturally most of the objects – some very fragile – and breakable structures, like steps and ablution slabs and brick benches, would be found. When this stage was reached, the digging would have to go much more cautiously and slowly.

Each *tourieh*-man would grab an empty rope basket from one or other of his attendant sprites, up-end it against his shins and in half a dozen swift movements of his *tourieh* draw into it all the sand it would hold. Then the child would pick it up and join the never-ending line of boys and girls moving towards the dump. These dumps had to be carefully sited, not too far from the work and yet not running over any hidden building. The children went to the far end of the dump, spilt their loads down the sloping chute, and quickly came back for more, swinging their baskets now, giggling and singing. Each dump began as a large mound of sand and then stretched out like a long straight dyke a few feet high, towards the desert; with the children running along the top, to and fro, to and fro, on a path beaten flat by their own feet.

It was wonderful how swiftly tons of sand were moved by this primitive method of human co-operation. The rubble seemed to melt away out of the rooms, and the children did not seem to tire. The pattern they made as they wound out of the house, up the dump, round the end and back again had the kind of nonchalant charm of a country dance. The cotton gowns of red and blue and green and orange and white fluttered along the grey-brown dump, the dust flew, and then the girls and boys passed back again into the house, with an occasional shy, brilliant glance up at us as they tossed the empty basket down for the hundredth time on father's toes.

'This is obviously a very fine house,' said John with satisfaction. 'Look at this.' He picked up something lying on the top of a low wall among cardboard boxes and notebooks. It looked to me like a very insignificant column base, just like the ones up at the house, but much smaller. I wondered why that made him think that this was a very fine house.

'It's so much smaller than the ones I've seen,' I ventured.

'Exactly,' he said. 'And whereabouts do you usually find column bases?'

'Well, on the floor, of course,' I answered, realizing that I was having an intelligence test.

'Exactly,' he said again, 'and we're nowhere near the floor of this house yet – a man found it almost as soon as we got the top layer off this morning – about three feet above ground level. What d'you make of that?' He and Hilda looked at me hopefully. I thought desperately. A small column base – but obviously nothing to do with the floor below, or it couldn't have been found where it was. Then I saw.

'Do you mean – could it have belonged to an *upper* floor and fallen through when the house became a ruin?'

'Yes,' they said together. 'And,' John went on, 'of course they had much thinner columns and smaller, lighter bases upstairs, so as to put as little pressure as possible on the ceiling of the room below. Ten marks. Come on, let's have lunch.'

I felt rather like Alice at the Mad Hatter's Tea Party. First going through a questionnaire, and then being suddenly invited to lunch in a waste of brick dust – the most unlikely place to find anything to eat. But at that moment old Umbarak appeared. He mounted the highest point of an old dump, holding a whistle; then, making sure that everybody could see him, he slowly drew out from his robes a colossal silver watch. (It was the *best* butter.) He gazed proudly at this for some time – I *think* upside down – and then took a swift unerring glance at the sun. Then he blew the whistle.

The hacking, scraping, shovelling, stopped. The children scampered down the dumps, screaming. The dust settled. The men stretched themselves, getting the kinks out of their spines, and then made their way slowly into the shade, settling down for an hour's rest with little bundles of bread and onions and dates and water-bottles. Tommy and Ralph and Hilary came towards us, looking hot. Another small procession was approaching from the direction of the house – John had seen it five minutes before – two of the big girls who had been taken on to do the water-carrying, laundry and odd jobs, followed by Young Abu Bakr. But whereas he went free of any burden, each girl was balancing on her head a large wooden box.

By the time they arrived, the six of us were sitting in the shade on the ground with our backs against a low wall. The girls yanked the boxes off their heads, laid them at our feet and retired giggling. Abu Bakr carefully unpacked and handed round the contents of one – a plate (hot), glass, fork, bread, even a paper napkin. The other box yielded an enormous cottage pie, still piping hot even after its long journey from the house. I looked inside the box afterwards and saw that there wasn't much Abd el Latif didn't know about the principle of haybox cookery. It was stuffed full of straw and tightly rolled wads of newspaper with a neat nest in the middle just big enough to jam the pie-dish into. He would have made a wonderful member of the Women's Institute…

My days were usually filled with office details of this kind; then there were accounts to do, and letters and reports to type, and objects to clean and perhaps mend. Sometimes I never got down to the dig at all for a day or two. I would look up from the typewriter through the window and see the yellow haze which always hung over the dig, and wish I were down there – sometimes, perversely, I might be happily slogging through a pile of prints, aware that I could polish them off before lunch if I kept at it, when there would be an unwelcome interruption; a message from the dig that I was wanted down there, and I would know that the job in hand would have to be shelved until after the evening's registration if it were to be finished the same day.

When something fragile was found, needing infinite care (and therefore time) and a light touch in handling, an appeal usually came up to the house, and either Hilda or I, or both of us if we could, went down to the dig. The *Guftis* were very clever at this work, but there wasn't always a *Gufti* available if delicate finds were turning up in more than one place at once.

It was one of those days. I was unscrambling the shorthand notes for the first report which John was sending to a London paper, when a shadow fell across the doorway behind me. Young Kassar Umbarak had run up from the dig with a note – although it was quite a mile, and a hot day, he wasn't even sweating. He stood there poised for the return flight, lithe and gay, his dark face alert. 'I think we've found a necklace,' said the note, 'can you come and deal with it, please?' Kassar flew off to say that I was on the way, and I collected a small drawing-board, pencils, brushes, tweezers, a knife, sun-glasses and a hat, waved farewell to the office, and set out, grumbling mildly, into the glare. When should I get at that report again? But as soon as I was on my way I began to think that it was rather a lark to be an odd-job person of this kind, slapping away at a typewriter one moment, and digging up ancient necklaces the next.

The house with the find had been cleared, except for a heap of rubble up against one low wall. Already some faience rings had been found in the heap, one bearing the cartouche of Nefertiti; and there were glazed beads to be seen here and there on the surface. And here, said John, pointing, was obviously the main part of a necklace to which most of these fragments probably belonged. Would I cope, while he moved the team to the next house? I said I would, took one look at the problem before me, and knew for a fact that the report, far away on my desk, would *not* be ready before nightfall.

I spent the afternoon working through the heap of rubble, picking up loose pendants which belonged to the necklace; the pace had to be slow, in case of disturbing yet another stretch of beads, perhaps made up in a different way; one ruthless jab with a knife into the rubble might bring down a shower of earth, and with it a stream of beads and pendants, carrying with them the secret of their shattered pattern, lost for ever. There was no such necklace, as it turned out, but I found one thing that belonged to the original one – a small flat triangular piece of cream-coloured faience, decorated with a small curving lotus flower in mauve and green. It had one hole pierced through at the apex and three close together along the opposite side. It was one of the two end-pieces of the necklace, each of its rows having once been fastened to one of the three holes; and the necklace must have been joined behind the neck by some kind of fastening, perhaps a thin cord, threaded through the hole in the apex of each end-piece.

At the end of the afternoon Kassar and another young *Gufti* carried the board up to the house without shifting a bead, and keeping perfectly calm; which was wonderful, really, as they had me nervously circling round them the whole way, rather in the manner of a cow with a new-born calf. They laid the whole thing in the antiquity room to await registration, and then trotted off to their evening meal. I had never felt grittier and sandier – or more elated. I asked Young Abu Bakr to bring a *tisht* (a flat tin bath, according to the manual) to my room as soon as he could. He went off to get it, respectful as ever, but with a sudden wild grimace which I had noticed before at the same request. It looked curiously like a hastily – but not quite hastily enough – concealed chortle. Once again looking the soul of decorum, he brought the *tisht* and lots of hot water, and retired; and it wasn't for weeks more that I learned that in his part of the country *tisht* meant frying-pan.

That was one difficulty in learning the language. The Egyptians were too polite to tell you when you went wrong; so long as they grasped your meaning, they would make no comment or correction, in fact even cheerfully use the wrong word back at you rather than upset you. Or perhaps, it wasn't so much politeness with these simple souls, as reluctance to end a good joke. I must have brightened life considerably for the Abu Bakr family while I was at Amarna. I can imagine Young Abu Bakr going back to the kitchen evening after evening and reporting to Uncle Abd el Latif that the lady was taking her bath in the frying-pan again, and Uncle doubling up in stitches every time, as he stirred the soup for the evening meal.

Necklaces were tricky because the threads had worn away, so that each pendant had to be lifted separately; and if a necklace had fallen in a heap before being buried, it was sometimes impossible to be sure that we had reconstructed the pattern correctly. Today we were lucky. I began by blowing away the surface sand very gently from the topmost beads – following the technique perfected by the *Guftis*, whom by now I had sometimes watched at just this kind of work. Through the thin veil of sand gleamed fragments of red and yellow and green and white. I brushed very lightly and then blew again – and there, lying on the sand, just as it had fallen more than three thousand years ago, was the main part of the necklace – a confused heap of beads at one end, to be sure, but happily a stretch of at least three inches lying quite flat, enough to show the pattern. The thread had perished, of course, but pendants and beads were lying exactly as if still threaded, in a fan-shape of three rows. If I were breathlessly careful, I could save this tiny piece of archaeological knowledge.

All the pendants were fashioned like fruit and flowers – there were enchanting white daisies, blue grape-clusters, mauve-tipped lotus petals, and rust-red pomegranates. Here it was again, this delight of Akhenaten's people in the beautiful simplicity of natural design and colour. I suddenly remembered, sitting back on my heels and gazing at it, a bead necklace I'd had as a little girl, which had completely fascinated me – small white daisies, yellow-hearted, linked together by fragile strings of tiny green beads. I felt sure that this necklace, too, had belonged to someone rather young, someone who had felt the same delight at wearing the pretty thing over her best white frock. I'd often wondered how the people of Amarna managed to lose so many of their possessions, as we picked up one thing after another out of the heaps of rubble – but after all, where was my daisy necklace now? Would some strange Wellsian creature, three thousand years hence, digging for history beneath the grassy mounds covering London, down through the collapsed rubbish that had once been Bloomsbury, come upon it, and finger it gently, and find it somehow pathetic?

But daydreams were a menace to neat field-work. I snapped out of it, and began to concentrate on the business of salvaging the necklace in good order. I made a diagram-drawing of the whole pattern on the drawing-board, writing in notes about the colour scheme, for some of the pendants were the same shape, but coloured differently. Then I began raising each pendant and small bead with tweezers, laying them out on the board beside the diagram in the correct order. This would save time when it came to rethreading the whole thing; but I still might need the drawing, for in the event of the necklace getting joggled out of position on its journey up to the house, or even by some misfortune spilled completely, it could still be correctly put together again by means of the diagram.

No one knew where Nefertiti's remains were laid, or indeed if any honour was paid to her in death. But now I knew this – that Nefertiti had lived close to this old house where we now sat talking about her; had passed the remaining few bitter years of her life, in the place that she made the last defiant stronghold of Atenism.

Our house, quite close to her northern dwelling that she named 'Castle of the Aten', was very large in comparison to many of the other private houses; perhaps it had belonged to one of her friends, or to a Minister of the new young Pharaoh.

Nefertiti must have known this house. It's not too fantastic to think that sometimes, long ago, people sitting as we were now, in this very room, may have heard the murmur of servants' voices out beyond the Central Room, speaking the lovely name as she drew near: 'Nefertiti. It is Nefertiti. The Beautiful Lady comes!' And in a moment she may have passed through this doorway, trodden this floor, and perhaps sat talking to her host with a small sandalled foot resting on this column base by my chair.

A little stooping now, ageing before her time, eyes shadowed with sorrow, the lid drooping rather more noticeably perhaps than it used to do over the impaired eye; the sweet mouth thinner and sharper than in the golden days when she was Akhenaten's 'Great of Favour, Mistress of Happiness, at hearing whose Voice one rejoices, soothing the heart of the king at home, Great and Beloved Wife of the King'. But still proud, still single-minded, very royal.

From *Nefertiti Lived Here,* 1930

This morning and tomorrow

H. V. Morton

Many travellers today fly into Luxor or Aswan and so have none of the pleasures of arriving there gradually by water or land, slowly waking up to Upper Egypt itself, as H. V. Morton did in 1938.

A TRAIN OF WHITE sleeping-cars leaves Cairo every night to go south to Luxor and Aswân.

When I glance from this train in the early morning, I see that we are steadily pounding along an embankment high enough above the surrounding land to lift it clear of the Nile's inundation. The sun is up; the sky is blue; the villages are awake. Donkeys come along the embankments with a mincing quick-step, bearing on their backs shrouded and rotund forms. At the corner of a patch of sugar cane I see a fox stealing home to his lair. Women in trailing robes stand at the wells, their water-pots held on head or shoulder; and in the villages among the palm trees, young and old sit warming themselves on the sunny sides of walls now streaked with the black, gigantic shadows of early morning.

No sooner does the warm light pour itself on Egypt than the whole land begins to wheeze, protest, and whine with a hundred aged voices like the sighs and groans of over-burdened men, for under tattered roofs of palm matting oxen slowly revolve as they make a circular journey which must have known a beginning perhaps before the Pyramids were built, but seems to know no end. And as they travel thus, without a hope of arrival, the wheezing, whining *sakiyeh* wheels turn as slowly as the mills of God, and a number of poised water-jars discharge their minute contribution to the welfare of the land.

Someday a learned man digging in the eloquent sands of this ancient country may come upon a carved stone bearing the design of the first *sakiyeh*, that most involved yet most simple of all man's inventions. With a gasp of delight he will discover in the neat language of hieroglyphs the name of the inventor – He-âth Rob-in-Son. For who can doubt but that the *sakiyeh* is really a joke that was taken seriously?

Men whose skins are the colour of mahogany and shine with a polished glow like Chippendale furniture, stand in mud trenches and pull down the slim, curved mast of the *shaduf*; dipping the bucket in blue water, they lift it dripping to the channel above. In a few hours' time, when the sun grows stronger, they will throw off their clothes and work like living statues of bronze.

Now and again, as the train presses southward, the Nile is seen hushed and windless in the golden morning, lying among the emerald embroidery of maize and sugar cane like a broad ribbon of palest blue. Upon the western bank the Libyan Desert rears itself in wild hills, sometimes the colour of a lion's skin, sometimes the colour of an orange; and in the valleys between these hills, and in their clefts and corries, the light is mauve, deepening to the misty blue of lavender in bloom.

The Nile twists and turns through the green land, often losing itself for a mile or two in groves of palm trees, then shining clear again, only to disappear into the green, its presence proclaimed by the tall sails of the *giyasat*, like the wings of white birds poised above the palm trees.

And now a man passes down the train, knocking at the doors and crying 'Luxor!' Tourists crowd to the windows, first at one side, then at the other, for they are nearing the great moment of travel in Egypt: Thebes, the Valley of the Tombs of the Kings, the Tomb of Tut-ankh-Amûn, the great Temple of Karnak.

I step from the train and select a smart little *'arabîa* drawn by two dapple-grey Arab ponies. We pass with a jingle of harness and a tinkle of bells through the streets of this growing town, dreary streets even in the eternal sunlight, and we come at last to one of the most exquisite places in the world – the banks of the Nile at Luxor.

There are two hotels on the bank, one hidden in a scented garden, the other on the riverside, like a ship in dock. A row of little shops faces the Nile: souvenir shops, shops full of fake antiques, English bookshops, and a pharmacy kept by a Scotsman who used to be a chemist in Chelsea.

I go to the big hotel on the riverfront. From the balcony of my room I look down on the river, which is twice as wide as the Thames at Westminster, but so smooth that the ferry-boat which is crossing to the west bank appears to be moving on a pale mirror.

The pink Libyan Hills shine against the sky on the other side of the river, their valleys and corries filled with blue shadows as if an artist who had been painting the bluebells at Kew had taken his brush and made a series of delicate little downward strokes on their tawny flanks.

It is that hour of the morning when the sound of Luxor is the prickle of water on tough leaves. I see gardeners directing hoses on exotic flowers that might be stamped from red velvet, on trailing banks of blue bougainvillæa, and on thousands of red and yellow rose trees. If they stopped for a month, the garden would wilt and go back to desert. Rain does not fall sometimes for sixteen years at a time, yet the constant effort of the men who pour Nile water on the garden makes it one of the greenest places in Egypt. No rain for sixteen years! Can you imagine what the sun is like at Luxor; how it springs into a clear sky every morning bringing long, golden hours, day after day, year after year, sinking to rest in the evening behind the Valley of the Dead, in a symphony of red, orange, lemon, and apple-green.

The certainty that tomorrow will be as lovely as today explains the sense of happiness and well-being which steals over you in this place.

From *Middle East,* 1941

Dearest Mutter

Lucie Duff Gordon

For seven years, the invalid Lady Duff Gordon made a house in the Temple at Luxor her home, from 1863 until she left to go upriver to Cairo and her inevitable death. There, the world came to call on her as foreign travellers followed the Nile south. But, possibly more important to her were the local people, who come alive again through her letters home to her husband in England. She tried to understand and came to love the Arabs' ways and told a friend from England that she had 'contrived to see and know more of family life than many Europeans who have lived here for years.' 'Weddings, funerals, marriage guidance, theological discussions, Arabic lessons – Lucie was game for anything; ready not only to understand but also to explain.' Thus Sarah Seawright writes of her in the introduction to her Letters from Egypt.

DEAREST MUTTER

I think I shall have an opportunity of sending letters in a few days by a fast steamer, so I will begin one on the chance and send it by post if the steamer is delayed long. The glory of the climate now is beyond description, and I feel better every day. I go out early – at seven or eight o'clock – on my tiny black donkey, and come in to breakfast about ten, and go out again at four.

I want to photograph Yussuf for you. The feelings and prejudices and ideas of a cultivated Arab, as I get at them little by little, are curious beyond compare. It won't do to generalise from one man, of course, but even one gives some very new ideas. The most striking thing is the sweetness and delicacy of feeling – the horror of hurting anyone (this must be individual, of course; it is too good to be general). I apologized to him two days ago for inadvertently answering the *Salaam aleykoum*, which he, of course, said to Omar [an Egyptian manservant] on coming in. Yesterday evening he walked in and startled me by a *Salaam aleykee* addressed to me; he had evidently been thinking it over whether he ought to say it to me, and come to the conclusion that it was not wrong. 'Surely it is well for all the creatures of God to speak peace (*Salaam*) to each other,' said he. Now, no uneducated Muslim would have arrived at such a conclusion. Omar would pray, work, lie, do anything for me – sacrifice money even; but I doubt whether he *could* utter *Salaam aleykoum* to any but a Muslim. I answered as I felt: 'Peace, oh my brother, and God bless thee!' It was almost as if a Catholic priest had felt impelled by charity to offer the communion to a heretic. I observed that the story of the barber was new to him, and asked if he did not know the *Thousand and One Nights*. No; he studied only things of religion, no light amusements were proper for an *Alim* (elder of religion); *we* Europeans did not know that, of course, as *our* religion was to enjoy ourselves; but *he* must not make merry with diversions, or music, or droll stories. (See the mutual ignorance of all ascetics!) He has a little girl of six or seven, and teaches her to write and read; no one else, he believes, thinks of such a thing out of Cairo; there many of the daughters of the *Alim* learn – those who desire it. His wife died two years ago, and six months ago he married again a wife of twelve years old! (Sheykh Yussuf is thirty he tells me; he looks twenty-two or twenty-three.) What a stepmother and what a wife! He can repeat the whole Koran without a book, it takes twelve hours to do it. Has read the Towrát (Old Testament) and the el-Aangeel (Gospels), of course, every *Alim* reads them. 'The words of Seyyidna Eesa [Jesus] are the true faith, but Christians have altered and corrupted their meaning. So we Muslims believe. We are all the children of God.' I ask if Muslims call themselves so, or only the slaves of God. ''Tis all one, children or slaves. Does not a good man care for both tenderly alike?' (Pray observe the Oriental feeling here. *Slave* is a term of affection, not contempt; and remember the Centurion's '*servant* (slave) whom he loved.') He had heard from Fodl Pasha how a cow was cured of the prevailing disease in Lower Egypt by water weighed against a Mushaf (copy of the Koran), and had no doubt it was true, Fodl Pasha had tried it. Yet he thinks the Arab doctors no use at all who use verses of the Koran.

M. de Rougé, the great *Egyptologue*, came here one evening; he speaks Arabic perfectly, and delighted Sheykh Yussuf, who was much interested in the translations of the hieroglyphics and anxious to know if he had found anything about Moussa (Moses) or Yussuf (Joseph). He looked pleased and grateful to be treated like a 'gentleman and scholar' by such an *Alim* as M. de Rougé and such a Sheykhah as myself. As he acts as clerk to Mustapha, our consular agent, and wears a shabby old brown shirt, or gown, and speaks no English, I dare say he not seldom encounters great slights (from sheer ignorance). He produced a bit of old Cufic MS. and consulted M. de R. as to its meaning – a pretty little bit of flattery in an Arab *Alim* to a Frenchman, to which the latter was not insensible, I saw. In answer to the invariable questions about all my family I once told him my father had been a great *Alim* of the Law, and that my mother had got ready his written books and put some lectures in order to be printed. He was amazed – first that I had a mother, as he told me he thought I was fifty or sixty, and immensely delighted at the idea. 'God has favoured your family with understanding and knowledge; I wish I could kiss the Sheykhah your mother's hand. May God favour her!' Maurice's [her son's] portrait (as usual) he admired fervently, and said one saw his good qualities in his face – a compliment I could have fully returned, as he sat looking at the picture with affectionate eyes and praying, *sotto voce*, for *el gedda*, *el gemeel* (the youth, the beautiful), in the words of the *Fathah*, 'O give him guidance and let him not stray into the paths of the rejected!' Altogether, something in Sheykh Yussuf reminds me of Worsley [an English friend]: there is the same look of *Seelen reinheit*, with far less thought and intelligence; indeed little thought, of course, and an additional childlike innocence. I suppose some medieval monks may have had the same look, but no Catholic I have ever seen looks so peaceful or so unpretending. I see in him, like in all people who don't know what doubt means, that easy familiarity with religion. I hear him joke with Omar about Ramadán, and even about Omar's assiduous prayers, and he is a frequent and hearty laugher. I wonder whether this gives you any idea of a character new to you. It is so impossible to describe *manner*, which gives so much of the impression of novelty. My conclusion is the heretical one: that to dream of converting here is absurd, and, I will add, wrong. All that is wanted is general knowledge and education, and the religion will clear and develop itself. The elements are identical with those of Christianity, encumbered, as that has been, with asceticism and intolerance. On the other hand, the creed is simple and there are no priests, a decided advantage. I think the faith has remained wonderfully rational considering the extreme ignorance of those who hold it. I will add Sally's [her English maid's] practical remark, that 'The prayers are a fine thing for lazy people; they must wash first, and the prayer is a capital drill.'

You would be amused to hear Sally when Omar does not wake in time to wash, pray, and eat before daybreak now in Ramadán. She knocks at his door and acts as muezzin. 'Come, Omar, get up and pray and have your dinner.' (The evening meal is 'breakfast,' the early morning one 'dinner'.) Being a light sleeper she hears the muezzin, which Omar often does not, and passes on the 'Prayers is better than sleep' in a prose version. Ramadán is a dreadful business; everybody is cross and lazy – no wonder! The camel-men quarrelled all day under my window yesterday, and I asked what it was all about. 'All about nothing; it is Ramadán with them,' said Omar laughing. 'I want to quarrel with someone myself; it is hot today, and thirsty weather.' Moreover, I think it injures the health of numbers permanently, but of course it is the thing of most importance in the eyes of the people; there are many who never pray at ordinary times, but few fail to keep Ramadán. It answers to the Scotch Sabbath, a comparison also borrowed from Sally.

Friday – My friend Seleem Effendi has just been here talking about his own affairs and a good deal of theology. He is an immense talker, and I just put *eywas* (yes) and *là* (no) and *sahé* (very true), and learn manners and customs. He tells me he has just bought two black slave women, mother and daughter, from a Copt for about £35 the two. The mother is a good cook, and the daughter is 'for his bed', as his wife does not like to leave Cairo and her boys at school there. It does give one a sort of start to hear a most respectable magistrate tell one such a domestic arrangement. He added that it would not interfere with the *Sittel Kebeer* (the great lady), the black girl being only a slave, and these people never think they have children enough. Moreover, he said he could not get on with his small pay without women to keep house, which is quite true here, and women are not respectable in a man's house on other terms. Seleem has a high reputation, and is said not to 'eat the people'. He is a hot Mussulman, and held forth very much as a very superficial Unitarian might do, evidently feeling considerable contempt for the absurdities, as he thinks them, of the Copts (he was too civil to say Christians), but no hatred (and he is known to show no partiality), only he 'can't understand how people can believe such nonsense.' He is a good specimen of the good, honest, steady-going man-of-the-world Muslim, a strong contrast to the tender piety of dear Sheykh Yussuf, who has all the feelings which we call Christian charity in the highest degree, and whose face is like that of 'the beloved disciple', but who has no inclination for doctrinal harangues like worthy Seleem. There is a very general idea among the Arabs that Christians hate the Muslims; they attribute to us the old Crusading spirit. It is only lately that Omar has let us see him at prayer, for fear of being ridiculed, but now he is sure that is not so, I often find him praying in the room where Sally sits at work, which is a clean, quiet place. Yussuf went and joined him there yesterday evening, and prayed with him, and gave him some religious instruction quite undisturbed by Sally and her needlework, and I am continually complimented on *not hating* the Muslims. Yussuf promises me letters to some *Alim* in Cairo when I go there again, that I may be shown the Azhar (the great college). Omar had told him that I refused to go with a janissary [guard] from the Consul for fear of giving offence to any very strict Muslims, which astonished him much. He says his friends shall dress me in their women's clothes and take me in. I asked whether as a concealment of my religion, and he said no, only there were 'thousands' of young men, and it would be 'more delicate' that they should not stare and talk about my face.

Seleem told me a very pretty grammatical quibble about 'son' and 'prophet' (apropos of Christ) on a verse in the Gospel, depending on the reduplicative sign (*sheddeh*) over one letter; he was just as put out when I reminded him that it was written in Greek, as our amateur theologians are if you say the Bible was not originally composed in English. However, I told him that many Christians in England, Germany and America did not believe that Seyyidna Eesa [Jesus] was God, but only the greatest of prophets and teachers, and that I was myself of that opinion. He at once declared that that was sufficient, that all such had 'received guidance', and were not 'among the rejected'; how could they be, since such Christians only believed the teaching of Eesa, which was true, and not the falsifications of the priests and bishops (the bishops always 'catch it', as schoolboys say). I was curious to hear whether, on the strength of this, he would let out any further intolerance against the Copts, but he said far less and far less bitterly than I have heard from Unitarians, and debited the usual most commonplace, common-sense kind of arguments on the subject. I fancy it would not be very palatable to many Unitarians, to be claimed *mir nichts dir nichts* as followers of *el-Islam*; but if people really wish to convert in the sense of improving, that door is open, and no other.

Monday, 7th – The steamer is come down [from Cairo] already and will, I suppose, go on tomorrow, so I must finish this letter to go by it. I have not received any letter for some time, and am anxiously expecting the post. We have now settled into quite warm weather ways, no more going out at midday. It is now broiling, and I have been watching eight tall fine blacks swimming and capering about, their skins shining like otters' fur when wet. They belong to a *gelláab* – a slave-dealer's boat. The beautiful thing is to see the men and boys at work among the green corn, the men half-naked and the boys wholly so; in the sun their brown skins look just like dark clouded amber – semi-transparent, so fine are they.

I rejoice to say that on Wednesday is Bairam, and tomorrow Ramadan 'dies.' Omar is very thin and yellow and headachey, and everyone is cross. How I wish I were going, instead of my letter, to see you all, but it is evident that this heat is the thing that does me good, if anything will.

From *Letters from Egypt, 1864*

Early Morning in Luxor Temple

Paul William Roberts

As I do when I visit, Paul William Roberts rises early to visit Luxor Temple before the city is properly awake, and the tourists have drifted out of their hotels. Then one can have it to oneself with only the workmen and the guardians.

WE ARRIVED AT LUXOR on Monday, 30 April, at 8.30pm. The moon was rising. We go ashore. The Nile is low, and there is quite a broad stretch of sand between the water and the village of Luxor; we have to climb the bank to see anything. On the bank, a short man accosts us and asks to be our guide. We ask him if he speaks Italian. '*Si, signor, molto bene*.'

> The mass of the pylons and the colonnades looms in the darkness; the moon, just risen behind the double colonnades, seems to be resting on the horizon, low and round and motionless, just for us, and the better to illumine the horizon's great flat stretch.

Gustave Flaubert, *Travel Notebooks,* 1850

In fact, Flaubert arrived on April 29, according to his diary. I quibble because one hundred and forty years later I arrived on the same date. If the name 'Thebes' conjured up visions of an incomparable past, that of Luxor reminded me of a cheap synthetic fabric. Essentially it is the Arab town that grew up around the ruins of

Thebes, sprawling mainly along the east bank of the purling Nile. My first sight, through that giant TV-screen window in my cabin, was a rosy-fingered dawn casting pale fuchsia light on the low mountain range of the west bank. Few buildings were visible there.

The ancient Egyptians called the west, the region of the setting sun, Amenti. It was the domain of Osiris, god of the dead, also known as Khentamenti, Chief of the West. Apart from that of Akhenaten, the heretical 'monotheistic' pharaoh, all burials in dynastic Egypt took place on the west bank. Within the mountain range I watched through dawn's mist lie the great pharaonic tombs: the Valley of the Kings, the Valley of the Queens, the Tombs of the Nobles, the Temple of Queen Hatshepsut, the Colossi of Memnon, the Ramesseum, and more. In fact, if you include the mighty Luxor and Karnak temple complexes on the east bank, Thebes and Luxor contain more than eighty-five per cent of the remains of ancient Egypt. Looking out across these western lands, I could comprehend the ancient Egyptian preoccupation with death as the goal and apotheosis of life. They were still forbidding yet powerfully attractive, hostile yet enticing.

I decided to go out alone in the early morning light, one of the best times to view and photograph the great Egyptian monuments. The ship was quiet, and so was Luxor. Thanks to construction engineers from China, there is now a new corniche along the water's edge rather than the broad stretch of sand Flaubert encountered. As I climbed the steps to street level, the breathtaking pylons and columns of the colossal Luxor Temple rose up, bathed in soft golden light filtering through a delicate mist, the shadows on its western side defining the exquisitely carved colonnades, massive hieroglyphic reliefs, rows of sphinxes, towering statues, and the serene harmony of the whole vast complex.

The low, rickety gates were locked, but in a booth nearby a hostile old man in a white turban, who looked as if he'd used tar as toothpaste for many years, growled at me, beckoning with a long, gnarled finger. 'Ticket ticket,' he said. With great effort, many groans and sighs, he walked the three yards to the temple entrance and unlocked a book-sized padlock to admit me.

The inner compound looked deserted – something to be

devoutly wished of Egyptian sacred sites – and even the surrounding town displayed few signs or sounds of life. Like most midnight ramblers, Egyptians are not early risers. As someone had advised, I avoided looking to my right at the temple entrance, walking to the left down the avenue of sphinxes that once stretched nearly a mile to the Karnak Temple of Amon, creating a sacred complex whose dimensions are not equalled on earth.

Now the avenue extends only a few hundred yards, and sphinxes in various states of ruin can be seen in fields, backyards, and dumps all the way to Karnak if you walk the ancient route. All the sphinxes, with their human heads on lions' bodies, appeared identical in size. One guidebook suggested they were so perfectly matched by the stonemasons that they looked as if they had been poured from a mold. This seemed true, too, until I noticed that their human faces were subtly different, one even distinctly fat and jowly. Like the gargoyles on Gothic structures in Europe, had the sphinxes been endowed with the characteristics of local personages? I wondered. Actually most of the faces are essentially that of one man, Amenhotep III, with the bodhisattva smile reminiscent of the great Indian sacred sculptures, or the tantalizing transcendent mystery implicit in the smiles of da Vinci's Mona Lisa and his Saint John the Baptist. That smile, reflecting a sublime inner secret, never changes on the sphinxes, but the face around it does – perhaps making Amenhotep III into Everyman?

Finally turning around, I faced the shattering magnificence of the temple's numinous entrance. Slowly I retraced my steps, picturing myself part of an ancient procession, the regularly spaced sphinxes on either side passing like the steady beat of enormous drums. Before the towering pylons, to the left, stands a single obelisk, once part of a pair. Flaubert explains what happened to its partner in his travel notes: 'The obelisk that is now in Paris was against the right-hand pylon. Perched on its pedestal, how bored it must be in the Place de la Concorde! How it must miss its Nile! What does it think as it watches all the cabs drive by, instead of the chariots it saw at its feet in the old days?' Flaubert was eleven years old when the obelisk was dismantled by French naval officers and engineers in 1832 to be transported to France. Its arrival caused enormous interest. In fact, since the ship carrying it sailed up the Seine from Le Havre to Paris, docking in Rouen for a few days, he might even have visited it on board, as many of his fellow citizens did. To me, the remaining obelisk seemed lonely, too, a widow at the end of a long and happy marriage. The colossus to the right of the pylons is of the ubiquitous Rameses II, and now, unobscured by the plundered obelisk, it looks all the more imposing. The wrecks of other colossi line the outer wall and are due for total restoration ... someday.

Across the length and breadth of this pylon wall is, as usual, a martial frieze in relief. This one, however, is exceptionally grand. One can only imagine how dramatic it would have looked when freshly carved and covered in vibrant colours. It depicts the Battle of Kadesh, an event, like so much of ancient Egyptian history, over which there is much dispute.

Rameses II, forewarned that a coalition centering on the Hittites and the nomadic Bedouin was forming itself in Anatolia (now Turkey) to invade his kingdom, gathered his army and marched through Palestine, intending to nip this nuisance in the bud. Outmanoeuvred by the enemy, betrayed and abandoned by his own army, we're told, Rameses prayed to Amon for assistance. Since no one had done more for Amon than Rameses, particularly in the field of temple-building, the god readily agreed to help him, descending into Rameses's body and giving him the strength to vanquish his foes single-handed, killing thousands and pitching chariots into the Orontes River. Yet, we learn, even after this total rout the battle somehow goes on for another fifteen years. Finally a peace treaty is signed and Rameses – evidently still working on his two hundred-odd children – takes a daughter of the Hittite king as wife, meting out other terms favourable to both sides. The problem all this raises is whether these events are to be taken literally or symbolically.

As in the legend of Cheops's burial in the Great Pyramid, there are again striking parallels here with the myth of Jesus. It's worthwhile quoting a section from Sir Alan Gardiner's translation of the invocation to Amon spoken by Rameses before the battle and carved beneath this scene on the pylons of the Luxor Temple:

> I invoke thee, O my father, Amon! I find myself in the midst of great multitudes of strangers; all the nations joined against me. My cohorts have forsaken me, not one of my charioteers has looked back to me, and when I summon, none harken to my voice. Yet I believe that Amon is worth more to me than millions of soldiers, and the hundreds of thousands of chariots, more than countless brethren and youths united with one heart! The work of many men is nothing! Amon is greater than all!
>
> My voice reaches unto Hermonthis; Amon responds to my call, he stretches forth his hand to me and I rejoice; he calls out from behind. 'I hasten to thee, to thee, Rameses Meriamon ["beloved of God"]. I am with thee! It is I, thy father, my hand is with thee, and I am of more avail than a hundred thousand men. I am the lord of strength, lover of valour. I have found a courageous heart and I am content. All that I desire will come to pass.'

That Amon has much in common with the Judeo-Christian concept of the one God is made clear by an incantation surviving in a Late Kingdom document called the Leyden Papyrus; Stanza 600 says of Amon that 'he gives birth to everything that is and causes all that exists to live.'

It's important to have this other perspective on the nature of ancient Egyptian beliefs, particularly if you find yourself as moved as I often was by the deep spirituality I found in the tombs and temples of Egypt, and particularly at Philae, Luxor, Karnak, and the Giza pyramids. Otherwise it is easy to become oppressed by these monuments and obsessed with the suffering one imagines was inflicted on the peasants and slaves who built them. The grandeur of Egypt quickly becomes a pile of stones, as one German tourist on the beach at Hurghada told me: 'You zee vun, you zee dem all.' In fact, there is no specific evidence to suggest that the Hebrews were ever enslaved in Egypt or that the Exodus occurred. There is no evidence of slavery in pharaonic times until comparatively late in Egyptian history. Only Cecil B. De Mille ever thought the Hebrews were forced to build the pyramids.

Thus, I entered the Luxor Temple looking not for pharaonic one-upmanship, but for evidence of spiritual concerns, arcane knowledge. That first morning I wanted just a first impression. The magnificent striding colossus of Rameses II with its unusually vivid sense of motion dominates the court he constructed. Now, incongruously, the same court also houses the little mosque of Abu al-Haggag, from which a muezzin starts his call as I pass; then the soaring colonnade, its twin line of pillars raising my spirits with their fluted stone all the way to heaven; Amenhotep III's Peristyle Court, broad, majestic, echoing with the invocations of a thousand years' devotion to union with God; beyond it the forest-like Hypostyle Hall, leading into a series of small chambers and the Inner Sanctuary itself, where the stones feel full of intense superhuman power; then, at the far end, another pillared hall leading to what is known as the Triple Sanctuary, the place where, according to some symbolist interpretations, Amon, the 'hidden', makes flesh out of spirit, the place where the Three-in-One of the New Testament are one and yet three. So impressed was the poet Rimbaud that here, up on the far right, he carved his name in bold capitals into the hard grey stone of a lintel.

I felt dazed at this point, my head spinning. I'd never realized the temples of Egypt were built on such a scale. It had taken me over an hour to walk through the complex. In comparison, anything in Greece seemed puny and lacking in resonance, in the mystic.

Wondering how to photograph myself for the family album in front of the entrance pylons in this magic light, I noticed a man halfway along the avenue of sphinxes surrounded by serious cameras. As I approached, I could see him scowl; he wanted to be alone here, too. I asked him if he'd mind taking a snap. He grunted, looking at my idiot-proof fully automatic Nikon as if I'd handed him a turd. I posed, then asked him where he was from, what he was up to.

A Swiss magazine had sent him to photograph a massive colour spread, he told me between gritted teeth. Did he like Egypt? At this he exploded, cursing everyone and everything he'd encountered – the dirt, the chaos, the hustlers, the incompetence, the bureaucracy. 'And now,' he shrieked, 'that idiot at the gate won't let me bring in my large-format because he says I have no permit for professional equipment!' I offered to find out if my government credentials pulled any weight.

'I been everywhere,' the photographer hissed, 'but I never encounter anything like this!' He must have meant 'everywhere' in Europe.

At the gate the turbanned official turned my documents sideways, upside down, back to front, then waved approval. The photographer hefted his mighty large-format from the hut where he'd been forced to leave it and sighed gratitude. I wanted to infuse him with what I felt, but looking at the professional baggage he was forced to lug around wherever he went, I decided he'd probably be incapable of appreciating any trip.

I sat for a while in the little garden behind the temple. Date palms, mimosas, broad-leaved banana trees, oleanders and lemon trees shaded me in deep green coolness from the ascending sun. Arabian jasmine diffused its perfume everywhere, and doves cooed under its leaves. Two old men sat puffing on a *narghile* as the city behind them came to rowdy life. Stalls full of fake antiquities and spurious papyri opened up; horse-drawn calèches packed with schoolchildren clip-clopped down to the corniche, horns honking, brasses jingling; roadside food stands cooked up *foul* beans and onions to be served in oven-fresh pitta halves. The sounds and the smells and the sights were intoxicating.

From *River in the Desert:*
A modern traveller in Ancient Egypt, 2006

On the Other Side with the Pharoah

Marta Bibescu

The Romanian princess recorded incidents, memories, flashes of imagination and ideas as she travelled. Men across the world were magnetised by her charms. Across the river from Luxor she enchanted the archaeologists and was enchanted by their discoveries. Now those discoveries are stored and displayed in the treasure house of the Cairo Museum.

'RAMESES, THE WELL BELOVED, has offered this monument in eternal tribute to his father Amen-Ra. He had a pillared hall built, vast and magnificent, in proud white stone. The centre group of columns is in flower, while those at the side end in tight buds. It will be a permanent place for his father to dwell.'

I find written there with hammer blows in the stone what I already knew from looking at the Luxor temple: that the architrave rests on the buds of water lilies *before* the Sun has touched them, and that the centre of the roof rests on the same flowers *afterward* when the Sun has opened them.

The joy of this corroboration.

The largest colossus in Egypt is here at the Ramasseum, mysteriously overthrown. Was it an earthquake or Christians? No one could tell me. The handsome head of blue granite is Rameses with his childlike lips full and smiling.

The men who carved the Sphinx of the great Pyramid and the blue colossus of the Ramasseum knew what a smile was made of.

Their faith in the puissance of life inherent in the human form shaped their language. The Egyptian phrase for sculpture is translated by: 'to give life to the face of the King', literally 'to animate' it.

Beneficent rays of the sun break out, fan-shaped, from under the cartouche effaced by that renegade sun-worshipper, Amen-hetep IV.

At the end of each ray blossoms a property to ease pain: a healing hand, a masseur's thumb, a dentist's forceps, a surgeon's scalpel, a druggist's scales, or the key to the breath of life ...

What a marvellous trademark for the ultraviolet rays of Doctor X – !

The Valley of Kings, Tuesday, January 26.

I visit Howard Carter, who is going to take me to the tomb of the Living King, whom American ladies at the Winter Palace dub familiarly 'the poor little man Tut'.

Carter had written to me to arrange a time. I call for him at his dwelling in the desert. It is just a cube of mud with a rectangular garden formed by the shadow of the house. His studio window opens out into the daylight. This is where he reads Balzac.

In the mountain necropolis, I am first honoured with admission to the laboratory. It is an empty tomb with fresco paintings, furnished with wooden tables, a stove, and a soldering-lamp. Carter works here to get the coating of rosin from his treasures.

Mr Lucas, his laboratory assistant, is heating the golden trappings of the mummy in a flame to melt the aromatic gums encrusting it. It is a long, patient task.

This spectacled sage shows me a bird on a golden plaque no larger than the nail on my little finger. The artificer had used five different enamels to colour the feathers.

At last here is little King Tut and all the things they found with him. Some are indifferent, and some are extraordinarily beautiful.

The jewels, for instance, are of two distinct types. First, there are the ready-made articles like those in the Cairo Museum, which come from the regular funeral establishments. It is astonishing to find them still intact, but they are common enough models, and I do not care for them. Second, there are the real things chosen from his own personal effects, things he used or wore during his lifetime. They can be recognised by that splendid something which, I suppose, would be called their reality.

Who threw them there in his coffin at the last second against all precedent? They are wrapped up, no matter how, like a furtive love-gift, defrauding the royal patrimony of the living King's real jewels.

There are five rings and two daggers, a crown, and rouge-boxes of singular beauty, besides toilet articles hermetically sealed, which pre-supposes a good valet.

Carter explained to me what I saw on the signet of one of the rings: the swift soul and the setting sun. The soul is represented by the largest of the swallows, which we call a swift. It is fastened to the sun of the dead, the setting sun. It is made so beautifully, so simply and starkly, out of a blood-coloured cornelian. A delicate allusion to the bird who always appears here, as in Europe, standing out against the setting sun.

These jewels do not resemble anything special; rather are they like the most beautiful things of every age and every country. They have such startling beauty that they have lost all national character.

The crown is very much like a Carlovingian jewel. The daggers bring to mind the most accomplished craftsmen of the Renaissance. Some of the objects suggest a Chinese source, some Indian, and others Persian or French. There are canes which match those of Marie-Antoinette.

National differences disappear when a certain plane of beauty is reached. I always remember the bold words of Montaigne, 'I have seen everywhere ruined dwellings, statues, land and sky. They are always man-made.'

One of the canes is a simple reed, topped with gold. It has inscribed on it these words, 'This has no value, but is a favourite of the King's, because it was cut by Majesty's own hands on the shore of his best-loved lake.'

The inscription has two interpretations. The first is the more sentimental. That is that the Queen is meant by 'Majesty'. But I much prefer the other; that the cutting of the little reed by the King himself was a memorable event in the life of a handsome youth so carefully guarded and served that he never did anything with his own hands.

I saw his bouquet also. I held it in my hands. They found it when they opened the tomb, placed upright at the foot of the sarcophagus.

It was made of olive and willow branches, cornflowers, blue nympheas and belladonna berries. They have all kept their form and have not quite lost their colours.

After the view of the jewels, canes, daggers and the bouquet we came to Him, lying under a veil of hospital gauze, the Living Image of God in his temporary coffin of wood. His little face, 'so sad', Carter said. His teeth, which betray his youth, give him a sorrowful smile. His lips, which I had seen in the mask at Cairo, so much alive, like a juicy fruit swollen with water and sugar pulp, are here dried up and dead.

I saw his death smile flickering over the windscreen of the Ford which took us back to the station, and in the wistful expression of the little Nubian chauffeur who looked enough like Tut-Ankh-Amen to be his brother.

From *Jour d'Egypte*, 1930

Luxor-Aswan return

Deborah Manley

THE STATION AT LUXOR did not look like the sort of place we would find out about trains. We decided to try elsewhere and set off through the dusty streets towards the Nile and Thomas Cook's office, nestling like a memory at the foot of the grand sweep of steps up to the reviving splendours of the Winter Palace Hotel.

No, they did not know about trains. Try the agency along the road.

I'm not sure if it was the right agency that we chose, but it had posters encouraging us to take the Blue Train to Nice as if it still existed and an immensely helpful man who gave us train times south up the river to Aswan: 7.00, 7.30 and 8.30 daily. The two hundred and ten kilometres would cost the equivalent of £1.50 – first class, air-conditioned.

By the temple of Luxor is the National Tourist Office. I went in to see what they had to offer. Three welcoming staff members and not a poster or leaflet in sight, so I asked again about trains to Aswan: 6.20 and 8.30 I was told. The smiling, cheery man added, 'But the trains are often late – half an hour – an hour – maybe two hours. They come from Cairo. Ask your hotel to check before you leave.'

Waiting in the hotel lounge seemed infinitely preferable to Luxor station after one morning, en route to visit the temple at Dendera, we had seen what must have been the 6.20 train racing towards Luxor after eight o'clock – or perhaps it was the 8.30 train an hour early.

Tickets, we discovered, could only be bought at the station, but it was obviously better to get tickets in advance. Back to the station. There were two queues: one long and one short. We were told authoritatively that one is for today, the other for tomorrow; that one is for daytime only, the other for night travel; that one is for first, the other for second, class. We decided to join the shorter queue.

'Two first-class tickets to Aswan, please, for tomorrow.'

'Why not come tomorrow then?'

'We would like to buy them today.'

'OK. Second- class.'

'No, first, please.'

'Air-conditioned?'

'Yes.'

The ticket seller marked a chart to book our places. There were not many places left. He selected the tickets and wrote on them. He rolled the date stamp for the next day, inserted it back into its brass holder and carefully stamped our tickets. Behind him the computerised ticket dispenser glowed dustily. The charge was the equivalent of £1.25 each to go two hundred and ten kilometres to Aswan and return. Perhaps it was not return. We cannot read Arabic and did not know. The man in the Nile-side agency had got one thing right: the train was said to go at eight o'clock. Time would tell.

As advised by the Tourist Office, we got the hotel to ring the station.

'Ring back in thirty minutes. We will know then.'

In twenty minutes we rang.

I know very little Arabic, but I understood the last phrase: 'Insh Allah.' The train, Allah willing, would be there at eight, in ten minutes' time. We rushed for a taxi.

It turned out not to be the eight o'clock first-class air-conditioned train but the 6.20 *wagons lits*: train 86, not 88.

'You,' the train steward said sympathetically, standing on the steps of the carriage, 'must wait for two trains. That will be your train.'

We pleaded, explained and almost despaired.

He stood back and let us aboard. 'If any official asks, you are travelling with Arc Tours from Cairo.'

'Our nationality? English? German?'

'French. You are French.'

'Oui, monsieur. Merci beaucoup.'

From the train we looked down into the backyard life of the villages. Black-dressed wives lay creamy flat loaves to leaven in the morning sun. Donkeys trotted along, man- or fodder-laden. Half-drowsing men watched cattle chew the cud.

In the early morning all is sand-beige or green-grey-green. The air is dust-laden below the blue sky. There is an occasional splash of other colours: an azure-painted house, a child's acid yellow robe; the black silhouettes of the women, the red letters TOYOTA on a white billboard, an ochre building reflecting the sun. The trunks of the casuarinas along the road that parallels the track are painted white, mirrored in the murky canal, which stands green-grey-green between the railway and the road. Red plastic buckets are balanced on the heads of straight black-clothed women as they climb from the canal edge.

Sometimes, as the train ran along, all was unrelentingly clay-beige, tints and shades of one colour: land, buildings, bricks laid out to dry row after row, flat or stacked in patterns so sun and breeze could bake them. Domed mausolea were clay-beige too.

Elsewhere all was green. Fodder green. Grain green. Palm green. Casuarina green. Lush green. Dry green. A child in acid green.

A working camel towered over his master bent to his crops. Camels work very little for their living, loaded no heavier than donkeys, slower moving, more arrogant. A scarecrow peered over the growing grain, *galabaed* arms outstretched, turban-headed. A crumbled railway carriage lay beside the track as dead as the Peugeots alongside the highway. The train sped up, swaying faster, as if to get away from the sight.

Most stations are small and unimportant places. We come to one more noble, pillared, carved with the symbol of a tied bundle of rods. It opens out directly onto the Nile. The name is only in Arabic, but we guessed it must be Esna. Tourist river-boats were tied up on the far shore where the ancient temple and the modern town are reached by a bridge. The train acknowledged it by stopping briefly and then swayed on south.

Music was inserted into the carriages from distant tapes. How can *Dirty Old Town*, the theme song of Salford, have come here? 'I kissed my girl by the factory door' and the dark streets of a cold northern British town loom across the miles.

At Kalabsha the buildings change. The houses – or many of them – are painted blue or ochre. They look well built and prosperous. The black-all-black of the women is covered now by a filmy over-wrap of white. The faces are darker as Nubia draws nearer.

Another wagon lay belly-side up, like a crumpled insect, beside the track.

'You would think,' we said to each other, 'that the metal would have had some use. In this climate it will never rust but stay there as a dust-gathering reminder like the wooden furniture of the Pharaohs in the museum at Luxor.'

The steward brought us coffee in good plastic cups. He told us that he was a qualified engineer but that he earned more money with tips as a steward on this train.

'But Egypt needs your skills!' we exclaimed.

'I know,' he said wearily, 'but my wife and children need this money.'

Occasionally factory chimneys belched black smoke into the clear air beyond our air-conditioned coach. They are as tall and slender as the minarets which dot the landscape, marking each village along the way. Very occasionally there is a church spire topped by the three-dimensional Coptic cross.

The permanent way undulates and the train swayed if it reached any speed. Even this superior, non-stop train was a slow train, taking almost four hours to cover the distance. But we were grateful that it did not hurry, for when it did we lurched from side to side and hoped it would not roll, belly-side up, off the track.

Twenty kilometres from Aswan the opposite bank of the Nile begins to close in. The fertile strip beside it narrows and sandy, rocky outcrops begin to loom, the sand orange-hued. Before long the land rises on both sides, squeezing the river between up to the First Cataract. The villages nestle at the foot of the hills, behind the fertile ribbon. The skyline is broken by the tall, angled masts of a flotilla of feluccas. It seems monstrous that, in this tiny strip of fertility – only 7 per cent of the land of Egypt – the road and the railway should have been allowed to eat up so much acreage. It is not that the road and the railway should not have been built, but they should not have been built here.

An announcement in English, French, German and Italian told us that we were arriving at Aswan. We were not to forget our personal belongings. We shook hands with the attendant and thanked him for all our care, and added *bakshish* to our words.

Aswan is wonderful to behold. The river runs strong through its narrow channel. The sun glints on the sparkling water and feluccas drift along with their great white triangular sails, posing for tourists. We spent the day enjoying it. Then we thought we might stay the night. But there were no beds to be had, at least no beds that we could find. We used the facilities of the Cataract Hotel all day: its veranda bar with imperial vistas, its pool, its loos, its buffet and its splendid views, but there were no beds.

We went back to the town to look for beds. The Happi Hotel, in the bazaar, had beds. Small wonder. The bazaar is Aswan. The city stands at the meeting point of two worlds – the Arabic and ancient Egyptian world and Africa proper. The powerful hand of ancient Egypt is lifted here and a new world, once held back by the three rocky surging cataracts of the Nile, are now calmed by two great dams, and Nubia has sunk below Lake Nasser. Tourism has flattened out the differences through the last century, but this, our first brief visit to Aswan, made us realise that Aswan was different.

The Abu Simbel Hotel looked OK, but the Yugoslavs had staked out their claim to its two-star luxury and the hotel was contentedly full, and we strolled on to the station – to see the Luxor-bound train being waved off by the friends and relations of its many passengers. Surely it had left fifteen minutes early? Or were we, perhaps, misinformed? Or was it, just possibly, an earlier train running late?

We queued up for tickets again. A girl ticket clerk could write out travel vouchers from right to left faster than I could ever do it the other way. Queuing in Egypt is obviously a skill. How can you move yourself from being behind someone to being in front of them without them seeing you? Is it best done left to right – or right to left? I let one person through and inserted my shoulder in the gap before a stout blue *galaba* had got there. We pressed against each other's shoulders until at last it was agreed that I was indeed in front.

The next train to Luxor is in two and a half hours, not one as we were firmly told. It is second class only, not first class. OK. Two tickets. The girl ticket clerk who wore a purple satin dress and a golden-yellow headkerchief very kindly wrote it all out for me: I had not even asked.

We went and sat benightedly on a station bench to gather our nerves. And what should appear but the morning's *wagons lits* and our friend who let us on that train. We told him our tale and he commiserated. We all laughed and wished each other well and once again shook hands.

We walked back to the Cataract Hotel for another hour with the sun setting over the desert, and then back to the station. The *wagons lits* were about to leave.

We settled down to watch it go and to wait.

'Can I help?' asks a distinguished-looking Egyptian.

'No, we had hoped to go by this train, but we cannot.'

'You have tickets?'

'Yes, but not for this train.'

'Come, perhaps I can help.'

And, once again, this time through the Egyptian dark, we travelled fraudulently – but we did buy tickets, we did ask for information and we didn't mean to cheat. It was Egyptian kindness that led us astray – and we still did not know what life was like on an ordinary Egyptian train.

Egyptian Villages and their Inhabitants

Winifred Blackman

A good anthropologist listens and so it was with Miss Blackman, who came to Egypt in 1923 and remained in the country off and on for a decade – listening with care and understanding to the ordinary people. Her writing brings the Nile villagers to detailed life.

THE NATURAL BARRIERS of Egypt have enabled the inhabitants, particularly those of the upper country, to live in comparative isolation throughout the whole of their history. On the north side lies the sea, along the east and west sides stretch vast, almost waterless deserts, while to the south ingress by way of the Nile is impeded by a series of cataracts. Their geographical isolation has doubtless been responsible for the characteristic conservatism of the Egyptian peasants. This conservatism is particularly apparent in their religious and social customs and their commoner industries, which have remained almost, if not entirely, unchanged from Pharaonic times.

The vast solitudes of the deserts are terrifying to the country folk, most of whom, up to the present day, cannot be induced to traverse even the lower fringes of those wastes after sunset. Fear of hyenas, and, still more, fear of *afarit* (spirits), forbids any man to venture beyond the cultivation at night. The ordinary peasant, unless he is obliged to remain in the fields either to protect his crops or to watch over his sheep and goats, returns to his village before sunset, remaining there until just before the dawn of the following day.

The deserts have proved themselves valuable defences against invasion, the peoples who conquered the country at different periods of its history having usually entered it from the north-east. These invaders do not seem to have left any very marked impression on the physical aspect of the Upper Egyptians at any rate; most of these still bear a striking facial resemblance to the ancient inhabitants of the land whom we see depicted on the walls of the temples and tomb-chapels and in the portrait-statues of the Old, Middle, and New Kingdoms. What really is beginning to affect the racial purity of the Egyptians is the presence among them of the descendants of negro slaves, who have been imported in large numbers by the Arabs in comparatively recent times. Many of them are now settled in certain of the villages, where they have married among themselves or with the *fellahin*, the result being that the population of such villages is almost entirely composed of black, or half-black, people. So far as I have observed, this negroid element is particularly marked in the Fayoum and Beni Suef, and on the edge of the cultivation in Minia and Asyut provinces, where large numbers of Arabs have been settled for several generations.

The influence of the deserts may be seen in Egyptian folk-tales, many of which tell of encounters there with *afarit* and other supernatural beings. Secret caves in 'the mountain', as the people call the steep, sometimes almost precipitous ascent to the high-desert plateau, also enter into the adventures recounted by the village story-tellers; these 'caves' are, of course, the ancient rock-hewn tomb-chapels with which the outer face of 'the mountain' is in some places honeycombed.

Egypt is a land of contrasts, the marked difference between the very fertile Nile Valley and the arid, waterless deserts on either side of it striking the eye of every visitor to the country. These physical features are, I think, reflected in the character of the peasants, for it is a remarkable fact that the most divergent traits of character can be seen in a single individual. The Egyptian peasants, in spite of much poverty and sickness, and with few amusements to break the monotony of their lives, are as a whole a wonderfully cheerful and contented people. They are very quick of comprehension, of ready wit, dearly loving a joke, even if directed against themselves, usually blessed with a retentive memory, light-hearted, kindly, and very hospitable; they are also very hard-working. At the same time they are very emotional, highly strung, most inflammable, generally very ignorant, and nearly always conspicuously lacking in self-control.

The fellahin form the bulk of the population of Egypt, and the larger number of them are Muslims. The Copts, who at one time were far more numerous than they are at the present day, are scattered about all over the country, though in a few towns and villages they may form the greater part of the population. The word 'Copt', it must be borne in mind, does not denote a racial, but rather a religious, distinction.

The Beduins (Arabic *Bedu*, singular *Bedawi*), many of whom still lead a more or less nomadic desert life, and the Arabs, who have settled down as cultivators of the soil, also form a not inconsiderable portion of the population. Their facial features and certain styles of dress distinguish them from the native inhabitants. Nubians, Sudan negroes, Turks, Greeks, Syrians and Jews are also to be found in large numbers, the four latter peoples chiefly in Lower Egypt, though they do not altogether confine themselves to the northern part of the country. Europeans of various nationalities have for many years past settled in Egypt, most of them being engaged in business connected with the production and sale of cotton, sugar, and the like.

The villages of Egypt, as seen from the railway-carriage or from points of vantage in the cultivation, present a most picturesque appearance. They are generally surrounded with palm groves, often very extensive, while palm trees also grow actually among the houses, affording a welcome shelter from the heat. These palm-girt villages are dotted about all over the cultivation, the brilliant green of which presents a startling contrast to the immediately adjacent, and seemingly endless, desert. Sometimes a village encroaches right on to the edge of the desert, the upper slopes of which tower above it, forming a most romantic background. During the period of inundation the villages, which stand on a somewhat higher level than the surrounding cultivation, appear like palm-encircled islands in a vast inland sea, a geographical feature also remarked upon by Herodotus.

Pigeon houses are prominent architectural features in a village. They are sometimes in the form of towers, with sloping, white-washed mud walls, surmounted by several layers of large pottery jars placed side by side in rows. Every jar has a hole in the base, for the ingress and egress of the pigeons. Sometimes the pigeon houses are painted with simple white designs. This is done, so I was told in one or two villages, because the birds like it, and it draws them back to their own houses! Pigeons are kept chiefly for the sake of the dung, which is considered to be a valuable fertilizer for the fields. Probably, however, more harm than good is done to the crops by the breeding of these birds, for they accumulate in large flocks when the corn is ripening, and are with difficulty dispersed by men and boys armed with slings and stones.

The houses of the peasants, in many cases mere hovels, are made of crude bricks, sometimes covered over with mud plastering. In the better houses there is generally a flight of steps leading to an upper storey, where there may be a sitting-room (*mandareh*), furnished with benches (called *dikak*, singular *dikkeh*), which are covered with rugs and supplied with cushions. The room in which the foodstuffs are kept is also usually in this upper story. The flat roof is a pleasant place on which to sit and watch the life in the streets below; it also serves as a hen-run, dog- and cat-run, a drying-ground, and is put to other utilitarian purposes. Here, for example, are stored huge bundles of sticks and dry maize-stalks (called *bus*), together with quantities of cakes of cow- and buffalo-dung, neatly stacked in rows, which are used with the sticks or *bus* as fuel. Here, too, are set up the household granaries.

The houses, especially the better-built ones, admirably suit the Egyptian climate. There is only one thing lacking to make them really pleasant places to live in, and that is greater cleanliness within the houses themselves and without in the streets. The salvation of the people lies in the fact that they lead essentially an outdoor life, the houses being regarded almost solely as places to sleep and cook in; otherwise the mortality would be considerably higher than it is.

I know how comfortable a well-kept house of the better kind can be, having lived in one for five months. This house stood on a high mound formed by the débris of earlier buildings; for in Egypt, when a house has collapsed or has been pulled down, the mass of rubbish is not necessarily removed, but when it has been sufficiently levelled another house is erected on the top of it. The whole of the upper floor of this house was placed at my disposal, my apartments consisting of a small bedroom and a sitting-room.

The latter had two unglazed but shuttered windows, from which I could look over the tops of the neighbouring houses and be a spectator of the varied life on the roofs. Outside the rooms was a partly covered passage, from which a glorious view of the sunsets could be obtained.

The villages are intersected by narrow lanes – in most cases they can hardly be dignified by the name of streets – progress along which is often impeded, sometimes almost entirely blocked, by piles of refuse and mud. In some of the larger villages there may be one or two broader streets, forming the chief thoroughfares. At the side of one of the narrow lanes there may be an open space in which palm trees grow, and here the village weaver often arranges the warp for his cloth, the threads being attached to the trunks of two of the trees. When this process is completed the warp is taken indoors and attached to the loom, which usually stands in a somewhat dark room, with mud-coloured walls, and so small in size that it is impossible to obtain a satisfactory photograph.

Itinerant vendors ply their trades up and down these tortuous village lanes, uttering their characteristic cries. For example, the onion-seller advertises his wares by calling out, 'Oh, onion, sweet as honey!' The cries are usually intoned in a minor key, sounding to the uninitiated more like a plaintive chant than the proclamation of goods for sale. Another hawker may trade in coloured cotton cloths, printed with various designs to suit all tastes. He usually conveys his goods about on a small hand cart. From such humble beginnings more than one fortune has been made, for the peasants are fond of hoarding their money, their daily living costing them but little. In time the small sums thus carefully put by amount to a considerable total, which may be profitably invested. Thanks to a lucky deal in cotton, or some other venture, the former humble itinerant vendor finds himself well on the way to becoming a man of substance.

The house doors are often decorated with a china plate or saucer fixed into the masonry above the lintel, as a charm against the evil eye. A house may also be decorated with coloured line-drawings of camels, boats, trains, trees and other objects, some hardly identifiable. Such artistic efforts denote that one or more members of the family inhabiting the house have performed the pilgrimage to Mecca, the design representing the various objects seen by the pilgrim on his way to the sacred city.

The interiors of the villages are often very picturesque, in spite of the dirt and squalor usually found in them. The Arabs are far more particular in this respect, their villages and settlements being much cleaner in every way than those of the Egyptian peasants. This difference between the two races is so marked that I can almost always tell if a village is Arab or Egyptian directly I enter it.

A mosque is to be found in every village, and in many places there are three or four such buildings. Five times a day a mueddin chants the call to prayer from each mosque – from the minaret if there is one – and the resonant voices of these officiants may be heard far beyond the confines of the village.

An old graveyard often stands in the middle of a village, probably indicating the older boundary, the houses built beyond it having been erected later owing to the increasing population. A whitewashed building, crowned with a dome, stands, perhaps, on the highest point of the burial-ground, indicating the last resting-place of a sheikh, or holy man, or, at any rate, erected in his honour. Candles are usually lighted in the building on 'the night of Friday' – i.e. the night preceding the Friday – in commemoration of the sheikh. Such lights are, in most cases, the only illumination out of doors to guide the late wayfarer. These buildings, and there are often several in or around one village, are prominent architectural features, standing up with their whitewashed walls and domes above, and in glaring contrast to, the mud houses and hovels of the peasants.

Shops of different kinds are situated in the wider streets or lanes, with open fronts which can be closed with wooden shutters when the owners are away. Through the open shop-fronts the tailors are to be seen making *galalib* (long blouses, singular *gallabiyeh*) for their customers, and in some villages one may watch the coppersmiths manufacturing bowls and jars. The vessels are hammered into shape over iron bars fixed in the ground. The iron bar is bent over at a right angle at the top, and flattened out so as to form a kind of anvil, on which the bowl or other vessel is beaten into shape.

Benches of bricks and mud (*masatib*, singular *mastabeh*) are found outside some of the houses, and on them is usually to be seen a collection of children, fowls, goats and even sheep, in happy promiscuity. Or perhaps a *mastabeh* may be occupied solely by an old man, spinning wool, or holding a rosary in his hand and slowly passing the beads between his fingers and thumb.

The Yusuf Canal flows past a village in which I have frequently resided, and there is a good deal of folklore connected with it. The water is believed to possess curative properties for sore eyes, fever, and other complaints. The canal, according to the peasants, was made in a miraculous way by the patriarch Joseph (Yusuf). They relate that he started one day to walk from Deirut, where the Bahr el-Yusuf (Canal of Joseph) diverges from the Ibrahimiyeh Canal, and as he went he trailed his stick behind him. Water began to flow along the course marked by his stick until he came to the lake Karun, at the north-west side of Fayoum Province, and into this lake the numerous streams in which the Bahr terminates disgorge themselves. Owing to this belief regarding the origin of the canal, its water is believed to contain much *barakeh* (blessing, healing virtues, good luck), and accordingly, on the day of Shemm en-Nesim, which coincides with the Coptic Easter Monday, the men make a point of bathing in the canal, for on this occasion the water is believed to be endowed with *barakeh* to a special degree.

From *The Fellahin of Upper Egypt*, 1927

The Inundation

William MacQuitty

Until the High Dam was constructed above Aswan in the 1960s the Nile poured northwards each year and flooded out onto the lands along the Nile.

DURING THE FIRST DYNASTY there were offices of the Royal Seal Bearer, the Royal Architect, the Keeper of the King's Vineyards and a Commander of the Inundation. The regulating of the flooding of the Nile was as important then as today. Even with the modern immensity of the High Dam the principle is unchanged. In spring the melting snows on the mountains of Central Africa and the heavy rains which fall in the lake districts of the Equator start rivulets, growing into torrents which come down in spate through Ethiopia. This water is held by a series of dams in the Sudan and Upper Egypt until it is high enough to spread in a shallow sea over the arable land of Egypt. Here it deposits the rich mud which it has carried on its long journey. In this manner every year, about mid-July, the flood begins. By September the waters start to subside. There may be a flush in October but by December the river returns to its normal level.

The success of the inundation depends on the ability of the farmers and controllers to flood as large an area as possible with the correct amount of life-giving muddy water. Too much is wasteful; too little will not permit the crops to grow. From the great flooding river out to the poorest farmer of the desert fringe, all must play their part in the delicate balance of irrigation. As the water flows farther away from the Nile the dams and sluices become smaller and smaller. Eventually, a spadeful of earth is sufficient to direct it from one channel to another in the plots of the small cultivators. The administration of such a complex operation reveals the high standard of government and control exercised by the early Egyptians. Apart from supplying fertility to this parched land, the Nile also indicated the rate of taxes that would be levied on the people. This was calculated by the height of the flood – the higher the flood, the more harvest and the greater the tax.

From *Abu Simbel,* 1965

When we will have no land …

Sayyid Qutb

To the peasant farmer and his family the land is all. To have to sell any part of it is a tragedy. To a child the idea of this happening holds almost unimaginable pain. Yet this is a threat that in this modern economic climate hangs over almost every peasant farmer as we, the travellers, watch him from boat, train or car as he plants and tends his harvests. We may see him as timeless. He is not, and cannot be, and some peasants have exchanged land for education and some have moved from the countryside to the towns and cities – even though the price of that change might be considered very high.

SHE LOOKED HIM IN THE EYES. It seemed as if she felt that her child had become a man and that the time had come to acquaint him with some of her worries, so she said to him:

'If I speak to you, sir, do you promise me that you will be a man?'

This word 'man' jolted him, for he wanted very much to grow up quickly, and he said:

'Most certainly.'

She said, 'Today your father sold a piece of land.'

Up to that time he had not really known the meaning of this. He had been sent to school when young and had been immersed in school life. He had not concerned himself with the conditions of agriculture or the *fellahin* as had others of his age in the village, who would have understood the meaning of that sentence if it had been uttered to one of them.

As he seemed somewhat puzzled about the meaning of this information and its connection with his mother's crying, she added: 'This means that our land is decreasing and, in fact, has decreased a number of times before by such sales, for your father sells a portion of our soil from one year to another, and if things continue this way the day will come when we will have no land, no fields, and no house, no animals, and nothing of all that you see now.'

Now he had understood – or sensed – the magnitude of the catastrophe that threatened him, threatened him personally. Would he lose this 'field' where he used to go on Fridays to run and jump merrily and play with the people who worked there and with those who took care of their animals? Their animals! Would he lose these animals? And especially, would he lose the cow that he cherished, which they kept even while they changed the other animals, because she had the special quality of providing milk and cream in abundance? More important than that was the firm friendship that bound him to her as it also did his sisters and his mother. She had been there almost the whole time he and his sisters were growing up and had become a 'personality' dear to him and to all in the house.

And the house … would he lose this house? At this point he felt for it affection such as he had never felt before. Their spacious, beautiful house. And the well that belonged to it, that well from which their animals and all the animals of the street drank. He took pride in this well because it was on their property and was needed by the people. These people complimented them when they brought their animals to its trough and flattered him in particular when he looked them and their animals over. He felt greatly elated that their house had this great and unique distinction, namely, that their cows and their other animals did not have to leave their property to drink as other people's animals did.

Then the 'oven porch', that room specifically set aside for the second-floor oven, to be distinguished from the oven on the first floor – and this was another special advantage, because other people had only one oven due to the limited space in their houses. Their house, however, which they were threatened with losing, had two ovens, one used in the winter for warmth, located on the first floor, and the other used only for bread in the summer. The latter was in a room whose ceiling had an opening to let the smoke out and whose wall was partly cut away for the same purpose. This allowed him and his older sister to jump off and back onto the wall where it was cut away while their younger sister tried but could not. So they would tease her a bit while she cried and then they would take hold of her together and pass her up and down between them.

Then there was the *makhash*, a very long, unroofed space along the side of the house where they stored the straw and the stalks of dry maize and the cotton stalks, so as to avoid the danger of fire that resulted from using the roof for storage as was the custom in the village. Their property was large enough to give their house this other special advantage, this *makhash* in which the piled straw brought one closer to the first-floor roof terrace. This enabled him and his older sister easily to jump from the roof of the first-floor onto the straw without danger and then race each other back up the ladder to the roof to jump again. Then there was the private alley in front of the house, which was his playground where he and his young playmates would play ball and the various simple village games.

Dozens of these beloved images passed through his mind in a fleeting instant. He wished he could put his hands around each one of these images and hold onto it for fear that it would slip away. Were they really in danger of losing all of this? He did not believe anything that had been said, and he turned toward his mother as if angry and said: 'But why is my father selling this land?'

She said: 'Because he owes money to people and has to repay it.'

But that answer was not adequate, for why did he owe people money? How could that be when the boy always saw plenty of money in his father's long white purse, with which he bought everything?

Perhaps she realized at that moment that she had made a mistake and told the small child these things too soon, so she tried to end the discussion and distract him from it, but he insisted on knowing. So she gave him a full explanation, which allowed him to understand that his father spent more each year than he took in and had to make up the difference by selling some of the land. Now he understood the whole situation and sensed the true nature of the danger, but it was more than his small mind could do to imagine the final outcome of things, so he said: 'No, mother. We will not sell our house and our field, or these animals of ours. And we will not sell our old cow!' His mother seemed to relax and take hope in these simple words of her child. She said: 'May God listen to you, my son.'

Then she clasped him to her, then pushed him away a bit and looked into his eyes. Concentrating in the tone of her voice all the warmth of her faith, she said: 'Listen, sir, you must get back what your father has lost!'

Although the warmth of her conviction penetrated to his heart, standing there in her presence he still could not understand how he could undertake such a marvellous task, and he looked at her seeking an explanation!

From *A Child from the Village*, 1946

Crawling into a Temple
Dr R. R. Madden

Over the centuries as the buildings of the ancient Egyptians fell into disuse, the sand blew in from the desert and heaped up in the interiors. Nowadays we can judge the heights the sand reached by the inscriptions carved by past travellers who stood on the sand. With the clearance of the temples this graffiti is now high above us on the columns and walls of the temples. Occasionally there is a hole – also now high up – cut through the stone to which a camel or donkey could be tethered. At Edfu in 1825 Dr Richard Madden was guided nervously into the temple on his hands and knees. When he emerged he met the renowned traveller and lexicographer Edward Lane and unwillingly returned with him into the temple.

AT EDFOU, which is about two and forty miles from Esnèh, we stopped a day to visit its celebrated temple. The situation of Edfou, the ancient Apollinopolis Magna, is beautiful; but the majesty of the finest temple in Egypt is insulted by a horde of filthy Arabs, who have made their miserable village on the roof, and who have blocked up the sanctuary with a dunghill: part of the splendid portico is converted into a stable, and the whole of the interior is so filled up with rubbish that it is deemed impossible to enter. An old man, to whom I gave some medicine, informed me there was a secret passage underground, which no Frank was made acquainted with, because hidden treasures were deposited there! I of course became deeply interested in the health of my old gentleman and of all his family; and in return for my courtesy, he consented to show me the passage, provided I carried none of the hidden gold away. Considerably below the surface of the adjoining buildings he pointed out to me a chink in an old wall, which he told me I should creep through on my hands and feet; the aperture was not two feet and a half high, and scarcely three feet and a half broad; my companion had the courage to enter first, thrusting in a lamp before him, I followed, and after me the son of the old man crept also; the passage was so narrow, that my mouth and nose were sometimes completely buried in the dust, and I was nearly suffocated. After proceeding about ten yards in utter darkness the heat became excessive, breathing was laborious, the perspiration poured down my face, and I would have given the world to have got out; but my companion, whose person I could not distinguish, though his voice was audible, called out to me to crawl a few feet farther, and that I should find plenty of space. I joined him at length, and had the inexpressible satisfaction of standing once more on my feet, commiserating, for the first time in my life, with the unfortunate serpent, who has to perambulate on his belly till doomsday. We found ourselves in a splendid apartment of great magnitude, adorned with sacred paintings and hieroglyphics; several rows of pillars supported the painted ceiling, and the plynth of the capitals I found by measurement exceeded that of the columns at Esnèh.

We were in the interior of the sanctuary of the temple, the exterior of which is encumbered with rubbish, fully three fourths of its height. The magnificence of this chamber exceeds that of any other temple in Egypt, not excepting Dendera. There are several doors, but they are blocked up with rubbish, so that we were forced to return by the same narrow chink through which we entered. Before we left the interior, I observed many animals represented which I had not seen elsewhere: among the rest one which appeared to me to be meant for the hippopotamus. We could not remain half as long as we desired; the fatigue of our entry, and the clouds of dust which almost prevented breathing, had excited an intolerable thirst, and all the antiquities in the world were nothing in comparison with the speedy prospect of getting a draught of cold water. Hamilton, I believe, attempted to get through this passage, but could not succeed; Belzoni, I have since discovered, made a similar attempt, and failed also. On the exterior of the vestibule I noticed a small figure of Harpocrates seated on a lotus, with his forefinger on his mouth, in the act of enjoining silence.

The propylons of this edifice are considered the largest in Egypt; and this temple is the only one I have seen which is surrounded like a fortress, by a wall of about six feet in thickness, and twenty in height. There is a smaller temple here, called the Typhonium, from its being supposed to have been dedicated to Typhon, the devil of the Egyptians: the figure of this multiform personage is represented on the capitals, neither encumbered with hoofs nor horns, but endowed with a most inordinate abdomen, and apparently possessed of the most amorous propensities. In one of the sculptures the hippopotamus is to be seen; which animal, as well as the crocodile, seems to have been an emblem of the evil principle.

On our return to our boat, we had the pleasure of meeting an English traveller, Mr Lane, who had been at Edfou, taking drawings of the temple, for some days; he was greatly surprised to hear of our subterraneous visit to the interior of the temple, as he had not been informed of any such entrance by the guides; he begged of me to conduct him to the passage, and this I did, after dark, when we had least reason to fear a surprisal by the Arabs. We took candles, and some jars of water with us, and proceeded to the spot; we left our servants, well armed, at the mouth of the aperture to prevent danger; for, had we not done so, we should have been subjected to no little annoyance from the natives.

We were dogged, however, by three or four fellows, just as we were about to enter, so we had no alternative but to make them acquainted with our intentions, and to promise them a present if they acted as our guides; only one had the courage to consent to enter, the others agreed to watch for us outside.

We had so much enlarged the passage, by our first entry, that we now got in with considerably less difficulty. After remaining in the interior for about an hour, we hastened to return; but as I first advanced, on all fours, I heard high words without, a loud threat that we never should come out without paying a large sum to the people of the fortress, for so they call the temple. I listened in silence, my reflections were anything but pleasing; the prospect of being immured in that horrid place, or of having my head broke if I advanced it through the chink, were not very agreeable anticipations. At last I resolved to advance slowly before my companions, and to emerge in silence, but with all the swiftness possible. I accordingly darted my body through the aperture, with all the force I could exert in so constrained a posture, and was soon in the midst of the Arabs, before they were aware of my intention: they offered me no violence; on the contrary, they assisted me to rise; I took my station by the aperture, and my companions came out in safety.

The Arabs now talked of nothing but the treasures we had found; a great number of them had collected to see what we came by night to take away; and, finally, it was only by giving *backsheesh* to half a dozen of them that we were enabled to get away.

From *Travels in Turkey, Egypt, Nubia, and Palestine,* 1829

Exploring the Cataracts

Sir William Armstrong

The famed Newcastle industrialist had a lifelong interest in water, how it works and how it can be used as a power source. His description in 1872 of the first cataract which broke the Nile as a south – north trade route reflects both his knowledge and his fascination.

THE CHIEF OBJECT of my voyage up the Nile with Mr Fowler was to examine the cataracts, in reference to an engineering work, proposed by him, for obviating the interruption to the river traffic, which occurs at that point. It was our business, therefore, to make a very minute inspection of that part of the river, and also of the adjacent shore. The Nile, at that part of its course, has forced a passage through a barrier of protruded igneous rocks, and in so doing has become divided into a multiplicity of channels, through which the water rushes with great rapidity and violence, but without any actual cascade. The islands formed by these numerous channels are all naked rocks, none of which are more than fifty feet in height. On the African side of the river, the banks are but little higher than the islands, but on the opposite side, the rocks rise in shivered peaks to a height of four hundred feet or more. Some of these peaks are rather difficult to climb, but afford fine views when the labour of ascent is accomplished. The spaces between them present the appearance of having been river channels, when the Nile flowed at a higher level than at present. The higher rocks are all of red syenite or granite, and are generally much disintegrated. The lower rocks, though all of the igneous class, vary much both in composition and colour. Amongst other varieties, there is a black rock, speckled with white, which is the hardest and toughest stone I ever met with, and yet it was worked by the old Egyptians, and may be seen in many of their sculptures. It is generally described as black granite, but I believe it would be more correctly designated a kind of porphyry. It is a curious circumstance that the lower rocks are, in many places, polished as smooth as an agate brooch. This fact was new to me, though I afterwards learnt that it had often been noticed before. I was much puzzled to account for it, but at length I was led to ascribe it to the drift sand acting for ages against the rock. Since my return to England, a process, depending upon the same principle, has been introduced for engraving glass or other hard substances. A jet of air, mixed with sand, is projected with great force upon the surface to be cut, the pattern being defined by a screen which protects certain parts, and leaves others exposed. Although the force of the wind is feeble in comparison with that of the artificial blast, yet time makes up for the want of intensity, and the delicacy of the touch results in an exquisite polish.

Mr Fowler and I having examined the lower parts of the cataracts by excursions from Aswan, proceeded to Mahatta, the higher shipping place, where a boat awaited us to convey us to the upper rapids. Our boat was manned by an experienced crew of cataract men, with the sheik of the cataracts at the helm. We paddled down till we came near to the crest of the first shoot. There we paused for observation, but kept slowly drifting towards the rapid. I thought we were getting rather too near, and expected every moment that the crew would use their oars to keep us further off. Instead of that, without the slightest warning, they launched us right down the surging current. The next moment we were in the midst of waves, whirlpools and broken water, and our little boat was tossed about in the most alarming manner, but on looking at the placid face of the steersman, and the confident air of the crew, I felt reassured; though I am not sure that I had reason to be so, for these fellows swim like ducks, and care nothing for being capsized anywhere. However, they would have got into a great scrape if they had drowned us, and would have lost their *backsheesh* into the bargain, so they would probably have felt it to be their interest to drag us out, even if we had been upset. Fortunately for our comfort, if not for our safety, we escaped immersion, and gaining courage from this successful performance, we volunteered to descend the succeeding rapid in a similar manner. Having done so in safety, we got quite to like the operation, and after that, no rush of water was too violent to restrain us. We spent two days amongst these rapids, in the course of which we passed down every channel and visited every island. After descending each channel, the boat had to be dragged up by the crew, who used a long rope for the purpose. On these occasions we went ashore and walked along the banks, or scrambled over the rocks on the margin of the stream. In one instance the efforts of the crew were insufficient to pull the empty boat against a rapid of more than usual force. At length the boat began to fill, and we nearly lost it, a result which would have been exceedingly inconvenient to Mr Fowler and myself, seeing that we were on an island, and were by no means qualified, like our boatmen, to swim across to the mainland. The boat was saved, but we had to go back, and make the ascent by another channel.

I never saw such a set of amphibious creatures as the people of these cataracts are; men, women and children are all alike in this respect, and are just as much at home in the water as out of it. If we wanted a measuring line carried across a foaming rapid, one of the crew would instantly take it in his mouth, and by the most extraordinary feats of aquatic agility carry it to the other side. Women and children ferry themselves across the quieter parts of the river, where the water is awfully deep, upon small logs of palm tree. In doing this they rest their stomachs upon the wood, and allow their legs and arms to descend into the water, to be used as paddles for propulsion. It is no easy matter to float upon a round log. Let any unexperienced person try to do so, and he will find himself head down and heels up in a moment. Still more difficult is it to prevent the log rolling over if you carry top weight, and yet it is quite common to see a woman thus crossing the river with a baby on her shoulders, and a bundle of grass on her cocked-up head. Once we saw a woman quietly seated on one bank, while her child, a boy of about eight years old, was coming across on a log which was to bear both him and his mother back to the opposite shore. We rowed up to the little navigator and stopped to look at him. He, in his turn, stopped to look at us, and when he had satisfied his curiosity he held out his hand and cried '*backsheesh Hawaghee.*' The first word I need not translate; the latter is the term which the natives apply to gentlemen in the garb of Europeans.

I never fully appreciated the volume of the Nile until I saw it divided at the cataracts into many separate courses. One sees that every channel contains as much water as would make a first-class English river, and thus an idea is formed of the enormous magnitude of the aggregate quantity. The river was nearly at its lowest when we were at Aswan. During the inundation, it rises, according to the nilometer at Elephantine, forty feet in perpendicular height above low-water level, and at that period nearly all the islands are submerged. The river, at the cataracts, is then no longer broken into a series of rapids, but flows in a smooth continuous stream, not too swift to prevent navigation. Even at low Nile, the rapids are not altogether impassable to small *dahabeeahs*, which, by a long train of men, can be dragged up one or two of the channels against the force of the current. Such vessels can also descend the cataracts but not without risk of being wrecked, as was evident from our seeing one abandoned *dahabeeah* sticking on the rocks, and the remnants of another not far off. As a rule, all merchandise is disembarked at the cataracts, and conveyed on camels between Aswan and Mahatta.

From *A Visit to Egypt,* 1874

Days and Nights at Ipsamboul

Florence Nightingale

For Florence Nightingale her journey to Egypt in 1850 was the beginning of her escape from the conventions and restrictions of upper-middle-class country life in England, which was to result in the realisation of her dreams and ambition to take up nursing. Her happiness and enthusiasm burst forth at Abu Simbel where she and her companions lingered for some days. To her the goddess Hathor was, significantly, the goddess of joy. In her musings at this wonderful place, can we hear the real beginnings of her chosen independence – and, one might say, her rebirth?

MY DEAREST PEOPLE.

Here we are arrived at the last and greatest point of our voyage – greatest it is in all respects – I can fancy nothing greater. All that I have imagined has fallen short of Ipsamboul (of the great temple of the Osirides), and thank God that we have come here. I can conceive nothing in Thebes to equal this, and am well satisfied to turn back now, for we are to go no further. We arrived here on the 15th, about nine o'clock, and climbed the bank immediately to the lesser temple to see that first. There is no effect about the exterior at all, you don't know where the rock ends, and the temple begins, the slanting lines of the face of the temple (none of them parallel) are ugly, and the six colossal figures between the slants impossible to see, as the bank slopes straight down from the temple door to the river. Yet I have a love for the place; it is so innocent, so childish, so simple, so like the Athor, 'the Lady of Aboccis' (the old name of Aboo Simbil) whom it represents. Athor means the habitation of Horus, and Horus means God; therefore Athor is nature, the world, in which God dwells, and which reveals Him. Her inscription calls her the 'nurse, who fills heaven and earth with her beneficent acts'. As such, she is identical with Isis. And her temple is so like nature, cheerful and simple, and to me at least, not very interesting, with her great broad innocent face and childlike expression, for it would not do if nature always kept us in a state of excitement. She is the same as the Grecian Aphrodite, yet how different – her simple, almost infantine, beauty to the more intellectual, yet at the same time more sensual, conscious beauty of the Greek Venus. It is the difference between Aspasia and Desdemona. She is also the goddess of joy, the lady of the dance and mirth, a sort of joy like that of children playing at daisy chains, not that of the feast of Epicurus. She is a secondary goddess, and her connection with the earth is more intimate than that of the real goddesses – her expression shows none of their supernatural serenity, but a simple enjoyment of her flowers and creatures.

The temple is small, the first chamber hewn in the rock and supported by six pillars, with the Athor head upon each; then a vestibule or *pro sekos;* then the *sekos* or sacred place, with her image in it. It was built by the Great Rameses, of the nineteenth dynasty, who reigned thirteen centuries and a half before Christ. The conqueror and Sesostris of the Greeks, and his figure, with those of his two queens, both evidently portraits, and one a most beautiful woman, are in *intaglio rilevato*, all over the walls. Everywhere Rameses's queens occupy as conspicuous a place as himself. One only of the representations interested me much. It was the Great Rameses crowned by the good and the evil principle on either side. What a deep philosophy! What theory of the world has ever gone farther than this? The evil is not the opposer of the good, but its *collaborateur* – the left hand of God, as the good is His right. I don't think I ever saw anything which affected me much more than this (three thousand years ago) – the king at his entrance into life is initiated into the belief that what we call the evil was the giver of life and power as well as the good. Tell Aunt M. I thought of her when

I looked at him, and of all she had taught me, and rejoiced to think how the same light dawns upon the wise from the two ends of space and of time.

The old Egyptians believed that out of good came forth evil, and out of evil came forth good; or as I should translate it, out of the well-ordered comes forth the inharmonious, the passionate; and out of disorder again order; and both are a benefit. The Romans, who were a more literal people, and we their descendants, never understood this, and have set our faces against evil, like the later Egyptians, and scratched his nose.

Some people have seen a portrait of Joseph in the ass-headed god with square ears: Ombte. I myself incline to this opinion, considering him under the later idea; as I never could bear Joseph for making all the free property of Egypt into king's property, the fee simple of all Egypt into leasehold, the cause of half the evil at this present day.

But I am in a hurry to get on to the great temple, the Temple of the Sun, as he stands side by side with the modest little temple of his daughter, the mistress of the West, the lady of evening, of the morning star (Athor), who receives him every night at the end of his course behind her mountain, when he sets into her resting place.

We clambered and slid through the avalanche of sand, which now separates the two temples. There they sit, the four mighty colossi, seventy feet high, facing the East, with the image of the sun between them, the sand hill sloping up to the chin of the northernmost colossus.

Sublime in the highest style of intellectual beauty; intellect without effort, without suffering. I would not call it intellectual either, it is so entirely opposed to that of the Jupiter Capitolinus; it is more the beauty of the soul – not a feature is correct – but the whole effect is more expressive of spiritual grandeur than anything I could have imagined. It makes the impression upon one that thousands of voices do, uniting in one unanimous simultaneous feeling of enthusiasm or emotion, which is said to overcome the strongest man. Yet the figures are anything but beautiful; no anatomy, no proportion; it is a new language to learn, and we have no language to express it. Here I have the advantage, for being equally ignorant of the language of any art, I was as open to impression from them as from Greek or any other art. The part of the rock smoothed for the temple face is about one hundred feet to the highest row of ornament. Over the door is the image of the sun, and on either side an intaglio figure of the Great Rameses, offering, not burnt sacrifices, not even flowers, nor fruit, but a figure of *Justice* in his right hand. 'Sacrifices and burnt offering thou hast not desired, else would I give it.' 'For what does the Lord require of thee, but to do justly.'

What more refined idea of sacrifice could you have than this? Yet inside I was still more struck by the king offering justice to the God who gives him *in return life* and *purity* in either hand.

The door, which is about twenty feet high, does not reach nearly up to the knee of the colossus. Alas! the sand is now as high as three feet below the top of the door, and into this magnificent temple you have to crawl on all fours. But I am not sure that the effect is not increased by it. When you have slipped down an inclined plane of sand twenty feet high which is like entering into the bowels of the earth, you find yourself in a gigantic hall, wrapped in eternal twilight, and you see nothing but eight colossal figures of Osiris standing against as many square pillars which support the rocky roof, their arms crossed upon their breast, the shepherd's crook and the *flagellum* in either hand, for he is here in his character of judge of the dead, Lord of Amenti, or the lower world of departed souls; and truly it looks like the lower world, the region of spirits; no light irritates your eyes, no sound annoys your ear, no breath of wind sets your teeth on edge; the atmosphere is much warmer than the outer air; this atmosphere, which is never stirred by anything but the beetle, the only creature light enough to tread this sand without being buried in it.

'Full of grace and truth', as his inscription bears, indeed he looks. I waited for him to speak; but he did not. Through two other halls I passed, till at last I found myself in a chamber in the rock, where sat, in the silence of an eternal night, four figures against the further end. I could see nothing more; yet I did not feel afraid as I did at Karnak, though I was quite alone in these subterraneous halls, for the sublime expression of that judge of the dead had looked down upon me, the incarnation of the goodness of the deity, as Osiris is; and I thought how beautiful the idea which placed him in the foremost hall, and then led the worshipper gradually on to the more awful attributes of the deity; for here, as I could dimly see through the darkness, sat the creative powers of the eternal mind: Neph, 'the intellect', Amun the 'concealed god', Phthah, 'the creator of the visible world', and Ra, 'the sustainer', Ra, 'the sun', to whom the temple is dedicated. The heat was intense, it was as if this were the focus of the vivifying power of those attributes; and before them stood an altar, the first and last we shall see – the real old altar upon which stood the sacred ark. As to having had sacrifices here, it is physically impossible in any part of the temple; the door of the Osiris hall is the only outlet, and there is no possibility of any others.

I turned to go out, and saw at the further end the golden sand glittering in the sunshine outside the top of the door; and the long sand hill, sloping down from it to the feet of the innermost Osirides, which are left quite free, all but their pedestals, looking like the waves of time, gradually flowing in and covering up these imperishable genii, who have seen three thousand years pass over their heads, and heed them not. In the holiest place, there where no sound ever reaches, it is as if you felt the sensible progress of time, not by the tick of a clock, as we measure time, but by some spiritual pulse which marks to you its onward march, not by its second, nor its minute, nor its hour hand, but by its century hand. I thought of the worshippers of three thousand years ago; how they by this time have reached the goal of spiritual ambition, have brought all their thoughts to serve God or the ideal of goodness; how we stand there with the same goal before us, only as distant as the star, which, a little later, I saw rising exactly over that same sand hill in the centre of the top of the doorway – how to them all other thoughts are now as nothing, and the ideal we all pursue of happiness is won; not because they have not probably sufferings, like ours, but because they no longer suggest any other thought but of doing God's will, which is happiness. I thought how, three thousand years hence, we might perhaps have attained – and others would stand here, and still those old gods would be sitting in the eternal twilight. Silent they sat and stern – and never moved; and I left them.

We shall never enjoy another place like Ipsamboul; the absolute solitude of it – the absence of a present, of any of one's fellow-creatures who contrast the past with that horrible Egyptian present. You look abroad and see no tokens of habitation; the power of leaving the boat and running up to the temple at any hour of the day or night, without a whole escort at your heels; the silence and stillness and freedom of it were what we shall never have again. At Luxor the present was such as to annihilate all pleasure in anything; and at Derr, where we stopped on the 13th for an hour, the cries and crowd were so insupportable that we saw the temple as quickly as we could, and I have no more idea of it at this moment than you have.

I came out of the penetralia and looked again upon the glorious colossi. I wish all my friends could see them once in their lives, if only for a moment; or that I could describe to anyone the look of intense repose in those faces. I think Europeans are perhaps better able to be judge of them than any others; to Europeans they must be always more peculiarly affecting, the revelation of an entirely new kind of life. To us toil and excitement and restless anxiety are so familiar, that we have even consecrated them in Christianity. To the Greeks intellectual activity seemed the highest god they could frame. To the Egyptians calm of soul was the characteristic of a Divine Being. Their Osiris is never represented (at least nowhere that I have seen him) as sharing in the agitations of humanity, though he took upon him their nature.

It is so touching to come thus to the 'ashes of their fathers and the temples of their gods', and even 'to the tender mother that dandled them to rest', for here is Rameses's Queen – that beautiful tender face – to descend into the bowels of the earth and find this revelation fresh and new, of a nation three thousand years passed away, that at first one is quite overwhelmed, and I assure you one is surprised to find oneself thinking of nothing at all, mechanically reading the names, which are alas scrawled over every statue, or counting the footsteps of the Scarabeus as he leaves his track upon the sand. It is like what one reads of people doing under a great blow, counting the fringe on the rug, or some such thing, instead of thinking of the event.

We went up to the top of the rock under which the temple is quarried, to look up the Nile. It is separated from the next cliff by a sand slip. I sighed for a walk in the Alps, the tropical Alps, and I walked round the valley and to the next mountain, and took a long last look south into Abyssinia, for further we were not to go. I saw nothing, met nothing, that had life, or *had had* life, but the whitened bones of a poor camel. And I reached the top of the next cliff. Oh, would I could describe that, my last real African view! The golden sand, north, south, east, and west, except where the blue Nile flowed, strewn with bright purple granite stones, the black ridges of mountains, east and west, volcanic rocks, gigantic jet-black wigwam-looking hills. If you can imagine the largest glaciers you ever saw, the Mer de Glace at Chamouni, with all the avalanches golden sand, and all the ridges purple granite, not one blade of green anywhere, except where a sunk fence, for I can call it nothing else, bounds the river, and is cultivated with lupins, that is Nubia. It reminded me perpetually of the philosopher's stone. The people tried to make gold, and prayed to the deity that he would turn all their soil to gold, and this must be the consequence. The banks of the rivers look like a beetle's back, green and gold, the rest of the country like one vast vein of metal ore.

They sent our Nubian steersman after their 'wild ass of the wilderness'; but he found a nice bank of sand in the sun, and lay down on his face to sleep. I thought he had had an apoplectic stroke (for you can see figures miles off, as large as life in this atmosphere), and hastened to his assistance; whereupon he got up, and carried me down the next sand avalanche like a child. They help you so beautifully, these Nubians, that your feet hardly seem to touch the ground; the sand is so fine and soft that you sink at every step almost to your knees.

We came back to the *dahabieh* for candles and went all over the great temple. Every inch of it is covered with sculptures, perfectly uninjured except the colouring, which is gone, but the outlines are as sharp as ever. But what is the good of attempting to describe that which is now as sharply cut in my memory as in the stone, but of which I shall give no idea to you? It seems to me as if I had never seen sculpture before, as if the Elgin marbles were tame beside them! As if I had now begun to live in heroic times. The great Rameses holds by the hair of the head eleven captives kneeling before him, in the presence of the god Ra, who decrees their destiny. Everything is done here in the presence of the gods. Rameses receives life and power from his patron Ra (after whom he is named), dedicates to him his victories, receives from him commands how his defeated nations are to be disposed of. It reminds one of another nation and another leader, whose name only differs by the omission of the first syllable from Rameses. But the most curious part of the thing is the sublime expression of this Rameses – I never saw so beautiful a countenance. It is not a man murdering other men; it is the type of power. The captives too are not bound, but with their hands free, and some even holding daggers, so that indeed everybody has seen in it only an allegory expressive of dominion over the enemies of his country.

Three types of face in the captives are quite distinct; a negro, an Ethiopian and an Eastern, showing that, at this early period of Rameses's reign, his conquests had extended into Asia and south Africa. If it is really a portrait of Rameses, he must have been a noble creature. His name means 'tried', or 'regenerated by Ra', as Thothmosis means 'regenerate by Thoth'. The last two syllables Mss (for, in the old Egyptian, as in Arabic and Hebrew, there are no vowels) immediately recall another name – and Moses does mean 'saved', 'regenerate', 'initiated'.

The two long sides of the Osiris hall are taken up by the battle scenes, which make even an heroic age run round in a peaceful brain like mine. Rameses in his chariot, hurried along by his galloping horses, the reins twisted round his waist, drawing his bow upon the foe, in full career, preceded by his constant lion. Rameses dismounted and killing a chief whom he holds by the arm, in the exact attitude of the Pætus and Arria, so that one would think the artist of that must have seen this. Rameses in his chariot commanding. These below, and a row of Rameses in conference with different gods above, occupy all the south wall, while the north is a series of small battle-chariots standing on their heads, on their tails, in every possible position, while Rameses sitting is receiving a deputation of conquered nations. One king dismounts from his chariot and holds the reins with one hand, while he makes an obeisance to Rameses with the other. All this north wall relates to the first year of his reign; and the temple appears to have been finished early in his reign, as an inscription relating to the thirty-fifth on the south wall was evidently added afterwards. He reigned from 1388 to 1322 BC and Egypt is covered with his monuments – the Augustan age of Egyptian art.

All these figures are in *intaglio rilevato*, very like Flaxman's outlines; the Rameses about ten feet high. But spirited as they are, I for one, am very soon tired of them. I never made much hand of chivalry or Homer, and I returned back to my beloved adytum.

In Ipsamboul you first know what solitude is. In England, the utmost solitude you can obtain is surrounded by human beings; but there in the depths of the rock, in eternal darkness, where no sound ever reaches, solitude is no longer a name, it is a presence. In the evening we made a great fire upon the altar, and while our turbanned crew fed it, we sat in the entrance on the top of our hillock, and enjoyed the sight and feeling of the ancient worship restored. But then I knew that I liked, yes, and appreciated the Egyptian worship much more now in its desolate grandeur than then in its pomp and show. I felt as if the temple was profaned, and the solitude of the 'Unutterable God' broken in upon – and I was glad when the blaze and glare were over.

Before sunrise the next day S [Selina Bracebridge] and I were sitting on the soft warm fine sand, watching for the first rays of his own bright Egyptian sun to illuminate that glorious colossus. It was very cold; but oh! the luxury of that soft warm bed, without creatures, without damp, without dirt, which shakes off directly. When you are cold you bury your feet in it, and it warms them; when you are tired, you lie down upon it; when your head aches with staring, you sit and watch the scarabei with their pretty tracks; no cries for '*Baksheesh*', and '*La Hawagee*' (you merchant) pester you, and you are as happy as the day is long. But the day broke; the top of the rock became golden – the golden rays crept down – one colossus gave a radiant smile, as his own glorious sun reached him – he was bathed in living light – yes, really living, for it made him live, while the other, still grey, shadowy and stern as a ghost, was unreached by the 'Revealer of Life'. We watched him till he too was lighted up, and then sat down over against the temple doors and looked in.

The Marys could hardly have been more surprised when they saw the angel whose countenance was bright as snow, and knew that He whom they sought was risen, than we were when we saw the resurrection which had taken place there. One spot of golden light on the third Osiris spread and spread till it lighted up the cheek of the second and first. They smiled in their solemn beauty, but did not speak – a flush came over their faces for a moment – it was an awful moment – it was only a blast of sand stirring outside in the golden sunlight, but the reflection had lighted them up, and in this morning eastern light I could go over all the sculptures in the temple, and see them quite plain; but still my heart yearned for the solitary four in the holy place, whom no light ever approaches. I was surprised to find them still sitting there – they are so living – yet there they have sat for three thousand years, for three thousand years the Osiridæ have seen the sun rise as they saw it that morning, and will for thousands of years more.

In the afternoon it was announced, to my unspeakable delight, that we were to stay another day at Aboo Simbil, another sun to see rise there, another evening to watch the stars, the only thing we wanted was a moonlight.

I climbed up into the lap of one of the colossi, the southernmost, who is quite uncovered, his knee is considerably above the doorway top.

To please them, I measured his middle finger, four feet. But to see my Hall of the Genii, my beloved Temple of Ipsamboul, all upon paper, with rule and line, brings it down to the level of Chatsworth in my imagination; and I won't give you the measurements of one of the colossi, I am afraid of getting like

Dante. What does it matter whether Rameses's ear is two or three feet long? Champollion has dreadfully spoilt one of the colossi by whitewashing its face. I never look at that one. Imagine painting one of the pinnacles of Westminster Abbey red. It is a dissight from afar off. All that day I spent wandering about within the temple, and in the evening the new moon, like a silver boat, rested on the surface of the cliff for a moment, and then set, leaving behind it the old moon, plainly visible upon the top of the rock, after the silver thread was gone, for some moments. I never saw that sight before.

The next morning we were there again at dawn, and again saw the wonderful light, the resurrection of those colossi, their own eastern sun saluting them. In what their beauty consists it requires a wiser eye than mine to tell you – their faces are rounded, their foreheads are low, their lips thick, nothing which generally gives expression or saves from monotony, is there. The figures are clumsy, the shoulders unmodelled, the hands resting on knees like flounders, excessively short from thigh to knee, the legs like posts. Yet no one would say that those faces were expressionless, no one that has seen them, but they will live in his memory as the sublimest expression of spiritual and intellectual repose he has ever seen.

The ceiling of the great Osiris hall came out in the morning light – huge overshadowing wings crossed it from side to side. 'He shall cover thee with his feathers, and under the shadow of his wings shalt thou trust.' I never understood the Bible till I came to Egypt. 'The Almighty shall overshadow thee;' and, 'as a mother will I nurture thee.' The vulture, whose shadowy wings are here portrayed, is the Egyptian symbol for a mother, and in this position, as protectress of men, she becomes a sublime representation. The king never goes out to battle, or 'runs' into the presence of the gods, without this beautiful Eilethyia hovering over his head to protect him (though in a somewhat different form, with wings folded round her, instead of outspread). When she is the protectress of the country, Eilethyia spreads her glorious wings and holds two ostrich feathers in her claws, as in this ceiling. She is the beautiful head-dress of Rameses's queen, whose portrait is all over the temple, and who stands behind him in the captive picture, the most lovely countenance, her black hair gathered together with a golden fibula on the side of her forehead, and then falling on her shoulders. The second queen, a somewhat pug-nosed female, is offering to Athor in her temple, where the first also appears. Everywhere she occupies the place which the most advanced Christian civilisation gives to woman – always the one wife, nowhere the face veiled, often the regent, the sovereign, or the co-ruler with a brother. Woman may be quite satisfied with her Christian position in old Egypt. The tricolor border of red, blue, and white runs round the ceiling, the sacred colours of light, wisdom and purity.

Egypt is beginning to speak a language to me, even in the ugliest symbols of her gods; and I find there such pleasant talk – philosophy for the curious, comfort for the weary, amusement for the innocent.

The sovereign of Egypt really deserved to be a sovereign; for he appears to have been chief in every act, just as the superior of a religious order was, at first, intended to be the superior only in every act of difficulty, self-denial or active benevolence; the king hardly ever appears carried by his fellow men on an ignoble throne, but driving his own chariot, fighting the enemies of his country, or running full tilt on his own feet into the presence of the assemblies of the gods. This is how one oftenest sees him.

But a little representation of him there is on the side of one of the great Osiris pillars in Ipsamboul, which pleased me more than any. He is offering Truth to Mau, the son of the sun, who expresses the insight, light, or pure intellect of God, and sometimes the world, the 'true image of God', but always 'the highest property of God in nature as well as man'. He is that property, if we may so speak, 'which proves the reality of God's attributes by the truth', or definiteness of the manifestations he makes of himself in nature.

It is a beautiful idea – is it not? – this offering *Thmei* (Truth) to the god, but more peculiarly interesting to us from its being the original of the 'Urim and Thummim'. The Egyptian judges, who were all high priests, wore a breastplate with Ra and Thmei, both in the dual (*lights* and *truths*), upon it; Ra in his double capacity of physical and intellectual light; Thmei perhaps as subjective and objective truth – i.e. truth as it appeared to the witness, and truth in an absolute sense. Now Urim and Thummim mean light and truth, the two lights and the two truths.

The judge gave judgement by touching one of the litigants with the figure as a token of the justice of his cause. I shall bring one home for Baron Rolfe. Dear Judge Coltman is gone where truths are no longer two (but all is one), and does not want it.

The king is represented so often with truth (or justice) as a fit offering for the gods; because, said the old Egyptians, this benefits your neighbours, while those pitiful other three cardinal virtues, prudence, temperance, fortitude, benefit only yourself. They knew a thing or two, those old Egyptians, don't you think so? When they spoke of a dead friend, they did not say, as we do, the 'lost', or the 'deceased', which is not true, as we all acknowledge in the Prayer Book, nor 'poor so and so'; but the 'justified' (*matu*); for the dead, who were found worthy, bore on their heads the feather of Truth or Justice, and took her hieroglyph.

I wish I could tell one half their philosophic ways. I must not forget the sacred boat in which people have seen Noah and his Ark, the Arkite worship, and all sorts of things, but which seems to be only a very natural emblem for a country which lived by its inundations, whose god Neph, 'the Spirit of God which moved upon the face of the waters', was called 'Lord of the Inundations', and was very likely, with the Egyptian want of imagination, to do this in a boat.

There are eight little chambers hewn in the rock, opening out of the Osiris hall, and covered with sculptures of offerings; but as these must be gone through with a candle, and it is impossible to enjoy anything in that way, I do not describe them. Some of them are left unfinished, as the workmen left them three thousand years ago – the line drawn but not cut.

The temple of Ipsamboul is the only thing which has ever made an impression upon me like that of St Peter's, yet how different. We bade him adieu at nine o'clock that morning. I never thought I should have made a friend and a home for life of an Egyptian temple, nor been so sorry to look for the last time on that holiest place.

We bade him goodbye, and turned our prow northwards, for we were to go no further. Our poor yard had been already taken down, and laid along from end to end. Our proud *Parthenope* no longer floated in the Nile breeze, and we, our eyes full of sand and tears (which made mud), very hungry, very sorry, very tired, watched from the deck the last of the colossi.

From *Letters from Egypt*, 1850

The Coming of the High Dam

William MacQuitty

The Nubia we see today was created within the lifetime of many of us. Before the High Dam the Nile flowed between high craggy hills; Lake Nasser did not exist. Thus the early travellers' accounts of Egypt are not the land we see. But the world was gathered together under the leadership of the United Nations to fund the preservation of the temples of ancient Egypt – that were seen to represent the history of us all. Thus, when we visit them today they are placed in positions as nearly as possible as in their original setting – though some are miles away from that setting. One of the great differences is that then the travellers met the people who lived nearby while now these areas are depopulated – the people of Nubia have been moved away.

THE FLOOD WHICH will result from the building of the High Dam at Aswan created international concern for the preservation of the Nubian and Egyptian monuments. The dam itself rivals the pyramids, and will require fifty-six million cubic yards of materials, enough to build seventeen pyramids the size of Cheops great monument at Giza. The ironwork alone would be sufficient to make fifteen Eiffel Towers. Much more important than the size is the greatly increased benefits which will flow from the harnessing of the river. For years the flood waters ran to waste in the sea. When the floods were high, twenty times as much water was lost as when they were low. The first dam at Aswan was built by the British in 1898. It was over a mile long, one hundred and fifty feet high and one hundred feet thick at the base. When the sluice gates were closed in winter, it flooded the Nile back to the Sudanese frontier over one hundred and sixty miles away. The High Dam can store the water over several years and release it as required. This will enable five million acres in the Sudan and two million acres in Egypt to be brought under cultivation. The water table in the surrounding area will be raised so that distant oases will become larger and more fertile. The permanent lake will cover under two thousand square miles. It will be three hundred miles long with an average width of six miles and will enormously facilitate navigation.

When finished the *Saddel-Aah*, as the dam is called in Arabic, will measure four thousand yards long, with a width of one thousand and seventy yards at its base and forty-five yards at its crest. The height will be one hundred and twenty yards. The layout of the dam is fairly simple. Through the east bank a deep diversion channel two thousand, one hundred yards long, forty-four yards wide, and ninety yards deep, has been cut in the solid rock. This leads to six tunnels sixteen yards in diameter and two hundred and fifty yards long. These tunnels will pass fourteen thousand cubic yards of water a second to the biggest hydro-electric power station in the world and thence to the irrigation of the land, both old and reclaimed. It is estimated that it will produce ten thousand million kw hours, or double the present supply, at economic rates. The old Commander of the Inundation would need all his powers to calculate the taxes that will ensue from this massive step towards industrialisation. To force the Nile through the canal a small coffer dam has been built upstream and a similar dam will be built downstream to prevent the river from flowing back into the area where the High Dam will be built. Although these dams are referred to as small, they are higher than the old British dam.

On 14th May, 1964, President Gamal Abdel Nasser and Mr Krushchev, amidst a cheering crowd of celebrities and workers, exploded a charge that breached the sand barrier at the entrance of the canal and the course of the river was changed for the first time in its long history.

Building the dam, like the pyramids, is a question of moving a great deal of heavy material, and the modern Egyptian worker has proved himself as adept as his ancient brother at this gigantic task.

From *Abu Simbel,* 1965

5

Desert Egypt

Siwa Town

Charles Dalrymple Belgrave

The oasis of Siwa in the Western Desert has fascinated people as a strange, distant place for centuries. Belgrave was stationed there in 1922.

'Through sun-proof alleys,
In a lone, sand hemm'd
City of Africa.'

SIWA TOWN IS LIKE NO OTHER PLACE that I have seen either in Egypt, Palestine or the Sudan. It is built on a great rock in the centre of the oasis, and from a distance it resembles an ancient castle whose rugged battlements tower above the forests of waving palm trees, and the rich green cultivation. It is somewhat similar to St Michael's Mount, but the inside of the town reminds one more of those enormous ant hills which are found in Central Africa. The houses are built of mud, mixed with salt, with occasional large blocks of stone from the temples let into the walls. The builder works without a line, gradually adding to the wall, sitting astride the part which he has completed, so few of the walls are straight. Another architectural peculiarity is that owing to the necessity of constructing walls thicker at the base than at the top most of the houses, especially the minarets of the mosques, become narrower towards the summit. The houses are built one above the other against the face of the rock, and the outer walls form one great line of battlements, pierced by little groups of windows, encircling the town, and rising sheer above the ground, in some places to a height of almost two hundred feet. The original site of the town was the summit and sides of two limestone rocks which rise abruptly from the level of the plain; but as the population increased more houses were built on the top of the old ones, and the town, instead of spreading, began to ascend into the air, house upon house, street upon street, and quarter upon quarter, till it became more like a beehive than a town. Fathers built houses for their sons above the parental abode, till their great-grandsons reached a dizzy height on the topmost battlements. The mud of which the walls were built gradually hardened and became almost of the consistency of the original rock.

In course of time the inside of the town has become a vast warren of houses connected by steep, twisting tunnels, very similar to the workings in a coal mine, where one needs to carry a light even in daytime, and two persons can scarcely walk abreast. This labyrinthine maze of dark, narrow passages, with little low doors of split palm logs opening into them from the tenements above, forms the old town of Siwa. In some places the walls are partly ruined and one gets little views of the green oasis, or the lower part of the town with its flat roofs and square enclosures, framed by the jagged ruined masonry. It took me nearly two years to know my way about this part of the town, at the expense of hitting my head many times against the palm log beams supporting the low roofs which are in most cases only about five feet high.

This human warren is surprisingly clean and free from the smells that one would expect in a place where there is such an absence of light and ventilation. One of the most curious things that one notices is the subdued hum of human voices, from invisible people, and the perpetual sound of stone-grinding mills, above, below and all around. When one meets people, groping along these tortuous passages, they loom into sight, silently, white-robed, like ghosts, and pass with a murmured greeting to their gloomy homes. It is a great relief after stooping and slipping and barking one's shins to reach the open roof on the highest tower of the town where, for a moment, the brilliant sunlight dazzles one's eyes, accustomed to the murky gloom of the lower regions. When, on rare occasions, I had visitors, I used always to take them up to see the view from the highest battlements, with a few stout Sudanese Camel Corps men to help pull, push and propel the sightseers. But most of them, especially the elderly colonel type, were too hot and exhausted to appreciate the view when they finally arrived, so I eventually kept this 'sight' for only the most active visitors.

High up in the heart of the town, in a little open space surrounded by tall grim houses, there is an ancient well cut out of the solid rock. It contains excellent water. Apparently there is a spring in the centre of the rock which supplies the well, and two smaller ones close by. Halfway down the well, about thirty feet from the top, just above the level of the water, there is a small entrance, wide enough to admit a boy, which leads into a narrow tunnel bored through the rock, terminating in the precincts of a mosque on the level ground. Nobody has traversed this passage for many years, owing to fear of snakes – which certainly exist, also *jinns* and *afreets*. The tunnel is about one hundred and fifty yards long, and must have taken years to complete, but it is difficult to guess its original object. This old well is specially popular with women, as by drawing water here they can avoid going out to the springs where they would necessarily meet with men. Often when I passed out from the narrow entrance of a passage I would see a dozen women busy with their pitchers, veils cast aside, laughing and chattering – in a moment, like magic, everyone would have silently vanished, and only the eyes peering from the adjoining windows would show any signs of life.

Below the old high town, huddled at the base of the mighty walls, there are more houses, and these, too, are surrounded by an outer wall. Beyond this more modern houses have been built when there was less fear of raids from hostile Arabs. Most of the sheikhs and the rich merchants have deserted the high town and built large, comfortable houses down below, or among the gardens in the adjoining suburbs of Sebukh and Manshia. Many of them have also country houses, where they retire in the summer when the heat in the town becomes intolerable, on their estates in different parts of the oasis. Residences of sheikhs and notables are distinguished by a strip of whitewash across the front, but woe betide a poor man if he decorates his house in a like manner. Tombs of sheikhs and holy men are whitewashed all over every year, at public expense.

From *Siwa: the Oasis of Jupiter Ammon,* 1923

The Lost Oasis – Arkenu

Ahmed Hassanein

Explorers and adventurers are an important category of travellers. While some were interested in tracking down the paths of rivers, others took up the more challenging task of desert exploration. But the job was rewarding. Beside collecting information, charting the obscure on maps and leaving their tracks behind on the sands, many explorers enjoyed the unmediated experience of the unknown, as did Ahmed Hassanein in the Western Desert in 1923.

WEDNESDAY, APRIL 18TH. Bu Helega had at last found two men, Bukara and Hamid, who would go with his camels. They were poor men and the money they would make loomed larger in their eyes than the danger.

Sayed El Abid sent three representatives to see us off. They brought a letter of farewell from him that touched my heart.

Bu Helega came to say goodbye. At the final moment there were tears in his eyes, and I do not think they were caused by fears for his camels or for the men whom he was sending with us. In spite of our controversy over the route, we remained true friends, with affection and respect for each other.

My men were greeted by their friends as though this was to be their last meeting. It was the most touching farewell of the whole journey. 'May God make safety your companion ... what is decreed is decreed and that will happen. May God guide you to the true road and protect you from evil.'

There was little about this parting of that sense of assurance which attends both those who go and those who stay behind when it is a case of starting for a holiday with some certitude of safe arrival. There were a few quivers in the last phrases of farewell, and knowing what had passed in the preceding days and the intimidation to which the men had been subjected, I could guess what was in their minds. Whereas I was excited by thoughts of the 'lost' oases and taking the unexplored road and going into the unknown, they were thinking that this might be the last time they would shake hands with their friends. There was even a pitying look on the faces of some of those who came to bid us God-speed as to doomed men, yet being Beduins they also felt: 'It is decreed that they should go thus.'

We recited the Fatha, the first chapter of the Koran: Praise be to God, the Master of the Universe, the Merciful, the Compassionate, the Lord of the day of Resurrection. It is You Whom we worship, and it is You Whom we ask for help. Guide us to the straight path, the path of those whom You have rewarded, not those upon whom displeasure has fallen nor those who have gone astray. Amen.

There followed the Call to Prayers: God is great and I testify that there is no God but God and that Mohammed is the Prophet of God. Haste to prayers, haste to that which is beneficent. Prayers are ready. God is great. There is no God but God.

It was upon the edge of the valley of Kufra where the oasis ends and the desert stretches out ahead. They had walked with us until then, and as we passed from the valley into the flat desert we looked back upon the date palms. The sun was setting, dusk falling and Kufra itself in the waning light was glimpsed as through the aperture of a camera. Those who had come to say farewell straightway returned and looked back no more. I was eager to get away from Kufra, and let my men turn their minds to the task ahead.

At last the real start had been made. Before me all was unknown, full of the mystery and the fascination that lie in those parts of the earth's surface yet untraversed by men from the outside world.

We started at 4.30 p.m. and halted at 8.15, making fifteen kilometres. It was fine and clear, with no wind. Hard sand covered with very fine gravel, slightly undulating. After leaving the date trees of Ezeila and Kufra, we crossed a zone of *hatab*, similar to that at Zieghen, and entered the *serira* at 5.45. At 6.30 we passed hillocks which form the south side of the Valley of Kufra. At 8.15 we arrived at Hatiet El Houesh, marked by dry *hatab*, which must once have been green. We left two men behind us to bring two loads that were to be carried on Tebu camels.

Our caravan comprised twenty-seven camels and nineteen persons – myself, Zerwali, Abdullahi, Ahmed, Hamad, Ismail, Senussi Bu Hassan, Senussi Bu Jaber, Hamad Zwai, Sad the Aujili, Faraj the slave, Bukara and his young brother Hamid, the camel man, Hassan, Mohammed our guide, and three Tebus.

We were delayed in starting through waiting for the two camels which had been left behind, and used the time in collecting *hatab*. It was very warm and the camels grew tired quickly because of the heat. The country was similar to that between Buttafal and Zieghen. With my new *hejin* I found it easy to fall behind to take observations without exciting suspicion. We had to camp early because of the condition of the camels.

This was the worst part of the journey for travelling, so far as temperature conditions were concerned. In the middle of the day it was too hot to march, and at night it was too cold. So we broke the trek into two parts, starting soon after midnight, and resting in the heat of the day. We had trouble with the baggage because of the difficulty of good packing and loading in the dark. The camels, however, went better on this day.

This was the fourth day of the lunar month. The Beduins observe the weather conditions on that day, believing that the weather for the rest of the month will be the same. It was to prove true in this case.

Saturday, April 21st. We started at 2.30 a.m. At 6 in the morning we came across stony and hilly country which lasted for twelve kilometres. We passed on our left the *gara* called Garet Kudi. At 9 we entered again into *serira*, with distant sand dunes on the right and left.

One camel fell ill shortly after our start and refused to go even when its load was taken off. Two Beduins were left behind to bleed it, but all efforts at cure were in vain, and it had to be slaughtered. I forbade the Beduins to eat its flesh. Later, after the midday halt, two Tebus dumped the loads from their camels and went back to dry the flesh and leave it until their return from Ouenat. They were to catch us up later. This all delayed us about an hour.

The men had little sleep the previous night and were very tired after sunrise. But it was chiefly the intense heat from noon to 4 o'clock that exhausted both men and camels. It was a very tired caravan that started again at 4.30 p.m. and moved slowly along.

I saw two hawks and fresh sleeping camps of birds on the sands.

Sunday, April 22nd. We travelled over flat hard sand, with occasional sand hillocks, three to ten metres high, covered with black stones. At 5.30 a.m. we sighted a chain of hills on our left running from north to south-west across our path. At 8 a.m. we entered into broken, hilly country, which continued all day. It was called Wadi El Maraheeg. We came across broken ostrich eggs.

We had better loading today, but the men were tired. Many of them fell out to snatch a half-hour's sleep, catching up the caravan when they woke.

Bukara brought me two little eagles which he had taken from their nest on the top of a *gara*. I ordered him to put them back and saw that it was done.

The *hejin* was ill and had to go all the afternoon without load or even saddle.

At the midday halt the men fell asleep immediately and snored heavily. This kind of travel is gruelling, tedious work. But we were getting on.

Monday, April 23rd. We started at 2.30 a.m., halted at 9.15 a.m., second start at 3.45 p.m., halt at 9 p.m., making forty-six kilometres. This was the most exhausting trek that I had yet known.

For eight days we had had only four hours of sleep a day. We had hardly started before the men with one accord fell back to snatch a half-hour's sleep, leaving the camels to follow the will-o'-the-wisp of the guide's lantern. I could not avail myself of this privilege, because of my anxiety for my instruments. The loading, done in the dark, was insecure and a slipped fastening may mean a broken instrument or camera.

At intervals one or another camel would halt and kneel and refuse to get up. Then a Tebu would come and press his thumb on a certain big vein in the camel's forehead and manipulate it. It seemed to give the beast relief.

We were having a hard time of it crossing the high steep sand dunes when suddenly mountains rose before us like medieval castles half hidden in the mist. A few minutes later the sun was on them, turning the cold grey into warm rose and pink.

I let the caravan go on and for half an hour I sat on the sand dune and let the sight of these legendary mountains do its will with my mind and heart. I had found what I came to seek. These were the mountains of Arkenu.

It was the outstanding moment of the whole journey. Any hardships I might have endured, any hardships that might still await me, were as nothing compared with the joy that filled me at the mere sight of those hills. It was not like going to seek a hidden treasure that had to be dug out of the ground. There they were standing right up high before me so that I might feast my eyes upon them. Up and down, up and down we had plodded across the sand dunes in the chilly greyness of the hours before dawn, until suddenly at the last dune it was as though somebody had rung up a curtain upon these magical hills of which I have not seen the like in the whole Libyan Desert. From the time I left Sollum until I reached this spot there had been nothing like the mountains of Arkenu. The sight of them so gripped me that for a while I dreamed that I was not in the desert any more.

Tuesday, April 24th, was the 111th day from Sollum and the 140th from Cairo. We covered broken country, sand covered with stones, undulating. At 5 a.m. heavy sand-dunes. After the dunes the country became stony again, and later there was hard sand covered with gravel.

North of Arkenu Mountain and only one hundred metres from it was a big sandstone hill about two kilometres long and one hundred metres or so high.

There was a glorious sunrise, with shades of red and gold splashed on the few grey clouds in the east. The cool wind soon dropped and it became close and warm.

Arkenu Mountain is a mass of granite, its grey surface weathered to a ruddy brown, rising uniformly along its length some five hundred metres from the desert surface. It is made up of a series of conical masses which run together at their feet, without intervals between them. We approached it at its most western point. As we came towards it, we could not tell how far it extended to the east. At the farthest point which we could see in that direction it rose into a peak. We marched around the north-western corner of the mountain mass and came to the entrance of a valley which runs to the eastward. There is one solitary tree of the species, called by the Goran *Arkenu,* standing in the desert here. From it the oasis takes its name. We made our camp near it. This was a bad spot for camel ticks, who lived in the shade of the tree and came literally running by the score when our camels approached. We were obliged to camp some distance from the tree, as the insects did not seem to care to forsake its shade, even to attack the camels.

I once picked up a tick that was like a piece of petrified stone. I hit it with a stick and it just clicked like a piece of stone. I turned away and pretended to be busy with something else. It took about three or four minutes before it gave any sign of life. The tick knows instinctively that safety lies in pretending to be petrified. Then, without warning, it scooted like lightning. When there are no camels these ticks live on nothing. They absorb the camel's blood, get inflated, and then they can live – the Beduins say years, but certainly a few months.

Immediately on our arrival the camels were sent into the valley to be watered and to bring back the supply of water of which we were much in need.

From *The Lost Oasis,* 1923

Red Sea to Nile

James Hanson

Travelling from India and across the Eastern Desert to the Nile with the retiring head of the East India Company Army in 1819, James Hanson paints both the hazards and the harshness of the experience of travelling through the desert lands. The harsh landscape and the fatigue of the journey become almost visible in his account. The wonderful relief of finally reaching the verdure leading to the river can, as anyone who has crossed desert lands know, be welcome after only a few hours – let alone days. Hanson was writing partly to pass on their experience to others who would follow.

FRIDAY, 26TH – At sunset, this evening, we anchored in Kossier roads, and were sheltered from a strong north-west wind, by a reef which extends about a quarter of a mile to the seaward of the town. The ship anchored close under this reef, in thirteen fathoms, and Sir Miles Nightingall having determined to land at Kossier, and pass through Upper Egypt, in consequence of the violent northerly winds which prevail in the Red Sea, I went on shore to wait on the Turkish governor, and ascertain the facilities we should be enabled to obtain in passing over the desert.

The Turkish governor, and indeed everybody on shore, was exceedingly civil; he apologized to us for the poorness of the place; but promised that everything Kossier afforded should be placed at our disposal. Camels were to be obtained in any number, as well as jackasses; but horses were not to be procured at all. He told us, therefore, we should be obliged to cross the desert either on an ass or a camel.

...The country in the neighbourhood of Kossier is indeed most barren; not a blade of grass or verdure is to be seen in any direction, and the water is very indifferent. The black arid tops of the mountains remind me of the summit of Goonong Cheremay, which environs a crater five hundred yards deep. We shall cross the desert to Khené without any difficulty. Khené is four days' journey from Kossier, and Cairo ten days' journey from Khené.

27th – Upon first coming on shore, the General paid his respects to the Turkish commandant, who received him with all the honours he could possibly show him, that is to say, he fired all the guns in his possession, and collected all the jannissaries under his command, to surround him in the hall of audience. In the evening, he returned the visit, and assured the General, that every arrangement was being made as speedily as possible for our departure.

… We are all of us exceedingly busy, as you may suppose, in our preparations to cross the desert; and every department of this little state is in active exertion to push us forward. As yet we have experienced nothing like unpleasant heat. The thermometer in our Arab mansion last night was down as low as 58°; and we are delighted with our sleeping contrivance, viz. a sea cot slung upon triangles, which fix in the ground, and keep us half a yard from its surface. The Bombay bottled water, which we brought with us for this journey, will be indeed a most valuable store, as the drinking water of this place is brought from the Nile, and necessarily smells very offensively. The water of Kossier is, I believe, too brackish, even for camels…

March 1st, 1819 – First day's journey across the desert.

Our first march was necessarily a very short one, as we started late in the day to get clear of the town; in fact to feel we had commenced our journey – we halted at Ambawajee, a valley about six miles distant from Kossier… Our caravan consisted of thirty camels, and about twenty jackasses. A very serious accident had nearly occurred to Lady Nightingall, before we had proceeded many yards upon our journey. The sort of basket in which she was to ride across the desert, was fixed to the side of the camel, and was to have a corresponding weight to balance it. The General took up his position as the *counterpoise*, but he found it so exceedingly uncomfortable, that he quickly abandoned this *elevated post*. Her ladyship was then balanced by two little girls, who were her servants; but the camels had hardly begun to move, when the ropes (being rotten) gave way, and they all came tumbling to the ground together, from a height of at least *seven feet.* We naturally feared that her ladyship would be very seriously hurt, particularly so, when I observed her to be somewhat confused as I raised her from the ground. We were gratified, however, to find that she quickly recovered, and had sustained no injury whatever.

The road lay, for the first part, in a westerly direction, and may be said to pass through a series of valleys, bounded by hills of the most wild and unfruitful appearance. The summits of these hills were in many instances as black as jet, and looked as if they had been burnt to cinders by the strong operation of fire. The road, however, was by no means so unpleasant as we expected. Instead of *fine sand,* we found nothing but *coarse sand* and gravel, and it was in every respect as fine a road as could be met with in any country. There was a slight ascent after we left Kossier, probably about one-tenth per cent. About half-past four we observed a stunted tree or two before us, and shortly afterwards, we arrived at a spring, where the people halted to refresh the cattle, and where we determined to remain during the night…

Upon tasting the spring at Ambawajee, I found it very brackish indeed, fit only for the refreshment of the cattle. The margin of the stream was encrusted with salt. Our tent was pitched in a narrow valley, with solid precipitous rocks rising upon each side of us, to the height of about three or four hundred feet. I would say that the road this day passed through a rocky gravelly desert, upon which any wheeled carriage might be driven with the greatest facility. The night was cold, but there was no dew. The thermometer at daylight 60°; distance five or six miles.

March 2nd, 1819 – Second day's journey.

We moved from our ground this morning at about seven o'clock. I forgot to mention that Lady Nightingall, apprehending a second misfortune yesterday, similar to that she had already experienced, determined to sit upon the camel *en cavalier* the remainder of the journey, which she found much less fatiguing than she had expected. The road continued through the same series of valleys, and became much more sandy. At about nine o'clock, we arrived at an extraordinary number of fantastic fissures in a mountain to the left, which would attract the notice of a traveller. It appeared as if an immense torrent of water had swept this huge and misshapen mass into the plain. After rounding a sort of projecting cliff, we arrived at two wells... From these wells we continued our journey a little to the southward of west, and proceeded to wind through rocky valleys, which communicated with each other in the most extraordinary way imaginable. We would fancy ourselves completely environed by mountains, without seeing the road ten yards before us, when suddenly we would arrive at a turn of the precipice, and see it traversing in quite an opposite direction.

At about a mile to the westward of these wells, we noticed an extraordinary range of mountains to our right, having the appearance of tombs. About twelve o'clock, we arrived at the entrance of a pass, which appeared to be defended in times of old, by a fort now in ruins. The fort was nearly square: about fifty yards each side, with regular bastions, but in a complete state of dilapidation. Inside the fort, there appeared to be the remains of a well, into which the earth had fallen; and the mountain that overlooked this fort was crowned by a watchtower, or rather by the ruins of a small building, which the people told us had been used for that purpose. They said these ruins were far anterior to their knowledge of the country. They believed they had been built by Europeans; but whether by French, English or Romans, they did not know.

After leaving this fort, the road ascended very considerably through the pass, which was not more than one hundred feet wide, and very serpentine. The ascent I should calculate to be about two per cent. Here our eye was in some degree refreshed by the appearance of vegetation, in the shape of a wild prickly thorn, which the camels eat with great avidity; and, upon clearing the pass, which was about two miles in extent, we occasionally passed trees of the bauble, or acacia kind, some of them measuring seven and eight feet in circumference.

The road still continued excellent; was composed of sand and gravel, and at about a quarter past three, we arrived at our halting place, which the people called Sayed Hajie Sooleman, and where the

Arabs procured most excellent water from the mountains; but I observed they used it only for their own refreshment, as they gave none to the cattle.

March 3rd, 1819 – Third day's journey.

We managed to get off this morning at a quarter past six o'clock, the camel men having become better acquainted with their loads, and more expert in placing them on the cattle. The road here took nearly a south-east direction for an hour, and wound in the same serpentine manner, through mountains of the most wild and savage sterility. We were constantly passing the same sort of watch-towers we had noticed yesterday… We also saw several deer, which fled to the mountains on our approach, and the General saw some larks and a *water-wagtail*!!! The ascent still continued very considerable, and the road lay to the northward of west. At one o'clock, we arrived at a *ghaut*, where the road became much more confined, but perfectly passable for all sorts of cattle. After passing this *ghaut*, the road continued over a sort of table land, until about a quarter past two, when we passed through another *ghaut*, and began to descend upon the other side of what appeared to be a range of mountains. At the foot of this *ghaut*, there was a sort of hollow in the rock, in which was deposited rainwater, but not of a very wholesome appearance. I observed the camels were not baited here. From this *ghaut* the road descended very considerably, and at about half-past four, we arrived at our halting ground, which the people called Hammamat. Here we encamped for the night. No water: distance twenty-seven miles; thermometer the following morning, 62°.

March 4th, 1819 – Fourth day's journey.

This was, indeed, a day of fatigue! We marched at a quarter past six, in nearly a north direction, but quickly turned to the west, at the top of another rocky pass, which was in like manner defended by one of these forts; but with this difference, that the fort appeared to have been much more considerable, extended from one side of the pass to the other, and was surrounded by the ruins of an extensive town. The road passed through the fort, and continued down a considerable descent, probably two and a half per cent. At ten o'clock, we had emerged from the pass, and entered upon a more open country. During our progress this morning, we saw abundance of partridge, pigeons, larks, etc.; and halfway through the pass, we observed some Egyptian hieroglyphics under a projecting part of the rock, on the left-hand side of the road. We passed another ruined fort, about ten o'clock, and saw the remains of a stone sarcophagus lying in the middle of the road, which the people told us was used as a trough for cattle to drink out of.

We also observed that extraordinary phenomenon which the French call *mirage*, and which appears in this barren desert to mock the feverish thirst of a weary traveller; in many instances I could have sworn we were near the margin of an extensive lake, so perfect was the deception.

The desert, as we proceeded, became exceedingly barren, and the road much more sandy and disagreeable. The heat was greater than any we had yet experienced, and we were certain, by the solicitude our guides expressed to get us forward, that we had a long day's journey before us.

At five o'clock in the evening, we saw the sun gradually descending to rest, without any appearance of a halt. The guides told us they were compelled to go forward to water, as the camels had not drunk for three days. We were, therefore, constrained to summon all our patience, and hope for a speedy relief. Lady Nightingall, who had now ridden *eleven hours*, began to complain of very considerable fatigue; and the General, who travelled upon a donkey, was so harassed by the motion of the animal, now completely knocked up, that he was obliged to alight and walk. At length, about half-past six o'clock in the evening, we discovered two buildings on the horizon, which the guides told us were the long-wished-for wells; and when quite dark, to our joy, we arrived at most capital water, which I quaffed with greater *gout* than I ever recollect to have experienced before.

March 5th, 1819 – Fifth day's journey.

We marched this morning at a quarter-past six o'clock, and passed over a greater desert of sand than we had yet seen; the road, however, was exceedingly good, and we saw several flights of remarkably fine plover… At half-past ten we were first gratified by the sight of trees and vegetation on the banks of the Nile; and at one o'clock we arrived at an Arab village, on the border of the cultivation, called Berambur, where the people flocked to us with milk, cheese, etc. etc. for sale; as Khenah was still four hours' distance in front of us, and as both men and cattle were considerably fatigued with the journey of the preceding day, it was determined to halt here for the night.

I am not capable of describing to you the sort of delightful sensation I experienced when I found myself surrounded by the rich verdure and cultivation of the Nile. The contrast between the white sandy desert we had been passing, and the rich corn and clover on the banks of this bountiful stream, is only to be imagined by those people, who like ourselves, had been traversing a dreary waste for four days, and then suddenly found themselves encompassed by the most luxuriant vegetation. I cannot convey to you the sensation I experienced when I saw water in abundance; when I felt that we were not obliged to use it sparingly; and that both men and cattle might drink their fill. In short, I refer you to that period when you will yourself, probably, pass by the same route, to understand what our feelings were when our tents were first pitched in the cornfields of Egypt. Nothing can be more strongly marked than the line of barrenness and fertility. You may literally stand with one foot in clover, and the other upon a barren desert, where neither the animal or vegetable world are capable of sustaining existence; where the eye on one side is fatigued with the boundless prospect of an eternal waste, and on the other refreshed by the most smiling abundance and fertility…

March 6th, 1819 – Sixth day's journey.

We moved from the village of Berambur this morning at four o'clock, in order to reach Khenah before the sun became powerful. The road continued considerably to the northward of west, and skirted the cultivation of the Nile, until within five or six miles of Khenah, when it passed between fields and villages; and we observed, with astonishment, the extent and richness of the cultivation.

At eight o'clock, we saw a party coming to meet us, apparently Turks, who were mounted upon asses. To our astonishment the principal person alighted from his donkey, and addressed the General in excellent French, presenting him a letter from Sir Thomas Maitland, which had been waiting his arrival at Khenah. The gentleman who gave the letter was Mr Anderson, whose good offices Mr Salt's communication had prepared us to receive. We accordingly proceeded to his house, in the town of Khenah, where we took up our abode…

From 'Routes of Lt General Nightingall', *India in Letters*, 1820

Centuries of Monastic Life

William Dalrymple

Far into the desert lands of Egypt, the early Christians withdrew to create monasteries that were the prototypes of such communities worldwide. Once almost totally isolated and only visited by the occasional pilgrim, these retreats can now be reached along the networks of desert roads. In 1994 William Dalrymple set off around the eastern Mediterranean to immerse himself in the monasteries and their histories, living alongside contemporary monks while becoming deeply aware of the generations of their predecessors.

THE STORY OF St Antony's life, which was written within a year of his death by Athanasius, the Bishop of Alexandria, was soon translated into Latin by Evagrius of Antioch for 'the brethren from overseas'; within twenty years it was being read and copied in distant Gaul. Not long afterwards, St Augustine, sitting in Hippo in North Africa, records that he was profoundly moved by a story he heard that two secret policemen from Trier (now part of Germany), having read *The Life of St Antony*, decided to leave their comfortable posts to become monks in Egypt. A century later monasticism was flourishing all over the West, and had become especially popular in Italy and southern France. By 700 it had reached even the Highlands of Scotland: around that time an image of St Antony under a palm tree was sculpted by Pictish monks on the windswept promontory of Nigg near Inverness, hundreds of miles beyond the Roman Empire's northernmost border.

The Monastery of St Antony – which is still, unlike most of its medieval Western imitators, flourishing – lies in the desert some three hundred miles south-east of Cairo, fifty miles inland from the barren shores of the Red Sea. Even today, when the monastery is linked to the outside world by a tarmac road, the drive is a long and dispiriting one, through a desolate wasteland: flat, shimmering with heat during the day, icily cold at night, impossibly inhospitable. Yet until forty years ago St Antony's could only be reached by a three-week journey, and it depended for all its supplies on a monthly camel caravan.

The monastery is so well camouflaged against its khaki backdrop that it is almost invisible until you drive up directly underneath it. Then, less than half a mile from your destination, the whole complex comes slowly into focus: out of the sand rises a loop of camel-coloured walls pierced by a series of pepperpot mud-brick bastions. Above these stand two enormous towers – the gatehouse and the Byzantine keep – beyond which you can see the tops of dusty palm trees shivering in the desert wind.

Inside the walls, the monastery looks more like some African oasis village than it does Tintern, Rievaulx, Fountains or any of the great medieval monasteries of Europe. Streets of unglazed mud-brick cottages with creaking wooden balconies lead up to a scattering of churches and chapels; occasionally a small piazza filled with a sway of date palms breaks the spread of cells. Over everything tower the wall turrets and the great castellated mud-brick keep. It is a deeply suggestive spread of buildings – to the European eye like some nineteenth-century Orientalist's fantasy – but to the Byzantines it must have sent out a very different message.

For the monastery's simple mud-brick buildings were constructed in the fourth century in a manner as crude and earthy as the buildings of Byzantine Alexandria must once have been refined and beautiful. This contrast was not accidental. St Antony and the monks who followed him into the Egyptian desert were consciously rejecting everything that Alexandria stood for: luxury, indulgence, elegance, sophistication. Instead they cultivated a deliberate simplicity – sometimes even a wilful primitiveness – and their way of life is reflected in their art and their architecture.

In contrast to medieval Western monks, the Egyptian desert fathers also tended to reject the concept of learning, the worship of knowledge for its own sake. St Antony was particularly scathing about books, proclaiming that 'in the person whose mind is sound there is no need for letters', and that the only book he needed was 'the nature of God's creation: it is present whenever I wish to read His words.' Many of St Antony's Coptic followers emulated his example, preferring a life of hard manual labour and long hours of prayer to one of study. A millennium of classical literary culture came to be forgotten as the works of Homer and Thucydides went unread for the first time; in the words of a monastic chant to the Virgin, 'the many tongued rhetors have fallen as silent as fishes.' As late as the mid-nineteenth century, this attitude to the classics seems to have lingered in Coptic monasteries: when the British bibliophile the Hon. Robert Curzon visited the Monastery of Deir el-Suriani in the Wadi Natrun, he discovered manuscripts of lost works of Euclid and Plato serving as stoppers in jars of monastic olive oil.

Modern Egyptian monks tend to be literate – in fact the majority are university graduates – but their energy is still consciously channelled away from scholarly study and into prayer and agriculture. The monks rise at three in the morning – just as the Cairo nightclubs and casinos are beginning to empty – and spend the next five hours praying together under frescoes of the desert fathers in the ancient early Byzantine abbey church. There then follows a day of gruelling physical activity as the monks attempt, with a certain degree of success, to get the desert around the monastery to flower.

Indeed they are such enthusiastic students of arid farming techniques that yesterday evening after vespers – the one period of the day when the monks are free to mill around – I saw several groups of fixated novices poring over seed catalogues and the latest issue of some obscure farming magazine – *Irrigation Today* or *Bore Hole Weekly* or some such – as excitedly as a gaggle of teenage schoolboys with their first girlie glossy. Because of this agricultural bent, conversation at mealtimes can turn surprisingly technical. Yesterday, when St Antony's Guest Master, Fr Dioscuros, brought me my supper, he produced a single boiled egg with as much flourish as a Parisian restaurateur might present some incredibly *recherché* piece of *nouvelle cuisine*. Then he waited while I tasted it.

'Very good,' I said, trying to rise to the occasion. 'It must be the most delicious boiled egg I've ever tasted.'

'That's hardly surprising,' replied Fr Dioscuros. 'It's an Isa Brown.'

Isa, the Arabic form of the name Jesus, is a common name among Copts, so I asked if the egg were named after some pioneering Coptic hen-breeder.

'No, no,' replied the Guest Master, looking at me as if I were some sort of halfwit. 'Not Isa – I.S.A.: *Institut de Sélection des Animaux* near Paris – the most famous poultry centre in the world. Fr Abbot visited it two years ago. Now all our animals are from the most modern and superior breeds.'

This obsession with state-of-the-art chicken-farming techniques is one of a number of ways in which the modern world has begun to knock at the gates of St Antony's. The abbey has recently abandoned candles in favour of its own electrical generator, and Fr Dioscuros turned out to have a portable phone tucked away amid the folds of his habit. More radically, the increase in the number of Coptic pilgrims visiting St Antony's has forced the monks finally to abandon their age-old practice of winching visitors into the abbey by a rope (a practice which began in the sixth century AD when Byzantine Egypt first began to be assaulted by Bedouin war bands) in favour of the relatively up-to-date option of a front gate.

Nevertheless, these concessions apart, the monks remain wonderfully Dark Age in their outlook and conversation. Exorcisms, miraculous healings and ghostly apparitions of long-dead saints are to them what doorstep milk deliveries are to suburban Londoners – unremarkable everyday occurrences that would never warrant a passing mention if foreigners did not always seem to be so inexplicably amazed by them.

'See up there?' said Abuna Dioscuros as I was finishing my egg. He pointed to the space between the two towers of the abbey church. 'In June 1987 in the middle of the night our father St Antony appeared there hovering on a cloud of shining light.'

'You saw this?' I asked.

'No,' said Fr Dioscuros. 'I'm short-sighted.'

He took off his spectacles to show me the thickness of the glass. 'I can barely see the Abbot when I sit beside him at supper,' he said. 'But many other fathers saw the apparition. On one side of St Antony stood St Mark the Hermit and on the other was Abuna Yustus.'

'Abuna Yustus?'

'He is one of our fathers. He used to be the Sacristan.'

'So what was he doing up there?'

'He had just departed this life.'

'Oh,' I said. 'I see.'

'Officially he's not a saint yet, but I'm sure he will be soon. His canonisation is up for discussion at the next Coptic synod. His relics have been the cause of many miracles: blind children have been made to see, the lame have got up from their wheelchairs...'

'All the usual sort of stuff.'

'Exactly. But you won't believe this' – here Fr Dioscuros lowered his voice to a whisper. 'You won't believe this, but we had some visitors from Europe two years ago – Christians, some sort of Protestants – who said they didn't believe in the power of relics!'

The monk stroked his beard, wide-eyed with disbelief. 'No,' he continued. 'I'm not joking. I had to take the Protestants aside and explain that we believe that St Antony and all the fathers have not died, that they live with us, continually protecting us and looking after us. When they are needed – when we go to their graves and pray to their relics – they appear and sort out our problems.'

'Can the monks see them?'

'Who? Protestants?'

'No. These deceased fathers.'

'Abuna Yustus is always appearing,' said Fr Dioscuros matter-of-factly. 'In fact one of the fathers had a half-hour conversation with him the day before yesterday. And of course St Antony makes fairly regular appearances – although he is very busy these days answering prayers all over the world. But even when we cannot see the departed fathers we can always feel them. And besides, there are many other indications that they are with us.'

'What do you mean?' I asked. 'What sort of indications?'

'Well, take last week for instance. The Bedouin from the desert are always bringing their sick to us for healing. Normally it is something quite simple: we let them kiss a relic, give them an aspirin and send them on their way. But last week they brought in a small girl who was possessed by a devil. We took the girl into the church, and as it was the time for vespers one of the fathers went off to ring the bell for prayers. When he saw this the devil inside the girl began to cry: "Don't ring the bell! Please don't ring the bell!" We asked him why not. "Because," replied the devil, "when you ring the bell it's not just the living monks who come into the church: all the holy souls of the fathers join with you too, as well as great multitudes of angels and archangels. How can I remain in the church when that happens? I'm not staying in a place like that." At that moment the bell began to ring, the girl shrieked and the devil left her!' Fr Dioscuros clicked his fingers: 'Just like that. So you see,' he said. 'That proves it.'

From *To the Holy Mountain,* 1999

Through Sinai to St Catherine's
Ahdaf Soueif

In her novel The Map of Love, *Adhaf Soueif recalls the long tradition of Sinaitic paintings which presented the peninsula as an obscure rugged place and animates the landscape with the presence of her two lovers, thus bringing the still pictures to life and evoking one of the classic connotations of Sinai. Her account is a fresh page in the history of Sinai that poses it as the meeting place for presumably opposed entities: a man and a woman, an Occidental and an Oriental, meet where the two continents of the classical world overlap.*

19 March 1901

OH HOW I WISH it were possible to go without sleep entirely, or that the hours of each day would be doubled, that I might have time to see and to feel all there is to see and feel, and then still have time to reflect on it, to let the impressions wind their way through my mind, settling here and there in small, shining pools, or merging with other thoughts and progressing towards some great conclusion! And then again I would have time to write it all down, to record it all, for in that act, I have found my thoughts clarify themselves and what starts as an hysterical burbling of impressions resolves into a view, an image as lucid and present as a painting.

I have never cared for the paintings of the Sinai that I have seen, preferring to them the intricate interiors, the detailed portrayals of domestic life. The paintings with grander ambitions never seemed to come to life for me and now I understand why. I have found myself thinking of the wonderful Turners hanging in Petworth, for surely no lesser genius than his could do justice in watercolours to the magnificence of these landscapes. And in oils, of all the painters I can think of, perhaps Corot comes closest to the possibility of rendering these mountains – and yet a painting would do justice only to that spot it depicted, and the viewer would be mistaken in thinking that now he had an idea of the whole of the Sinai. For each day brings us to a different aspect of this amazing land, this conjunction of the two mighty continents of the Ancient World. One day it is a bare gravel plain stretching as far as the eye can see, and then you are surprised by a small stream and thorny acacias digging deep into the sand for the little water that will help them sustain the small life that is their lot; the next day you find yourself amid stupendous ranges of solid rock, some black, some purple, some red, and you are treading the same land in which the Ancient

Egyptian laboured to extract copper and turquoise – indeed, you can see the remains of his excavations still. You then come out on an open plain by the Red Sea and there you are joined by huge flocks of birds, pausing, resting for the night on the shore where you are camped, and as the sun rises, while the men perform their morning prayers, the birds too rise. They soar and wheel and call out to each other and set off in a great swooping cloud across the sea and towards their summer homes in the North. And then, opening out among cliffs more than a thousand feet in height, a *wadi* lies before you and life is plentiful again, with gardens of tamarisk and apple trees and fields of wheat and barley. What one painting could even suggest all this?

Tonight we are camped a single day's ride from the Monastery of St Catherine and in full view of the mountains of Sinai. We rode, Sharif Pasha and I, through the most spectacular pass, called the Nugb Hawa, so precipitous and narrow that camels cannot go through it but have to be sent the wider and more level route through Darb el-Sheikh. Sharif Pasha put the question to me: would I prefer the spectacular route or the easier one? And naturally I chose the first. He said, 'It can only be done on horseback. And since we have only two horses, we would have to go alone.'

I said, 'You will have to convince Sabir,' and he smiled.

For the first time Sabir consented to leave my side, and Sharif Pasha and I broke off from our companions and rode off into the narrow pass of Nugb Hawa. The granite cliffs on either side of us rose to fifteen hundred feet or more and at times, by leaning slightly to one side or the other, I could have touched both walls of the pass with my hands. Sometimes it seemed that we were riding towards a solid rock face, but as we drew near, an opening would miraculously appear and we would turn into it. The incline meanwhile was for stretches so steep that only the most sure-footed and even-tempered of horses would have climbed it without harm to his rider. Our mounts were willing and agile, however, and we rode on, mostly in single file with me at the front, but sometimes my companion drew abreast and with the briefest of looks satisfied himself that all was well with me.

It was on one of those occasions, and sensible that this was the first time we had had a possibility of private conversation, that I started to tell him how grateful I was for all he had done for me and assured him that I was well aware of the great inconvenience this must have caused. But he cut me short with '*C'est rien*. You would have made the journey anyway.'

'I would have tried,' I said, 'but I think I would have met with a tour in Suez and travelled with them, and that would not have been the same thing at all.'

'Why not?' he asked, seeming surprised. 'You would have travelled in comfort and without the necessity of disguise.'

'I would have …' I did not quite know how to put this. 'I would have remained within the world I knew. I would have seen things through my companions' eyes, and my mind would have been too occupied in resisting their impressions to establish its own –'

'Have you always been like this?' he asked.

'Like what?' I said, surprised in my turn.

'So insistent on making up your own mind.'

'You make me appear wilful.'

'And are you not?'

'I have not given free rein to my will before,' I said. And with that the pass narrowed and he pulled in his horse and fell behind. He had not said it was no trouble, nor assured me that he did not find my company irksome, but I was not displeased with our exchange – and I was glad that I had thanked him.

Nugb Hawa ended as abruptly as it had begun and suddenly we emerged from the dark cool of the pass and into a bright open plain with the majestic mountains of Sinai in full view before us. We were rejoined by the men on camel-back and Sabir greeted me with smiles and with no evidence of any anxiety. I believe he now trusts that I am in safe hands. Indeed, as the days pass and we go deeper and deeper into Sinai, I am quite frightened (although I would not for the world admit this other than to my journal) to think that I tried to do this with only Sabir for company. I had not spoken falsely when I said to Sharif Pasha that I had thought I would meet with a company of Cook's travellers in Suez and perhaps travel with them, but there was a strong part of me that did not wish to be in the company of my own kind here. As though I had an instinct that their conversation, their presence itself, would preclude my truly entering into the Sinai. And I know now that it would indeed have been so. The encompassing silence and the ease (or indifference) of my companions have left my soul free to contemplate, to drink in the wonder of this place. How fitting it is that it should have been here that Moses heard the word of God! For here, where Man – if he is to live – lives perforce so close to Nature and by her Grace, I feel so much closer to the entire mystery of Creation that it would not surprise me at all were I to be vouchsafed a vision or a revelation; indeed it would seem in the very order of things that such an epiphany would happen. I have found myself, every time the men stopped for prayer, offering up prayers of my own; simple offerings in praise of Him who fashioned all this and who sent me here that I might see it. I have also prayed for His mercy to be visited on the soul of my poor Edward, for I have fallen, from time to time, to thinking that if he had come here as a pilgrim instead of going to the Soudan as a soldier, he might have been alive today and at peace.

21 March

It is afternoon and the monks have retired to prayer and we to our siesta.

We have been to the summit of Jebel Moussa and have watched the dawn break to the accompaniment of the melodious chant of the muezzin calling for prayer.

The air is dry and light and its effect on the mind is similar to that of a glass of champagne before dinner.

I have not written anything of this Monastery where we are lodged. The Father is very kind and – as the men are encamped outside the walls – Sharif Pasha has told him who I am on the grounds of it being wrong to accept hospitality under false pretences.

The building is rather like a medieval castle and was established in the sixth century and soon afterwards, as the Moslem armies advanced westwards from the Arabian Peninsula, somebody had the prescience to build a small mosque in its courtyard to guard against it being burned or demolished. At the time of the Crusades it was the turn of the monastery to protect the mosque, and so it has been down the ages, each House of God extending its shelter to the other as opposing armies came and went.

Last night it was early when we all retired, and I thought to try on Layla's gift. It is a lovely, loose gown of deep-green silk, and even though there is, naturally, no mirror in my cell, I was happy to be wearing it.

I went out into the dark garden. I knew we would rise early, but the night was not much advanced and I thought there could be no harm in slipping out for a breath of air.

I saw him come out of the Chapel. He too had doffed his desert attire and was in plain trousers and a woollen jersey with his head uncovered to the night air.

I fancied he started when he saw me. He came towards me and I thought he would be angry that I had ventured out, and that in my woman's dress with the *kufiyya* draped loosely about my shoulders. And indeed his first words were *'Que faites vous ici?'* I said I needed air as my room was close and he said, 'You should go in.' But presently, when I did not move, he gestured towards the seat and upon my giving him leave, he sat himself down beside me. That he was troubled I could tell without even looking into his face. We sat in silence but there was that about his posture, his air, that betokened a restlessness, a disquiet, and eventually I ventured:

'Could you not sleep?'

'I have not tried.'

'You were in the Chapel,' I said. And he heard the question in my voice.

'I was looking at the monks. The old ones. The bones,' he said, and his voice was harsh and bitter. He sat stooped forward, his elbows on his knees, gazing into the darkness.

I could think of nothing to say. Indeed, all I was conscious of was a desire to put out my hand and touch that arm that was so close to mine, to put my hand upon that troubled head – a desire that grew in intensity so that I folded my arms about myself. He turned.

'You are cold?'

'No,' I said.

'But you are shivering.'

'No, not really.'

He studied me for a moment, then turned away. 'What brought you to Egypt, Lady Anna?' he said into the night air.

It was the first time he had said my name.

'The paintings,' I said. And when he turned to me I told him about the paintings in the South Kensington Museum, about their world of light and colour. I told him about my visits there when Edward was sick. When he was dying.

'You have been very unhappy,' he said.

'Yes,' I said. 'He did not need to die like that.'

'Like what?'

'Troubled. Not at peace.'

'But he did what he believed in, surely? He believed he should fight for his Empire.'

'It was an unjust war.'

'But he did not know that.'

'I think – I believe he knew. But he knew too late. And it killed him.'

There was a silence. It was the first time I had said this to anyone. Perhaps it was the first time I had put the thought so clearly to myself. I was shivering in earnest now and had he put his arms around me I believe I would have allowed myself – but he stood up and said, 'You must go in.'

'No,' I whispered, shaking my head, and with an impatient sound he strode off. I thought he was going away but he strode about the garden, then he came back to a stop in front of me and said:

'So. Tell me. What do you think? Which is better? To take action and perhaps make a fatal mistake – or to take no action and die slowly anyway?'

I considered. I tried to consider, but it was hard with the trembling upon me and he standing tall in front of me, blocking my view of anything but himself. At last I said, 'I believe you have to know yourself first – above all.'

'So. She is wise, as well as beautiful and headstrong.'

I shook my head and kept my eyes on the ground. There was a mocking tone to his voice. But – '*aussi que belle*' – he had called me '*belle*'.

'What if you know yourself too well? What if you do not like what you know?'

I was silent.

Within moments he had collected himself: 'Forgive me. It is all those skulls and bones in there. The dead monks. So –' He sat down again. 'You came to look for that world you saw in your museum. And you have found it?'

'In your house, monsieur,' I said.

'Ah, there are other houses like mine,' he said dismissively. 'We must arrange for you to see them.'

I did not know whether to be pleased or disappointed. He was sending me somewhere – but he was sending me away.

'What is the matter?'

'Nothing.'

'I did not mean to frighten you earlier. Forgive me.'

'I am not frightened.'

'Then why are you shaking?'

'It is grown – rather cold.'

'Then you must go inside. Now.' He stood. 'Will you go or shall I have to carry you?'

'You are a bully, monsieur,' I said. But I stood up.

'Yes,' he said, 'I have been told.'

At my door I held out my hand and he took it in both of his. 'Will you be warm enough?' he asked.

'Yes,' I said.

'Then sleep well. Sleep well, Lady Anna who is never afraid,' he said. He raised my hand and for a fleeting moment I felt on it the pressure of his lips. And even though I was warm, I cannot say that I slept well.

From *The Map of Love*, 1999

6
Travellers and Writers

The Traveller
Robin Fedden

PTOLEMYS AND CALIPHS, Turks and British residents may come and go, but the traveller in Egypt never fails. Herodotus broke the ground, and after him followed a host of avid Greeks to whet that admirable Aegean curiosity. Later the Romans came flocking to take the cure and leave their names on public monuments. In the Middle Ages Von Suchem was moved to wonder at the 'little green parroquet birds' on the Nile, and Antoninus Martyr piously visited the tombs of Alexandrian saints. Sandys climbed the Great Pyramid in the year Shakespeare retired to Stratford, and on his heels came the leisured eighteenth-century gentlemen. The Cairo 'season' was almost in sight.

We know, and have been told, that travel broadens the mind; but, given human nature, such a fact in itself would hardly be likely to account for the popularity of travelling. Travel does more than this; it primarily provides an escape from real life:

Time for soul to stretch and spit
Before the world comes back on it.

The traveller has no age, no fears, and no reputation. No facts and figures hem him in; he is free from the idiotically repeated scene and there are no relentlessly familiar faces. His personality, like elastic, can stretch from point to point. He has for a while the great illusion that he is nowhere pegged in time. Some countries can achieve this blessed disembodiment of the personality better than others; among the former Egypt, with its weirdness, age, and unreal contrasts, is exceptional. Thus for two thousand and more years it has been the traveller's goal.

In the latter half of the nineteenth century the traveller in Egypt combined romance with comfort perhaps better than he ever did before or will do again. If you were a person of consequence, or had one or two letters of introduction, you could dine cross-legged in oriental Turkish splendour, picnic off gold plate beside the Sphinx, and enjoy the sight of barefoot *syces* in red velvet running before your carriage. If you were really a notability and showed the necessary enthusiasm your hosts arranged that you should discover a tomb which, with oriental accommodation, they took the trouble of preparing overnight. Even for the nonentity there were crocodiles to shoot and mummies to be bought in every town. Though nowadays this romance has been lost, and time and money do not so often launch those private *dahabiehs* on their leisurely explorations towards Nubia, the twentieth century has its own advantages. Communication is quick and easy; the British Consul at Suez no longer gets his drinking water by boat from India as he did in the 1950s, and Belon oysters come regularly by air from France. Though you will not sit cross-legged or dine off Turkish plate, helpful waiters will hover round you in admirable hotels, and comfortable pullman-cars whisk you to your destination overnight. Your range is from Damietta to the Sudan. In the midday sun you can lie in the gardens of Luxor or under the fretted shade of oasis palms. Egypt has preserved her eight thousand years for you, and the twentieth century presents them with a minimum of effort and trouble.

The rest depends, as it has always done, upon the traveller. Taste and intelligence will make or mar any landscape. A certain gentleman on his honeymoon organized a vast display of fireworks for his bride in the moonlit Temple of Karnak, and Queen Alexandra's lady-in-waiting recorded in her diary her reaction to the past: 'Saw another old temple, the name of which I am not certain.' Such travellers undoubtedly exist, but would probably achieve the stimulating effects of travel equally well nearer home, and with far less expenditure of energy. For the judicious enthusiast, however, every day will bring experiences that he will not forget, and places of whose names he will remain certain. Egypt will imprint itself upon his memory, as it has done upon the memory of former travellers. The beauty of its landscape and its past does not change, and the traveller is able to share the same enthusiasms as his daring eighteenth-century prototype. The tales that he brings back will not differ much from those that stirred the imagination of Bonaparte. Having watched the sun burn the mist off the Nile at dawn, and heard the songs of the boatmen, having stood in the shadow of the Colossus of Memnon, and walked in the mortuary temple of Hatshepsut, having seen twilight in the Tombs of the Mamelukes, and moonrise in the desert – standing on the Great Pyramid and looking down, he may well echo an earlier traveller and exclaim *O soveraigne of streams, and most excellent of countries.*

From *The Land of Egypt*, 1939

The Story-teller's Tale

Winifred Blackman

THE MODERN EGYPTIAN PEASANTS are as fond of stories as were their ancestors in the days of Herodotus. Since few of the older people can read or write they have largely to depend for such entertainment on the public recitations of story-tellers. Most villages possess at least one story-teller, who, as a rule, has some trade with which he is engaged during the day. In the evening the male villagers are in the habit of congregating in one another's houses, or in some shop or café. To such a gathering the story-teller is a welcome addition, and he tells his tales in return for very small sums of money presented to him by members of his audience. The story-teller may have taken years to collect his tales, or he may have inherited them from his forebears. The peasant is an excellent *raconteur*, possessed of great imagination, very dramatic, and entirely free from self-consciousness.

Among my village friends are two or three story-tellers, and from them I have collected and written down a large number of tales. Some were related to me in my brother's desert camp the first year I was in Egypt. I would appoint a day for the story-teller to visit me, and, as the hour approached, I would see him and the schoolmaster who came with him to assist me in my translations of the stories riding across the lower desert on donkeys. On their arrival coffee was brought, and, when they had partaken of this refreshment, the story-teller seated himself cross-legged on the ground, drew his robe around him, and, after some minutes' reflection, began one of his tales.

One of my story-teller friends, a cheery person, was a dyer by trade as, indeed, was made evident by the state of his hands, which were stained almost as dark a blue as his cotton clothes. When he was a young boy he was apprenticed to a firm of dyers, and he would listen to stories told to his fellow-workmen as they plied their task. Having a retentive memory, he stored up all these tales, which he now relates to the people of his village in the evening. He also tells his tales to his customers, who often wait while he is dying the cloth which they have brought him. Thus some tedious hours of waiting are pleasantly whiled away.

When he first came to me he was somewhat shy, but after a while, seeing that I was really interested, he would start off without hesitation. Sometimes he would consult the schoolmaster as to what he thought would be most to my taste, giving him a short epitome of two or three stories. Then, when a suitable one was chosen, he would go ahead without further delay. Several stories were recited at a sitting, and occasionally I was writing them down for three or four hours on end. Our servants would often stand near, listening in breathless attention as the plot developed.

The next year I engaged another man, who was a water-carrier by trade. I was then living in tents near an out-of-the-way village in Upper

Egypt, and the *'omdeh* (headman of the village) kindly placed his reception room at my disposal. Wealthier villagers would drop in from time to time and take a seat at a respectful distance from me, while humbler folk stood at the doorway, or squatted on the threshold, all alike listening enthralled, and from time to time uttering ejaculations of appreciation.

I was assured that these tales had never been committed to writing, but had been handed down orally.

The two shoes of Henen

Once upon a time there was a shoemaker whose name was Henen. An Arab came to him and wished to buy a pair of shoes, but they did not agree about the price, and quarrelled with each other, and Henen was much annoyed and desired to take his revenge on the Arab.

So when Henen learnt that the Arab was going to cross the desert he took a pair of shoes and went along the road on which he knew the Arab would go. As he went he put one of the shoes on the ground; the other shoe he placed on the road a mile away from the first. Then he hid himself in a tree near where the second shoe lay.

When the Arab passed by the first shoe he said to himself that it was like Henen's shoe, and he left it on the ground and did not take it. He then went on his way till he found the second shoe a mile distant from the first. Whereupon he said to himself, 'I must leave the camel here and go back to take the first shoe.'

So he went back. And after he had turned back, leaving his camel, Henen came down the tree and led the camel off to his house. When the Arab returned to the place where he had left his camel he found it had disappeared, so he took the pair of shoes and went to his house. When he arrived there his family said to him, 'What have you brought?' He replied, 'I have brought back the two shoes of Henen instead of the camel.'

And this proverb, 'I have returned with the two shoes of Henen', is quoted when anyone returns with small things in exchange for large ones.

From *The Fellahin of Upper Egypt*, 1927

Seeing the Sights
Anthony Sattin

Anthony Sattin calls into the present the experiences of travel in the past. He brings to life the complex but necessary preparations needed for a long journey into a strange land.

> '... what is going on in all the *canges* that are fitted out like ours? English ... gentlemen with ladies – albums displayed on round tables – they will be talked about in green parks ...'
>
> Gustave Flaubert, *Travel Notebooks,* 1850

DURING THE EVENING of 2 October 1872, Phileas Fogg, the eccentric hero of Jules Verne's *Around the World in Eighty Days*, left his companions at the Reform Club in London, took his Bradshaw's *Continental Railway Steam Transit and General Guide*, collected his servant and a carpetbag containing £20,000, and caught the 8.45 p.m. train from Charing Cross Station. Crossing over from Dover to Calais, he then took the express train to Brindisi via Mount Cenis, boarded the P&O iron steamer *Mongolia* and, only seven days after leaving London, arrived at the southern end of the Suez Canal at eleven o'clock in the morning, exactly on time. The steamer docked at Suez for a few hours and Fogg used the time to go ashore and obtain a *visé* for his passport from the British consular agent. Having fulfilled this formality, he returned to the wharf, was rowed back to the steamer and waited for it to leave for Bombay. 'As to seeing the town,' Verne explained, 'he did not think of it, being of that race of Englishmen who have their servants visit the countries they pass through.'

Although Gustave Flaubert, when he declared that the temples bored him, proved that even a man of learning and sensibility could tire of seeing the sights in Egypt, many people who passed through the Suez Canal did want to stop off in Egypt and, of those, most wanted to do some sightseeing. But in the second half of the nineteenth century, the problem for the hurrying visitor wanting to go up to Aswan or Abu Simbel was that the distances involved were formidable and the available transport slow. So when the railway was opened between Alexandria and Cairo, the old steamer route along the Mahmoudieh Canal and the Nile was immediately abandoned by most travellers. However, even starting from Cairo, where *dahabiehs* to let were tied up along the quay at Boulak, Abu Simbel was still nearly eight hundred unpredictable miles away. The Egyptian season traditionally started in November because not only was the weather just right – cool enough for Europeans to travel in comfort and still much warmer than a northern winter – but also, this was when the winds usually changed and began to blow from the north. Eight hundred miles with the wind and Allah behind you still took four to six weeks. But if the winds failed, the boat had to be pulled or rowed up the river, at three miles an hour if the going was good. Obviously patience was an essential requirement for a Nile journey where the word *Inshallah* – God willing – was added to the end of each itinerary. So, although it was unheard of to have adverse winds for three consecutive weeks, it was obviously helpful to leave Cairo when the winds were behind you.

The first thing to be done, usually even before hiring a boat, was to find a dragoman. The word is derived from the Arabic *targuman*, which literally means 'interpreter'. The dragoman, however, was more than merely a linguist; he was also a guide and organizer. He knew better than his employers where they wanted to go and how they were going to get there; and along with the *rais* or captain of the boat he was the person who left the greatest impression on the traveller. A dragoman was usually indispensable, but the relationship between him and his employer was a delicate one: he had the knowledge but they had the money; they were the masters but he was their leader. Obviously it was important to get on with him from the start. Cook's *Handbook* for 1906 advised that 'It often requires considerable moral courage to keep these individuals in their proper places, for the more useful and capable they are the more easy it is for their employers to lose control over them.' It was essential to keep control of this man for he in turn usually kept the captain of the *dahabieh* in check.

Dahabiehs were one of the larger sort of Nile boat and, for a long time before Europeans visited the country were used by wealthy Egyptians and Turks to travel along the Nile. Rather like cars in our own time, *dahabiehs* were status symbols, a visible assertion of wealth, and a pasha would have at least one for himself and one for his harem. Later, *dahabiehs* were rented out to foreigners – Florence Nightingale's boat, for instance, had never taken Europeans before, but had been for the exclusive use of a wealthy pasha's harem. *Dahabiehs* were also the most comfortable boats on the river at the time and when the Nile cruise became a popular and fashionable thing for Europeans and Americans to do, the number and variety available for hire increased greatly so that when Amelia Edwards arrived in Egypt for the first time, twenty-three years after Florence Nightingale, she had nearly three hundred of them to choose from at Boulak. 'Now, most persons know something of the miseries of house-hunting,' she wrote, 'but only those who have experienced them know how much keener are the miseries of *dahabeeyah*-hunting.' The first problem was that they all seemed to look the same. Some were a little longer and others a little shorter, some newly painted and others weather-worn, but their layout was usually the same. Even the crews tended to look alike to the travellers. A system of testimonials had been introduced whereby people who had previously hired a boat gave a written recommendation or condemnation to help future passengers, but even these – which every captain seemed to have – all appeared to be similar and sometimes were indeed the same sheet of paper passed on from one boat to another. 'All this is very perplexing,' Amelia admitted, 'yet it is as nothing compared with the state of confusion one gets into when attempting to weigh the advantages or disadvantages of boats with six cabins and boats with eight; boats provided with canteens, and boats without; boats that can pass the cataract, and boats that can't; boats that are only twice as dear as they ought to be, and boats with that defect five or six times multiplied. Their names, again – *Ghazal, Sarawa, Fostat, Dongola* – unlike any names one has ever heard before, afford as yet no kind of help to the memory.'

The *dahabieh* they eventually hired, which Amelia described as being 'more like a civic or an Oxford University barge, than anything in the shape of a boat with which we in England are familiar', was a large one, one hundred feet long, with eight sleeping cabins. 'These cabins measured about eight feet in length by four and a half in width, and contained a bed, a chair, a fixed washing-stand, a looking-glass against the wall, a shelf, a row of hooks, and under each bed two large drawers for clothes.' In addition, there was a dining saloon, a bathroom, and another small saloon in the stern which they used for storage. 'For the crew,' Amelia added, 'there was no sleeping accommodation whatever, unless they chose to creep into the hold among the luggage and packing-cases.'

Some *dahabiehs* were even larger than this, like the khedival boat at the disposal of the Prince and Princess of Wales when they toured Egypt in 1869, just before the opening of the Suez Canal. The fittings on Ismail's *dahabieh* were beautiful and expensive and the carpets were rare and thick. It was bigger than most Nile boats, too, and the Prince and Princess had a bedroom, two bathrooms and two dressing-rooms for their own use, and even the Hon. Mrs William Grey, the Princess's companion who recorded their journey, had two cabins of seven feet by seven for herself and one each for her maid and her dresser. Because this was a royal party, locomotion was not left in the hands of the weather and, instead of unfurling the lateen sail, the royal *dahabieh* was towed up the Nile by a steamer, the *Federabanee*. This does seem to be missing some of the point of travelling by *dahabieh*, namely the sense of peace which settles over the boat as the wind fills the sail and passengers settle into armchairs under the awning on the upper deck …

When a *dahabieh* had been chosen and a price agreed, a contract was drawn up which safeguarded both sides – foreigners could be sure that they would get to where they wanted to go and the crew knew they would be paid for taking them there. At first these were registered with the passengers' consulate, but as the number of foreigners in Egypt increased this become impractical and tourist agencies took over. Having arranged the formalities, the boat was taken across the river to the bank at Gezira or Giza where it was sunk to rid it of rats and whatever else was living on it. Murray's

Guide stressed the importance of moving off that side of the river as soon as possible after the boat had been refloated, for otherwise the vermin simply climbed back on board and the process had to be repeated. After its submersion, the boat was dried, redecorated and fitted out with rugs, mattresses, bedding and whatever else the owners had agreed to provide. In the days before Cook's tours and travel representatives, it was as well to pay attention to these details at the beginning of a trip and make sure the work was done properly and that the boat was carrying the necessary equipment and stores. John Gardner Wilkinson, the Egyptologist whose guide to the country formed the basis for Murray's Guide, suggested a list of requirements which would fill the average modern home. Among the equipment he listed were mats, carpets, towels, sheets, cloths, pillows and cases, horse-hair mattresses, blankets and mosquito nets – preferably the invention of an earlier traveller in Egypt, Mr Levinge, who devised the curious hanging mosquito tent. This was considered indispensable, as were a national flag, pots, kettles, curtains, table and chairs, thermometer, two sheets of Mackintosh, a medicine chest, water filter and even a donkey, or at least a donkey saddle. The list of foods the passengers were advised to take with them was even more extensive. Of course, as more tourists went up the river, it became easier to procure the sort of provisions they would enjoy in towns along the way, but before that time it was necessary to make an expedition to the bazaars in Cairo, usually under the guidance of the dragoman.

'A rapid raid into some of the nearest shops, for things remembered at the last moment – a breathless gathering up of innumerable parcels – a few hurried farewells on the steps of the hotel – and away we rattle,' Amelia wrote of her departure from Shepherd's. With the *dahabieh* decorated and filled with their bags and provisions, all that was needed for them to start was a fair wind. Sometimes, if there was only a slight wind, the *dahabieh* was towed or rowed away from its mooring into the middle of the river before the great sail was unfurled. But if, as on this occasion, the wind was up, the captain stood on the upper deck, the steersman at the helm and all it took was a push from the sailors and the crowd which always gathered on the wharf when a boat was leaving. Their departure was then announced by several rounds fired from the dragoman's pistols. It was not a racing start, but a slow, sedate, stately progression.

From *Lifting the Veil: British Society in Egypt 1768-1956*, 1988

The Sitt of the Theban Palace

Sarah Searight

'I LONG TO BORE YOU with travellers' tales,' Lucie Duff Gordon wrote to her husband Alexander in 1863 in one of her memorable letters, written after her first winter in Egypt.[1] She neither bored him, however, nor did she really long to do so; Lucie's *Letters from Egypt*, first published in 1865, with three reprints the same year, were superbly crafted and intended as such, in order to pay the expenses of her sojourn to Egypt. This, it was hoped when she set off from England in 1861, would assuage the terrible effects of her tuberculosis.

There are countless books about nineteenth-century Egypt – discoveries and rediscoveries, on archaeology and anthropology, the political assessment often leading to the patronisingly imperial tract. Plenty for Alexander Duff Gordon and Lucie's many other readers to choose from if they wished. But Lucie handled her readership with an astuteness cultivated by years of literary association in England and on the continent. Her seven years in Upper Egypt were the longest any European woman had spent in that part of the world (sadly for Alexander and her children) and she put them to good use: the fresh, uniquely sympathetic but acute observations on life in her adopted country, which she made in her letters home, painted a portrait of that country dramatically different from previous accounts

[1] Lucie Duff Gordon, *Letters from Egypt* (London, 1902), November 14th, 1863.

and from many since. The word 'dramatically' is particularly appropriate to Lucie's letters; her descriptions of her meetings with a vast range of Egyptian life often read like scenes from a play.

Lucie was born in 1821, the daughter of John and Sarah Austin, a serious-minded couple with all the right connections. John was an academic lawyer who wrote books on jurisprudence and bequeathed to Lucie that 'innate bent to exactitude', as George Meredith put it,[2] so apparent in the letters; her mother supplemented a meagre income by translations of German literature. Their friends were radicals of the day – Bentham, John Stuart Mill, Macaulay among them – and Lucie grew up as an only and precocious child in their midst. London proving expensive, the family moved to the Continent, travelling in France and Germany, as a result of which she read French and German fluently; during a stay in Boulogne they were befriended by Heinrich Heine. She had a spell in a hated boarding school and at the age of eighteen, met and married the handsome Scottish baronet, Alexander Duff Gordon, well connected but not so well paid as a minor Treasury employee.

They were a handsome and popular couple. Judging by her portrait by Henry Phillips, painted around 1851 (in the National Portrait Gallery), she was remarkably beautiful, Alexander her match in looks. They attracted to their Westminster house and later Esher an intelligentsia that stood Lucie in good stead when she embarked on her literary career, initially following in her mother's footsteps as a translator. George Meredith was among their friends, much in love for a while with Lucie's elder daughter Janet and later author of a memoir of Lucie. Several other friends had travelled in the Near East – Kinglake whose *Eothen* appeared in 1884, Thackeray whose *Cornhill to Cairo* was published in 1844, Elliot Warburton whose *The Crescent and the Cross* was published in 1845. Their accounts are witty, mocking and self-deprecating, popular with the Victorian armchair traveller, still entertaining reading today and a contrast to the earnest tomes

[2] Meredith wrote an introduction to the 1902 edition of Lucie's Letters.

produced by such as the worthy Harriet Martineau.[3] But you would not be much wiser about the world they travelled through; in this particular respect their approach is very different to what Lucie's was to be.

In the late 1850s Lucie developed a hacking cough, perhaps the result of nursing her dying father in a cold and damp cottage at Weybridge. One winter she nearly died of bronchitis and soon after that appeared the first signs of the dread tuberculosis. In 1860 her doctor told her she was too ill to spend the winter in England and that autumn she set sail for South Africa, leaving her family in England and writing lively letters to them about her travels. Her health was not sufficiently improved; she was warned she should on no account spend another winter in England and so the decision was taken to experiment with Egypt. The year before Janet her daughter had married Henry Ross, a middle-aged banker in Alexandria. Lucie, perhaps guided by Kinglake or Thackeray, decided she would be less cut off from family and friends if she tried wintering in Egypt.

The 'unveiling' or development of modern Egypt stemmed from the French invasion in 1798 but even more from the policies of the first post-Napoleon ruler, the Viceroy (as he became) Muhammad Ali who governed the country as a semi-autonomous province of the Ottoman Empire. Muhammad Ali was a military adventurer who with European assistance remodelled the Egyptian army and administration on more European lines. This in due course brought about radical changes in society, culture and politics in Egypt which his successors were in general unable to control. Their growing dependence on European finance replaced Ottoman rule with the far more onerous burden of the Briitsh and French interference as creditors, the burden borne on the whole by the Egyptian tax payer, as Lucie frequently noted. The almost medieval city life described vividly by Edward Lane in his *Manners and Customs of the Modern Egyptians* (published in 1836) was a far cry from the scene of rural deprivation that Lucie described.

[3] Lucie criticised Harriet Martineau's *Eastern Life Past and Present*, published in 1843, as having excellent descriptions 'but she evidently knew and cared nothing about the people here'. (February 7th, 1864)

Muhammad Ali's successors, in particular his nephew Ismail who became viceroy in 1863, just a year after Lucie's arrival, had even greater delusions of grandeur. Railways, harbours, cotton plantations, above all the Suez Canal were designed to elevate Egypt in the eyes of Europe as well as enrich the viceroy and a good many European hangers-on. Many of those who came to Egypt meant well – Lucie's son-in-law, the banker Henry Ross worked for the bank in Alexandria founded by Samuel Briggs, an entrepreneur who persuaded Muhammad Ali to introduce cotton and to improve communications between Cairo and Alexandria by excavating the Mahmudiyyah Canal (Lucie steamed along it on her initial journey to Cairo). Not all were as scrupulous as Briggs, however. On his accession to power Ismail was soon on the way to impoverishing the country irreparably. Lucie's letters are a sad commentary on this state of affairs.

She steamed across the Mediterranean in the late summer of 1861, arriving at Alexandria to find her daughter off on a hunting expedition; loathing the noise and dirt of that city Lucie soon set off for Cairo which initially she loved: 'I write to you out of the real Arabian Nights,' she wrote to her mother early in November 1861. 'Well may the Prophet (whose name be exalted) smile when he looks on Cairo. It is a golden existence – all sunshine and poetry, and I must add, kindness and civility.'[4] Sadly the city was not so kind to her health and as soon as the weather cooled she rented a Nile boat, known as a *dahabiyah* (£25 a month, including crew) and headed upriver to Abu Simbel. It was while staying in Luxor on her voyage northwards that she first conceived the idea of living there. That summer she returned to England for a brief sickly three months; while there she was encouraged by Meredith and Alexander reluctantly to allow publication of the letters she had written from South Africa, on the grounds that it would help pay for the expenses of her Egyptian sojourn. *Letters from the Cape* was published in 1864.

Lucie's letters home thereafter, mostly from the rickety house she rented in the heart of the village that nestled in the ruins of the Great Temple of Luxor, but also from her regular visits to Cairo, are

[4] November 11th, 1862.

among the most acute observations of local life, and her participation in it, made by foreigners in Egypt in the nineteenth century. Her 'Theban palace' had been built into the ruins of the Temple of Luxor by that great looter of Pharaonic stones Henry Salt (and occupied by later generations of looters), but to Lucie 'it seems more and more beautiful,' she told her husband, 'a lovely dwelling … Some men came to mend the staircase, which had fallen in and which consists of huge solid blocks of stone.' A workman crushed a finger 'and I had to operate on it', another of Lucie's many first aid occasions.[5] Rather more of the house collapsed by the time she came to leave it.

Rare among foreigners she went to great lengths to learn Arabic. Within a few days of her arrival in Cairo she had mastered a few words of colloquial Arabic, then in Luxor she acquired a teacher for the classical language. 'Oh dear what must poor Arab children suffer in learning A B C,' she wrote later,[6] complaining of the difficulty of writing backwards. But speaking Arabic obviously made all the difference to her relations with all those around her: she tended the sick, dined with the local great and good, listened to complaints, and at times of famine and cattle disease (both frequent misfortunes) fed all and sundry. Knowing the language was crucial to her understanding of the problems around her. 'One must come to the East to understand absolute equality,' she writes with upper-class confidence; 'money and rank are looked on as mere accidents, and my *savoir vivre* was highly thought of because I sat down with Fellaheen and treated everyone as they treat each other.'[7] John Stuart Mill would surely have approved.

She was attended throughout by a faithful servant, Omar. In April 1864, the hottest time of year, she sailed upriver to Philae, which she like most European visitors adored. Omar tended her against heat exhaustion and sang sad Turkish songs, but '"Do not rub my feet, oh Brother, that is not fit for thee,"' she told him to which he responded, '"The slave of the Turk may be set free by money but how shall one be ransomed who has been paid for by

[5] January 13th, 1864
[6] November 21st, 1866.
[7]May 12th, 1863.

kind actions and sweet words."' And she forgave Omar when her almost as faithful maid Sally gave birth to Omar's child. The maid was dismissed; Omar stayed.

One relishes too the descriptions of her sheikhly visitors, one of whom was her teacher Sheikh Yusuf, 'a graceful, sweet-looking young man, with a dark brown face and such fine manners', 'a perfect darling'. Interest in the language of Islam encouraged an interest in the faith itself: visits to mosques, to saints' shrines, attending feasting at the end of Ramadan. She attends the departure of the *mahmal*, the covering for the Kaabah in Mecca, and the *hajj* or pilgrimage heading from Cairo also to Mecca … 'all those men prepared to endure such hardship.'[8] Her role treating the sick was particularly important: 'Yesterday was Bairam [the feast at the end of the Muslim month of fasting] – she writes – I rejoice to say and I have lots of physic to make up, for all the stomachs damaged by Ramadan.'[9] On one occasion she runs out of medicines, including Epsom salts. She writes of her tolerance of the petitions for help, her readiness to respond to the petition, of the tolerance of her Muslim friends towards a Christian, though she found that Copts were less sympathetic. She attends harvest festival, a great celebration when the harvest is good as it was that year.

She also tells tourists not to shoot pigeons which are private property (housed of course in those splendid pigeon houses which are such a feature of the Egyptian landscape); in 1906 such shooting at Dinshawai in the Delta would develop into a major political incident. Tourists are generally less welcome, especially after the publication of the first batch of Egypt letters in 1865 turned her into a celebrity; the women always want to borrow Lucie's side saddle rather than make do with the local saddle: 'last year five women on one steamer all sent for my saddle, besides others – campstools, umbrellas, beer etc. etc.'[10] Particularly important is the fact that as a woman she could make friends, and did, among the local women; medicines, her Arabic and her sex were an invaluable combination.

[8] April 13th, 1863.
[9] April 1865.
[10] January 22nd, 1867.

She did like certain visitors: Edward Lear was 'a pleasant man and I was glad to see him',[11] the artist Marianne North and her father, the Prince and Princess of Wales whom she liked, especially the princess – 'the mostly perfectly simple-mannered girl I ever saw', the prince too, 'quite respectful in his manner', as well he might be, given Lucie's reputation (but also extreme fragility) at the time of their visit in 1869.[12] Above all her ne'er-do-well son Maurice whose manners are so much improved by consorting with the locals. There's a poignant moment as she says goodbye to Maurice just a month before her death, for he mustn't think of coming out again, 'he must begin work now or he will never be good for anything.' Right to the end Lucie remained a most artful letter writer.

She was unique in another significant respect, the one European to note the effect of the Khedive Ismail's commitment to the construction of the Suez Canal on the rural population of Egypt. This major construction project demanded not only a huge increase in taxation but also a vast workforce, extracted from the countryside by a forced levy known as the *corvée*. 'Everyone is cursing the French here,' she wrote on February 11th, 1863. 'Forty thousand men always at work on the Suez Canal at starvation point does not endear them to the project.'[13] Ismail was forced to abolish the system before the completion of the canal but not before Lucie had reported the appalling impact on the countryside. The radicalism of her childhood comes to mind: 'I should like to see person and property safe which no one's here is (European's of course excepted),' she wrote to her mother. 'Food … gets dearer and the forced labour inflicts more suffering.' She goes on: 'What chokes me is to hear English people talk of the stick being "the only way to manage the Arabs", as if any one could doubt that it is the *easiest* way to manage any people where it can be used with impunity.'[14] In 1867 she wrote to Alexander (February 5th), 'I cannot describe to you the misery here now, indeed it is wearisome to think of: every day some new tax', and later the same year she compared an earlier

[11] Ibid.
[12] February 11th, 1869.
[13] January 9th, 1864.
[14] January 5th, 1864.

view from her window (of 'the lovely smiling landscape') with the 'dreary waste now' before her.

Lucie's story, like that of so many consumptives in the nineteenth century, is as poignant to us today as it was to her contemporaries – far from family, far from a husband who showed no anguish for her plight, surrounded by local people who adored her. Lucie's penultimate letter to her husband easily reddens eyes, written from Boulak on the Nile outside Cairo on June 15th, 1869, a month before her death:

> Dearest Alick,
> Do not think of coming here. Indeed it would be almost too painful to me to part from you again; and as it is, I can patiently wait for the end among people who are kind and loving enough to be comfortable, without too much feeling of the pain of parting…

And on July 9th, just four days before dying:

> I wish I had seen your dear face once more – but not now, I would not have you here now on any account…

Such a farewell casts quite a spell and was intended to do so; it does Lucie no harm to suggest that was indeed her intention. It is a spell that has lasted a hundred and fifty years, since the first edition of letters, those of 1863–65 edited by Alexander and Lucie's mother, Sarah Austin, was published in 1865 and reprinted three times that year.

From the introduction to *Letters from Egypt*, 1983

The Dragoman's Experiences

Mohammed Aboudi

Through this book we have heard the voices of travellers and of writers from Egypt and the world beyond. Here, Aboudi's voice tells of their relationship to the dragoman – the guide, the interpreter – who brings travellers to his country and his country to the travellers.

I STARTED AS DRAGOMAN to the travellers on the Nile steamers of Messrs Thos. Cook & Son during the season of 1905, a position of great responsibility. I organise the sightseeing trips on shore, and lecture upon them. Each night while the passengers are at dinner, I enter the saloon and clap my hands to call attention, then announce the particular places which will be visited on the morrow, mentioning distances and giving the necessary information with regard to donkeys, cars and carriages and boats prepared in readiness for the excursion. In the daytime, while the steamer is proceeding on its course along the classic river, I point out the various places and objects of interest on the banks, particularly drawing attention to the unique characteristics of the landscape, with the green fields in the foreground, the unchanging desert beyond, and in the distance, the pink-tinged hills in the recesses of which are hidden the tombs of the Pharaohs of old.

During the years of my service I have been privileged to come into close contact with many distinguished persons: Egyptologists, and leading lights of learning and science, from all parts of the world. I have studied hard to acquire a certain knowledge and understanding of the history and mythology and antiquities of my country and I have been able largely to increase my knowledge through my intimate association with the many famous Egyptologists who have made the Nile trip during the extended period of my service. During the summer months, I take engagements as a private courier in Europe in order to enlarge my knowledge and make myself more proficient in foreign languages, of which I am acquainted with six.

A specimen of my evening announcements in the dining room is as follows: 'Ladies and Gentlemen, subject to your approval, you will be called tomorrow at 8.30. Breakfast will be at nine. We shall leave the steamer at 9.30, and proceed by car or donkey for about half an hour to the Great Temple of Karnak which stands on a thousand acres of ground. After thoroughly viewing the temple, we shall return to the steamer in good time for lunch. The many beauties and interest of the scenes which we shall visit cannot be described in words, but must be viewed to be appreciated, as you will be able to judge for yourselves tomorrow. One word more. I have learned to trust you, and I hope that this trust will not be betrayed tomorrow. I therefore expect to see each of you go forth on this excursion to the Great Temple of Karnak armed with his Temple ticket. Please do not forget this ticket.'

On the steamer I answer the various questions addressed to me by the tourists concerning everything connected with the excursion, the inhabitants of the Nile valley, scenery, monuments, donkey boys and *baksheesh*. When we are on shore I shout to the donkey boys, trying to keep them in order so as not to confuse the tourists. During the excursion I must keep to the rear, in case someone falls from his donkey, so that I may be able to give him immediate assistance, and the clouds of dust make my throat dry to suffocation, in spite of which, when we have reached the temple I start explaining everything and never leave a detail neglected.

From *Egypt: Aboudi's Guide Book*, 1946

The Tourist

Alan Bennett

The playwright and writer was briefly in Egypt for the making of a film. He catches a moment which has been enjoyed daily by thousands over the decades.

15 January, 1987 Luxor.

TEA ON THE TERRACE of the Winter Palace Hotel, a brown stucco building no different from the Winter Gardens of many an English seaside town because built around the same time and nowadays as rundown and deserted as they are. We watch the sun set over the Nile, a scene captured by dozens of tourists with film cameras, who wait as if for the passage of royalty.

From *Letters Home*, 1987

A Chronology of the Extracts

c. 1190	Ibn Jubayr
c. 1330	Ibn Battuta
c. 1560	Leo the African, Amin Maalouf's novel
1817	Dr Robert Richardson
1819	James Hanson
1825	Dr R. R. Madden
1833	Robert Curzon
1835	Ahmad bin Tuwayr al Janna
1850	Florence Nightingale
1852	H. J. Ross
1864	Lucie Duff Gordon
1872	William Armstrong
1901	Ahdaf Soueif's novel
	Muhammed Aboudi
1909	Pierre Loti
1911	Lady Evelyn Cobbold
	Taha Hussein
1922	Charles Dalrymple Belgrave
1922	E. M. Forster
1923	Ahmed Hassanein
1927	Winifred Blackman
1928	Constance Sitwell
1929	Princess Marta Bibescu
1930	Mary Chubb
1938	H. V. Morton
1939	Robin Fedden
1943	Penelope Lively

1946	Sayyid Qutb
	Jean Said Makdisi
1965	William MacQuitty
1978	Amitav Ghosh; Naguib Mahfouz
1980	Deborah Manley
1982	Michael Haag
1987	Alan Bennett
1993	Penelope Lively
1994	William Dalrymple
1998	Max Rodenbeck
2006	Paul William Roberts

Biographies of the Authors

Sahar Sobhhi Abdel-Hakim

Dr Abdel-Hakim is an Associate Professor at Cairo University. She specialises in travel studies and has contributed many critical essays in both English and Arabic languages on a wide range of cultural topics that deal with travel writing such as travel and translation, women travellers, the construction of gender, exhibitions and museums as travel texts, negotiations of identity through writing, the traveller and Arab traveller accounts. Together with Deborah Manley, she published *Travelling through Egypt* and *Travelling through Sinai.* They are both founder members of ASTENE (The Association for the Study of Travellers in Egypt and the Near East).

Mohammed Aboudi (fl. 1930–1945)

Aboudi worked as a tour guide or dragoman for Thomas Cook's and published his own guide book to Egypt and the Nile.

Sir William Armstrong (1810–1900)

Armstrong was an important Victorian inventor and lawyer, his inventions including 'a water pressure wheel', 'a hydroelectric machine', 'hydraulic crane' and several types of rifle. The account of his Nile journey was given as four lectures to the Newcastle Philosophical Society in 1872. It shows his fascination with how things work – how could the pyramids have been built? – how did the ancients carry such huge weights? His journey to Egypt combined pleasure with work. As the excerpt shows, he was travelling with 'Mr Fowler' – probably the civil and railway engineer Sir John Fowler (1817-1898) – to look at the flow of the Nile and the cataract above Aswan that limited trade within Egypt. Today his residence at Cragside is famed for its early use of electricity in a domestic setting.

Ibn Battuta (1304–1377)

Born into a Tangier family, Ibn Battuta set out on pilgrimage in 1325 with the hope that he would meet famous scholars along his route. His passion for travel took over and he determined to travel throughout the Earth. He went twice to Mecca, and visited Egypt, East Africa, Asia Minor, the Crimea, Constantinople, and even India and China. He returned to Mecca in 1348 and on this journey also visited Spain and West Africa before finally settling in Morocco.

Alan Bennett (1934–)

The actor, playwright and writer visited Egypt in 1987 to film *The Fortunes of War*. At Luxor on 15th January he sat overlooking the Nile and wrote a diary entry later published in his *Writing Home (1994)*.

Sir Charles Dalrymple Belgrave (1894–1969)

Stationed at the oasis of Siwa in the Western Desert in 1920-1, in charge of a section of the Camel Corps, Belgrave also acted as the government District Officer there. He spent as much time as he could discovering the history of Siwa and learning about the manners and customs of the local community. He later became adviser to the Sheik of Bahrain (1926-57) and wrote an account of the Persian Gulf. His book, *Siwa: the Oasis of Jupiter Ammon (1923)*, is illustrated with his own charming watercolours.

Princess Marta Bibescu (1888–1973)

The Romanian aristocrat and patriot Princess Bibescu was regarded as one of the outstanding women writers in the French language. Her writings embraced travels and biographies (of Proust and Churchill). Her rare beauty and great style caused many men to fall in love with her – as did the archaeologist Howard Carter when she was recuperating from illness in Egypt in 1930.

Winifred Blackman (1872–1950)

The eldest daughter of a clergyman, Winifred Blackman read Anthropology at Oxford where she began her lifelong focus on Egypt. She worked on research about the Fellahin in 1920-1 and for the next decade was in charge of anthropological research expeditions in Egypt. She published *The Fellahin of Upper Egypt* in 1927 and wrote numerous articles in archaeological and anthropological journals. Unlike other travellers to Egypt, Miss Blackman's purpose was to listen to, learn from and write about the ordinary people of the country talking about their lives and customs. Her records have led another traveller, Anthony Sattin, to write about the continuity of ideals, beliefs, customs and rituals along the Nile.

Mary Chubb (1903–)

In 1928 Mary Chubb joined the staff of the Egypt Exploration Society in London, and was sent as secretary to the field director of the dig at Tel el Amarna – home in about 1370 BC of the pharaohs Akhenaten and the beauteous Nefertiti. She also worked in Iraq at Tel Asmar. Later she wrote of her experiences in *Nefertiti Lived Here* (1954) and *City in the Sand* (1957) which have both been re-issued.

Lady Evelyn Cobbold (1867–1963)

Having spent long periods in the early days of her life in Morocco, Lady Evelyn Cobbold found herself drawn to the Muslim world. In 1911 she travelled in the Fayoum with a friend and their two maids

– who also became drawn into their adventure. Later she became a Muslim and went on the Haj – an experience she described in *Pilgrimage to Mecca* (1934).

Robert Curzon (1810–1873)

Briefly a Member of Parliament, Curzon lost his seat in 1831 and went travelling to the eastern Mediterranean. His underlying purpose was to discover ancient manuscripts in the libraries of monasteries.

William Dalrymple (1965–)

Born and brought up in Scotland, Dalrymple has wandered the world to become the great travel writer of this generation since his early twenties. His first book, *Xanadu*, was published when he was twenty-two. He lived for four years in Delhi undertaking research for his next book, *City of Djinns. From the Holy Mountain* for which he travelled to monasteries from Greece to the Eastern Desert of Egypt, has been described as 'a rich stew of history and travel narrative spiced with anecdote, opinion and bon mots.'

Lucie Duff Gordon (1821–1869)

In 1862 Lucie Duff Gordon withdrew from cultured London society to travel in the hope of conquering tuberculosis. She lived for a time in South Africa and then for seven years in Egypt, mainly in a house in Luxor temple where she drew around her a new social circle of visiting foreigners and the important Egyptians of the area, who saw her as a great lady 'who was just and had a heart that loved the Arabs'.

Robin Fedden (1908–1977)

Born in France, Robin Fedden lived in, travelled in and wrote about the Near East and Egypt. Returning to England, he worked for the National Trust, rising to become Deputy Director and editing the

National Trust Guide – a description of all the properties then owned by the Trust.

E. M. Forster (1879–1970)

The novelist E. M. Forster was stationed in Alexandria as a Red Cross volunteer during the First World War. During that time he wrote *Alexandria: A History and a Guide,* in his words 'after the fashion of a pageant, to marshal the activities of Alexandria during the two thousand two hundred years of her existence'. It was published in Egypt and in the USA in 1922, but not until 1982 in Britain.

Amitav Ghosh (1956–)

Growing up and educated in India, Ghosh won a post-graduate research scholarship to Oxford in 1978. His subject was social anthropology and his field research was carried out in the Nile Delta, a couple of hours from Alexandria.

Michael Haag

Photographer, writer, creator of guide books on Egypt, Michael Haag has a long-time love of and deep knowledge of Egypt. His book *Alexandria: City of Memory* (2006) looks at that city in both width and depth.

James Hanson (fl. 1815–1825)

An officer in the East India Company army, Hanson travelled from India to England accompanying the retiring East Indian commander, Lieutenant-General Sir Miles Nightingall and his wife and their entourage. He published his accounts of the journey under the patronage of the redoubtable Lady Nightingall.

Ahmed Hassanein (1889–1946)
Born in Cairo and educated at the universities of Cairo and Oxford, Ahmed Hassanein then served as an Egyptian diplomat. In 1923 he went on an expedition to discover the lost oases of the Egyptian-Libyan desert. He was the first to discover the long-lost oases of Arkenu, Uweinat and Kufra. He recorded his perilous exploratory trip in *The Lost Oasis* (1925).

Taha Hussein (1889–1973)
Born in the provincial city of Menya in Upper Egypt where he received his early education in traditional schools, Taha Hussein moved to Cairo to study at Al-Azhar University, then later to France were he read for his PhD. He lost his eyesight at an early age, yet despite this and many other impediments, he played an epoch-marking role in Egyptian cultural life. He became acknowledged as Dean of Arabic Literature, a title that has remained his exclusively to this day. He was a pioneer in Egyptian reform and advocated free education for all citizens – an achievement which leaves all educated Egyptians indebted to him. He is also remembered for his efforts to modernise Egyptian culture and educational institutions. His fictional writings and biography, *The Stream of Days (1948)*, are classics of Arabic literature and of Arabic literature in English.

Ahmed bin Tuwayr al-Janna (fl. 1830–1835)
A Mauretanian scholar who went on pilgrimage to Mecca, Tuwayr al-Janna wrote a record of his journey: a mixture of narrative, poems, pious thoughts, anecdotes and observations on the Mediterranean world.

Ibn Jubayr (1145–1217)
Ibn Jubbaya is one of the better known Arab travellers. A renowned poet and writer, he served as scribe to the Governor of Granada. In 1187 he set out for Mecca to perform the Hajj. Yet, in the manner of many medieval Arab travellers, he stopped, lived and worked in

many places. He arrived in Alexandria by sea, travelled down the Nile and left the country through Port 'Aizab on the Red Sea, heading for Jedda. He kept a diary which became known as *The Travels of Ibn Jubayr (1952)*, one of the most celebrated Arab travel accounts. It is remarkable for its adaptation of the diary form in travel writing and for its recording the critical period of the Crusades and hence inclusion of impressions of the controversial character of Salah el-Din.

Roger Lancelyn Green (1918–1997)
A British writer, stage actor, librarian and schoolmaster, Green developed an interest in myths and legends at an early age. His passion for mythology led him to collect ancient myths which he then, with skills as a story-teller, retold.

Dame Penelope Lively CBE *(1933–)*
Prize-winning writer of both children's and adult's books, Penelope Lively spent some of her early years in Cairo, about which she wrote in *Oleander, Jacaranda: a childhood perceived* (1994). She also writes short stories and scripts for television and radio.

Pierre Loti (1850–1923)
A long-serving French naval officer, Loti started his writing career with travel accounts and then moved on to publish romantic novels about the countries in which he was stationed. Returning to his home in France, he led an increasingly eccentric life.

William MacQuitty (1905–1990)
MacQuitty's working life took in some years of business in the Far East and then, returning to Belfast, he became involved in making films and, in the late 1950s with television. In 1962, while planning a film on General Gordon in Sudan, he visited Abu Simbel to see the temples before they would be flooded by Lake Nasser. He became involved in

the plan to save them and was invited to write a book, *Abu Simbel*, about the temples.

Dr R. R. Madden (1798–1886)

The Irish-born Dr Richard Robert Madden deserves far greater recognition for his work across the world for human rights and against the exploitation of labour. He travelled in the Levant and Egypt between 1824 and 1827 and in 1840 returned to Egypt to raise the subject of slavery. He worked in the Caribbean and West Africa, published an account of his Near Eastern travels and a study of Pasha Mehemet Ali, and served in Australia where he exerted himself on behalf of the Aborigines. In 1850 he returned to his native Ireland to work for the improvement of conditions for the Irish peasantry.

Naguib Mahfouz (1912–2006)

The Egyptian novelist wrote many novels based in his home town of Cairo. *Miramar (1978)*, from which our excerpt is taken, however, is based in Alexandria. He won the Nobel Prize for Literature in 1988.

Amin Maalouf

A Lebanese-French writer, Amin Maalouf started his career as a journalist in Lebanon but then moved to live in Paris where he wrote fiction and established himself as 'a voice which Europe cannot afford to ignore' (*Guardian*). *Leo the African*, *Samarkand* and his recent *Origins* are among the best known of his fictional works. He is known for his technique of mixing historic facts with fantasy and spicing them with a hint of philosophy.

Jean Said Makdisi

Jean Said Makdisi was born in Jerusalem. She spent her childhood and educational years in Cairo before moving to the United States for her higher studies. She has written two memoirs. *Beirut: A War Memoir* records her experience in Lebanon during the civil war; *Teta, Mother and Me: An Arab Woman's Memoir* describes, what it means to have grown up in Cairo as a Palestinian emigrant. She now lives in Lebanon.

Deborah Manley

Deborah Manley has lived in India, Australia, Canada, Nigeria and Cameroon, and her native England. She has worked in publishing, written children's books and a biography of Henry Salt, a Consul General in Cairo and collector, and has published collected travel writings about the Trans-Siberian Railway and Egypt. This is the third book on which she and Sahar Abdel-Hakim have collaborated.

H. V. Morton (1890–1975)

Entering journalism in 1910, Morton worked for several major newspapers. His *In Search of…* books began to appear in 1927, after a series of collected essays on London. He was a correspondent in Egypt at the time of the discovery of the tomb of Tutankhamun. His books on the Near East greatly enlightened people who found themselves there during the Second World War. He eventually left England to live in South Africa.

Florence Nightingale (1820–1910)

When Florence Nightingale visited Egypt in 1849-50 she was on the verge of achieving her life's ambition: to study nursing. On her way back to train in England she visited Kaiserwerth Institution in Germany. In 1854 she was sent to the Crimea to supervise nursing during the Crimean War and her achievements there assured her of historic status. In the excerpt here one can almost feel her preparing herself for the break with her past.

Sayyid Qutb (c.1910–1966)

Sayyid Qutb wrote in 1946 of the village life of his childhood in the early twentieth century. As everywhere, some of the ways of village life have changed but much is preserved and continues. Yet as he writes, 'well-off city people have hardly any conception of them (village people) whether as things in real life or even in imaginary things.' He grew up in an educated village family and was one of the first pupils at the local state primary school, in contrast to Taha Hussein's traditional education. He trained and worked as a teacher and civil servant. A contemporary of Hussein and Naguib Mahfouz, Qutb was a radical Islamic writer and activist. He was first published in 1924 and published many poems and articles and two novelettes. After studying in America, he returned to Egypt and became deeply involved in radical politics, but after the Muslim Brotherhood was banned in 1954, he spent much of the rest of his life in prison, and was executed for his political activities in 1966.

Dr Robert Richardson (1779–1847)

In 1816 Dr Richardson was invited to become personal physician to the Irish Earl of Belmore and his family as they set off to cruise around the Mediterranean for the next two years. His *Travels* (1822) give very interesting observations and insights into the countries around the Eastern Mediterranean. Richardson then set up as a Physician in London, and was often consulted by travellers he had met in Egypt.

Paul William Roberts

Born in Wales, Roberts is now based in Toronto as a writer, film producer and film-maker and researches Jewish and Arabic history and religions. He writes for various prominent magazines and has published a number of accounts of his travels, including *Journey of the Magi: Travels in Search of the Birth of Jesus.*

Max Rodenbeck (1960–)

Max Rodenbeck moved to Cairo from Virginia with his parents when he was two in 1962 and, after absences, returned to live in Cairo in 1980. He worked as a cartographer, tour guide and development consultant before settling into a career in journalism. He became *The Economist's* Cairo correspondent in 1989 and has been its Middle East Bureau Chief since 2000.

H. J. Ross (1820–1901)

Born in Malta, Ross joined the consular service and spent years in Mesopotamia (where he worked with Layard at Nineveh), Asiatic Turkey and Alexandria, returning to Turkey during the Crimean War and continuing to travel in the Near East for some years. He married Janet, the daughter of Lucie Duff Gordon, and they settled in Alexandria until they retired to Italy, where he grew orchids.

Anthony Sattin

A journalist and travel writer with a special interest in North Africa and the Near East, Anthony Sattin has written a number of books about travellers in the region and in India. He discovered Florence Nightingale's *Letters from Egypt* (1987) which, perhaps for the first time, gave real and personal insights into a period in which this great woman prepared herself for her future life.

Sarah Searight

Another founder member of ASTENE, Sarah Searight has travelled and worked all over the Middle East writing about the history of travel there in *British in the Middle East* and *Steaming East*. She wrote the introduction to Virago's re-issue of Lucie Duff Gordon's *Letters from Egypt* – which can be bought in most bookshops on the Egyptian tourist routes. Her re-assessment of Lucie in the light of this collection was published in ASTENE's *Women Travellers in the Near East*.

Constance Sitwell (1888-1974)
Constance Sitwell was the daughter of a tea planter in Ceylon who became a British Member of Parliament. She travelled in Egypt first with her parents (a visit described in *Bright Morning*, 1942) and then again in 1927, evoked so beautifully in her *Lotus and Pyramid* (1928). She wrote other travel memoirs and one novel.

Ahdaf Soueif
Born in Cairo and educated in Egypt and England, Ahdaf Soueif is probably the best-known modern Egyptian writer. Her publications include *Mezzaterra,* a collection of political and cultural writings (written between 1981 and 2004, and described as 'perceptive, fearless, intelligent and necessary'), and her acclaimed, dream-like novel of time-spans, *The Map of Love* (1999), which was shortlisted for the Booker Prize.

Acknowledgements

We would like to thank all of the authors for making this collection possible by allowing us to use their material, and gratefully acknowledge permission to reprint copyright material as follows:

The American University in Cairo Press for the extract from *The Fellahin of Upper Egypt* by Winifred Blackman; Syracuse University Press for the extract from *A Child in the Village* by Sayid Qutb; Anthony Sattin for the extract from *Lifting the Veil: British Society in Egypt 1768-1956*; Little, Brown and J.C Lattes for the extract from *Leo the African* by Amin Maalouf; I.B Tauris for the extract from *River in the Desert* by Paul William Roberts; Egmont Books for the extract from *Going Back* by Penelope Lively; Random House for the extract from *Tales from Ancient Egypt* by Roger Lancelyn Green; HarperCollins and Holt for the extract from *From the Holy Mountain* by William Dalrymple; Saqi for the extract from *Teta, Mother and Me: An Arab Woman's Memoir* by Jean Said Makdisi; Macmillan for the extract from *Cairo: The City Victorious* by Max Rodenbeck; Yale Univeristy Press for the extract from *Alexandria: City of Memory* by Michael Haag; Anchor for the extract from *Miramar* by Naguib Mahfouz; Granta and A.M Heath for the extract from *In an Antique Land* by Amitav Gosh; Andre Deutsch for the extract from *Alexandria : A History and Guide* by E.M Forster; Longmans Green & Co. for the extract from *The Stream of Days: A Student at the Azha*r by Taha Hussein; *Nefertiti Lived Here* by Mary Chubb; Methuen for the extract from *Middle East* by H.V Morton; Parkway for permission to reproduce a letter written by Florence Nightingale in *Letters from Egypt: A Journey on the Nile*; Bloomsbury for the extract from *The Map of Love* by Ahdaf Soueif; Batsford for the extract from *The Land of Egypt* by Robin Fedden; Oxbow for the extract from *Women Travellers* in the Near East by Sarah Searight; and Faber for the extract from *Writing Home* by Alan Bennett.

Bibliography

Aboudi, Mohammed, *Egypt: Aboudi's Guide Book*, Luxor, 1963
Armstrong, Sir William, *A Visit to Egypt in 1872*, Newcastle-on-Tyne, 1874
Belgrave, Charles Dalrymple, *Siwa: the Oasis of Jupiter Ammon*, John Lane, The Bodley Head, London, 1923
Bennett, Alan, *Writing Home*, Faber, London, 1994
Bibescu, Marta, *Jour d'Egypte*, Flammarion, Paris, 1929
Blackman, Winifred, *The Fellahin of Upper Egypt*, London, 1927
Chubb, Mary, *Nefertiti Lived Here*, Bles, London, 1954 and re-issued Libri, 1998
Cobbold, Lady Evelyn, *A Wayfarer in the Libyan Desert*, London, 1912
Curzon, Robert, *Visits to Monasteries of the Levant*, London, 1849, re-issued Century Publishing, 1983
Lucie Duff Gordon, *Letters from Egypt*, London, 1865, re-issued Virago, 1983
Fedden, Robin, *The Land of Egypt*, Batsford, London, 1939
Forster, E. M., *Alexandria: A History and a Guide*, 1922, re-issued Michael Haag, London 1982
Ghosh, Amitav, *In an Antique Land*, Granta, London, 1992
Hanson, James, 'The Route of Lt-General Sir Miles Nightingall' India in Letters, London, 1820
Hassanein, Ahmed, *The Lost Oasis*, London, 1925, re-issued American University in Cairo Press, Cairo, 2006
Hussein, Taha, *The Stream of Days: A Student at the Azhar*, Longman, London, 1948
Ibn Battuta, *Travels in Asia and Africa 1325-54*, trans. by Sir H. Gibb, Routledge, London, 1958
Ibn Jubayr, *The Travels of Ibn Jubayr*, trans. R. J. C. Broadhurst, London, 1952
al-Janna, Ahmed bin Tuwayr, *The Pilgrimage of Ahmas: Son of the Little Bird of Paradise* tran. and ed. H. T. Norris, Warminster, 1970
Lancelyn Green, Roger, *Tales of Ancient Egypt*, Bodley Head, London, 1967
Lively, Penelope, *Going Back*, Heinemann, London, 1975
Loti, Pierre, *Egypt*, (trans. from *Egypt: La Morte de Philae)* T. Werner Laurie, London, 1909
MacQuitty, William, *Abu Simbel*, Macdonald, London, 1965

Madden, Dr R. R., *Travels in Turkey, Egypt, Nubia and Palestine*, London, 1829

Mahfouz, Naguib, *Miramar*, trans. Fatma Moussa Mahmoud, American University in Cairo Press, Cairo,1978

Maalouf, Amin, *Leo the African*, trans. from French Peter Sluglett, Quartet, London, 1988

Makdisi, Jean Said, *Teta, Mother and Me: An Arab Woman's Memoir*, Saqi, London, 2005

Morton, H. V., *Middle East*, Methuen, London, 1941

Nightingale, Florence, *Letters from Egypt: A Journey on the Nile*, ed. Anthony Sattin, Barrie and Jenkins, London, 1987

Qutb, Sayyid, *A Child from the Village*, trans. John Calvert, American University in Cairo Press, Cairo, 2006

Richardson, Dr Robert, *Travels along the Mediterranean*, London, 1822

Roberts, Paul William, *River in the Desert: A modern traveller in ancient Egypt*, Tauris Parke Paperbacks, London, 2006

Rodenbeck, Max, *Cairo: The City Victorious*, Picador, London, 1998

Ross, H. J., *Letters from the East*, London, 1902

Sattin, Anthony, *Lifting the Veil: British Society in Egypt 1768-1956*, Dent, London, 1988

Searight, Sarah, from *Women Travellers in the Near East*, Oxbow, Oxford, 2006

Sitwell, Constance, *Lotus and Pyramid*, Cape, London, 1928

Soueif, Ahdaf, *The Map of Love*, Bloomsbury, London, 1999

Index